The
NEWPORT &
NARRAGANSETT BAY
Book
A Complete Guide

Craig Hammell

THE
NEWPORT &
NARRAGANSETT BAY
BOOK
A Complete Guide
With Block Island

Pamela Petro

Photography by
Craig Hammell

Berkshire House Publishers
Stockbridge, Massachusetts

The Newport & Narragansett Bay book: A Complete Guide
Copyright © 1994 by Berkshire House Publishers
Cover and interior photographs © 1994 by Craig Hammell and other credited photographers and sources.

Library of Congress Cataloging-in-Publication Data

Petro, Pamela.
   The Newport & Narragansett Bay book : a complete guide / Pamela Petro ; photography by Craig Hammell.
      p. cm. — (Great destinations series, ISSN: 1056-7968)
   Includes bibliographical references and index.
   ISBN 0-936399-40-6 : $16.95.
   1. Newport (R.I.)—Guidebooks. 2. Narragansett Bay Region (R.I.)—Guidebooks. I. Title. II. Title: Newport and Narragansett Bay book. III. Series.
F89.N5P46   1994
917.45'70443—dc20   93-44660
                                                        CIP

ISBN: 0-936399-40-6
ISSN: 1056-7968 (series)

Editor: Sarah Novak. Managing Editor: Philip Rich. Original design for Great Destinations™ series: Janice Lindstrom. Original design for Great Destinations™ cover: Jane McWhorter. Production services by Ripinsky & Company, Connecticut.

Manufactured in the United States of America
First printing 1994
10 9 8 7 6 5 4 3 2 1

No complimentary meals or lodgings were accepted by the author and reviewers in gathering information for this work.

The GREAT DESTINATIONS Series

The Berkshire Book: A Complete Guide
The Santa Fe & Taos Book: A Complete Guide
The Napa & Sonoma Book: A Complete Guide
The Chesapeake Bay Book: A Complete Guide
The Coast of Maine Book: A Complete Guide
The Adirondack Book: A Complete Guide
The Aspen Book: A Complete Guide
The Charleston, Savannah & Coastal Islands Book:
A Complete Guide
The Gulf Coast of Florida Book: A Complete Guide
The Central Coast of California Book : A Complete Guide
The Newport & Narragansett Bay Book: A Complete Guide
The Hamptons Book: A Complete Guide

The Great Destinations™ series features regions in the United States rich in natural beauty and culture. Each Great Destinations™ guidebook reviews an extensive selection of lodgings, restaurants, cultural events, historic sites, shops, and recreational opportunities, and outlines the region's natural and social history. Written by resident authors, the guides are a resource for visitor and resident alike. Maps, photographs, directions to and around the region, lists of helpful phone numbers and addresses, and indexes.

Contents

CHAPTER ONE
Of Rhodes and Rogues
HISTORY
1

CHAPTER TWO
Between the Bridges
TRANSPORTATION
20

CHAPTER THREE
Sleeping by the Sea
LODGING
34

CHAPTER FOUR
The Gilded Age and All That Jazz
CULTURE
77

CHAPTER FIVE
Of Jonnycakes, Cabinets, and Quahogs
RESTAURANTS & FOOD PURVEYORS
123

CHAPTER SIX
At the Helm
RECREATION
182

CHAPTER SEVEN
Not a Mall in Sight
SHOPPING
223

CHAPTER EIGHT
The Nitty-Gritty
INFORMATION
249

Acknowledgments

A lot of people have contributed to this book and all deserve my heartfelt thanks: none more so than Marguerite Harrison, my steadfast friend and official *Newport & Narragansett Bay Book* fact-checker and researcher, with whom I shared countless fried seafood dinners and research jaunts in the rain. My parents, Pat and Steve Petro, also put in some heroic days in the heat of a brutal July, scouring the antique shops of Newport with trained eyes. Thanks to them and to my cousin, William Thompson, for his erudite round-up of art galleries.

Mary Diaz — who with Tom Ferguson put me onto the best Italian ice I've ever tasted — is responsible for a last-ditch effort at the Providence Public Library without which I may never have finished. Cindy Roberts, of Bed & Breakfast Newport, deserves special thanks for outstanding advice; and without assistance from innkeepers Shirley Kessler, Neva Flaherty, Barbara Nyzio, Alva from the Chamber of Commerce, and my parents' neighbors Dot and Nancy Van Court, I'd still be cycling around Block Island. Thanks are also due to my uncle, Morton Snowhite, for his all-encompassing knowledge of libraries, and to the indefatigable team of appetite-ready restaurant reviewers upon whose palates and stomachs Chapter Five rests: Paula and Casey Knynenburg, Nelson and Nancy Vieira, Annie Garthwaite (clam chowder taster extraordinaire), Karen Caniglia, Lori Dalesio, and Ellen Douglass and Jessie Biddle. Special commendations are in order for Dick Newman for braving the Jazz Festival in the heat and for his African-American contributions; Carole Pace, mistress of the East Bay, not only for eating above and beyond the call of duty but for her expert reading of the *History* chapter; and my dear pals Lora Urbanelli and Bill Rae: thanks for eating Italian out, for helping on Block, and for all the encouraging phone calls.

Finally, it must be said that without the invaluable input of Craig Hammell — the *Newport & Narragansett Bay* photographer — this book wouldn't exist. I thank him for his wonderful photos and good humor, and extend the latter appreciation to the staff at Berkshire House as well, notably Sarah Novak, who stuck with the project despite an intense schedule, and especially Philip Rich, who has a miraculously calming influence on his writers. And last but not least, thanks to my car, a 1987 Volkswagen Fox wagon, for not breaking down.

Introduction

The symbol of Newport, Rhode Island is the pineapple. Legend holds that when Yankee sailors returned home from long voyages in exotic climes, they stuck a pineapple on their gate post or front door so that neighbors would know they were home and come to visit. That's how this spiny fruit came to be known as a symbol of hospitality, which certainly explains its presence in the City by the Sea. More families in Newport have opened their homes to guests, offering visitors from New York to Australia the comforts of a bed and breakfast, than any other city in the United States. If that's not hospitality, then pineapples aren't prickly.

When I received the assignment to write this book, I made an effort to tell everyone I knew of my good fortune, and nearly everyone replied, "Oh yeah, Newport. That's where the mansions are, right?" Newport is where the mansions are — or rather "cottages," as they were called by their Gilded Age owners — but as I discovered, the mansions are just a small part of this city's charms. Ask yourself why people like the Vanderbilts and the Astors built summer homes here, and you'll begin to appreciate the range of attractions, both natural and man-made, that make Newport such an hospitable place. As usual, Henry James put his finger on it in his memoir, *Notes of A Son and Brother:*

> Newport was and still is a unique place. One of the most beautiful towns in America, it is at one and the same time a colonial city of singular distinction and a well-known summer resort of long standing; to walk through Newport is to walk through three hundred years of American architecture, much of which is beautifully preserved, used, and lived in still.

"Lived in still" is the phrase that gets to the heart of it. Newport may welcome tourists but it's not a "tourist town," in the sense of a city that has come to live principally on the sale of its charms. The clean, foaming, crashing waters of Narragansett Bay and the endless winds that blow above them have insured that residents of Newport and her sister towns up and down the Rhode Island coast have always had more to do than simply sell T-shirts to visitors. Over the years these occupations have included everything from harvesting quahogs — Rhode Island's favorite crustacean — lobsters, and mussels to designing and building some of the fastest and most graceful yachts ever to race the seas, notably at the famed Herreshoff shipyard in Bristol.

And that's another thing: the Herreshoffs built their America's Cup defenders not in Newport, arguably the sailing capital of the world, but in Bristol, a fishing town of Greek Revival houses and Portuguese bakeries, about twenty minutes north of Newport by car. While the City by the Sea may be the focal point of Narragansett Bay, it certainly doesn't have a stranglehold on beauty, history, or eccentricities (Rhode Island's trio of attractions), all of which are found in abundance on both shores of the Bay. How else but venturing beyond Newport would you find one of only two chicken memorials in the world (to the Rhode Island Red), set in the pristine countryside of the Sakonnet region, or eat honest-to-goodness West Bay jonnycakes (a Rhode Island delicacy) at Jigger's Diner, a 1917 dining car in East Greenwich?

Beyond the Bay, off by itself in the open ocean, is Block Island. It was named by the Nature Conservancy as one of the "12 Last Great Places in the Western Hemisphere" (an honor it shares with the likes of the Amazon rain forest), and in a snit once tried to abdicate from Rhode Island (needless to say, a brief flirtation with joining Colorado came to naught). Block is a quirky, lovely, timeless place, even by Rhode Island standards. Any community that can move a lighthouse — after almost 10 years islanders succeeded in having the landmark Southeast Light moved back from an eroding cliff face — is worthy of hearty respect. Residents have even limited development to protect the island for the future — perhaps the supreme act of hospitality, this time to the Earth itself. As one resident put it, "We've got to have the open space, or where's the rain going to fall?"

Pamela J. Petro
Providence, Rhode Island

THE WAY THIS BOOK WORKS

ORGANIZATION

This book is divided into eight chapters, each with its own introduction. If you are interested in one chapter or another, you can turn to it directly and begin reading without losing a sense of continuity. You can also take the book with you on your travels and skip around, reading about the places you visit as you go. Or you can read the entire book through from start to finish.

If you're interested in finding a place to eat or sleep, we suggest you first look over the restaurant and lodging lists in the Index (organized by area and price); then turn to the pages listed in the general index and read about the places that most interest you.

Some entries, most notably those in the lodging and restaurant chapters, include specific information (telephone, address, hours, etc.) organized for easy reference in blocks in the left-hand column. The information here, as well as the phone numbers and addresses in the descriptions, were checked as close to publication as possible. Even so, details change with frustrating frequency. It's best to call ahead.

Entries within most of the chapters are arranged alphabetically by towns under **five regional headings:** "West Bay," "East Bay," "Aquidneck," "Sakonnet," and "Block Island." A map showing the entire coast divided into these five regions appears at the end of this Introduction.

LIST OF MAPS

Newport & Narragansett Bay, with Block Island
Newport & Narragansett Bay Access Maps
West Bay and Acquidneck
East Bay and Sakonnet
Newport
Block Island

PRICES

Since prices are subject to constant change, I've avoided listing specific rates and have instead indicated a price range. Lodging price codes are based on a per-room rate, double occupancy, in high season (roughly Memorial to Labor Day); I've noted only when breakfast is *not* included. Low season rates are likely to be 20 to 40 percent less. Again, it's best to call. Remember that lodging prices do not include tax.

Restaurant prices indicate the cost of an individual meal including appetizer, entree and dessert, but not including cocktails, wine, tax or tip. Restaurants with a prix-fixe menu are noted accordingly.

A final word about prices. Like the Gilded Age, the penchant for conspicuous consumption that went with it has long since disappeared. Today's visitors to the area — and their hosts — appreciate the importance of frugality. Even the finest and most formal of establishments consciously seek to offer patrons a good value for their money. Therefore, the use of the word "Expensive" here, in connection with some establishments, is intended for comparative purposes only — not as a value judgment.

PRICE CODES

	Lodging	Dining
Inexpensive	Up to $50	Up to $15
Moderate	$50 to $100	$15 to $25
Expensive	$100 to $180	$25 to $35
Very Expensive	Over $180	Over $35

Credit Cards are abbreviated as follows:

AE — American Express	DC — Diner's Club
CB — Carte Blanche	MC — Master Card
D — Discover Card	V — Visa

AREA CODE

All of the Rhode Island telephone numbers cited in this book begin with the 401 area code, with a few exceptions, in which cases the correct area code is provided.

AUTHOR'S NOTE

While *The Newport & Narragansett Bay Book* claims to be a "Complete Guide," the subtitle is more of an aspiration than an accomplishment. A truly complete guide would be encyclopedic in scope and require wheels to make it portable. This book is the result of my personal research and selections, and is complete only in the scope of its concerns. Enjoy extending its boundaries.

The
NEWPORT &
NARRAGANSETT BAY
Book
A Complete Guide

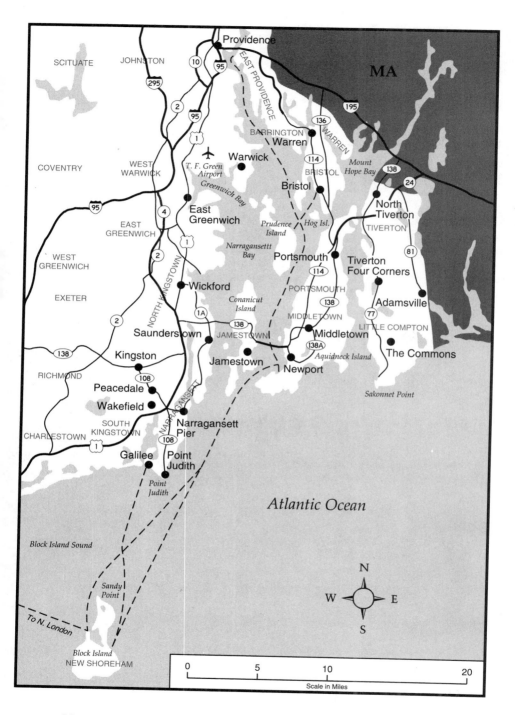

Newport & Narragansett Bay, including Block Island

CHAPTER ONE
Of Rhodes and Rogues
HISTORY

Most of the big shore places were closed now and there were hardly any lights except the shadowy, moving glow of a ferryboat across the Sound. And as the moon rose higher the inessential houses began to melt away until gradually I became aware of the old island here that flowered once for Dutch sailor's eyes — a fresh green breast of the new world.

— F. Scott Fitzgerald, *The Great Gatsby*

It was no accident that the film of *The Great Gatsby* was made in Newport, Rhode Island. Even though the novel was set in New York, no place illustrates Fitzgerald's fable of the American Dream quite like the City by the Sea.

Newport occupies the southern tip of Aquidneck, a long, slender island that rises from the water like the great backbone of Narragansett Bay. The city is famous as the showplace of all that money can buy, in particular the "summer cottages"

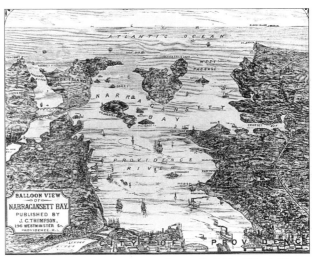

Courtesy Rhode Island Historical Society

A "Balloon View" of Narragansett Bay from 1882.

of the Gilded Age rich — aptly described as crosses between Grand Central Station and the Palace of Versailles. Yet it doesn't require a leap of imagination by moonlight to imagine Aquidneck and neighboring islands as they were when Verrazzano sailed into the Bay in 1524. Pockets of that old New World, still fresh and green, remain just a car or boat ride away from those famous new copies of Old World splendor.

Mrs. Astor once decreed that it took money three generations to "cool off." You couldn't get into turn-of-the-century Newport society without a lukewarm pocketbook. And yet the host city of the nation's most frivolous, though nonetheless grueling, social caste system — remember: never overtake anyone of higher status when you're out in your coach — was one of four original Rhode Island towns founded by free-thinking radicals in the name of such principles as religious tolerance, freedom of speech, and separation of church and state (Providence, Warwick, and Portsmouth were the others). From the first, Rhode Island was a haven for iconoclasts unacceptable elsewhere — rogues to everyone else. Today that policy seems courageous and forward-thinking: at the time Cotton Mather called Rhode Island "the sewer of New England." Newport welcomed the first Jewish congregation in the country (Touro synagogue is the oldest on the continent), and the colony hosted other suspect groups such as Quakers, French Huguenots, and Baptists. Gatsby himself, the loner with ill-gotten money and no pedigree, would have felt at home in colonial Newport.

In fact, he would have fit right in. Newport, and to a lesser extent other seaport towns on Narragansett Bay such as Bristol, Warren, and Providence, reaped a fortune from the colonial slave trade. The money made Newport one of the supreme cultural and economic centers in the colonies. Recently a desk crafted in the city's famous 18th-century Townsend-Goddard workshop fetched $11 million at auction: the highest price ever paid for a work of art other than a painting.

When the nouveau riche began to arrive in town in the 1870s, they hoped that some of this high-toned colonial culture would rub off on them. Few realized that the quaint cobbled streets and stately public buildings of the old city had been paid for by a tax slapped onto the slave ships. Like Fitzgerald's great American novel, Newport's history is laced with irony, not least of which is that many mansions are now open to the public (the ultimate come-down). And yet, the city embodies the vicissitudes of the American Dream for one basic reason: its unique position at the mouth of Rhode Island's greatest natural asset — the source of so many of its pleasures, riches, headaches, and historic events — Narragansett Bay.

NATURAL HISTORY

THE OCEAN STATE

Rhode Island wasn't dubbed the Ocean State for nothing. Over one-fifth of its total area is taken up by Narragansett Bay, the state's premier physical feature and natural resource. The Bay is 28 miles long from its mouth at Newport to its head in Providence, roughly two-thirds of the distance from the sea to Rhode Island's northern border with Massachusetts. At its southernmost, Narragansett Bay stretches 12 miles from the town of Narragansett in the west to Little Compton in the east; its width narrows to about three miles in the north. Though the Bay is full of dozens of small islets, three major islands congregate in the center: Aquidneck, Conanicut (better known as Jamestown), and Prudence. This has the effect of splitting the Bay into two unequal halves with the bulk on the western side, and just a slender filament two or three miles wide on the eastern side, known as the Sakonnet River.

What Rhode Island lacks in land mass — it's been said that two hundred Rhode Islands could fit into Texas — the Bay makes up for in nearly 400 miles of irregular shoreline. Its coastal lowlands include sandy beaches, marsh flats, brackish pools, and dramatic, rocky promontories where the wind never quits. For the past several decades, watchdog groups like Save the Bay have helped to reduce pollution dramatically in upper Bay waters (though the once-thriving oyster farms near the mouth of the Providence River are gone for good) and to protect the integrity of the lower Bay. Lobsters are the mainstay of the state's small commercial fishing fleet based in Galilee and Point Judith, though scallops, soft-shell clams, quahogs, blue crabs, and mussels are on hand as well. Game fish include tuna, shark, striped bass, swordfish, white marlin, bluefish, cod, mackerel, and flounder. Whales, porpoises, and seals are also found in coastal waters.

CLIMATE CONTROL

One of the results of a large body of water sitting in the midst of a small state is that it regulates temperature extremes. The Bay retains warmth in winter and coolness in summer, casting a weather force-field over the areas covered in this book. When it snows in Providence it rains in Newport; when it reaches 90 degrees in Providence it's invariably only 80 in Newport. Not a bad trade-off, if you live on the Bay. There are exceptions — in 1799 Narragansett Bay froze solid, so that farmers were able to run oxen-teams over the ice from Newport to Fall River. On February 23, 1934, Professor Ellsworth Huntington announced at Yale that he had discovered that Newport, Rhode Island had the best weather in the country, and proposed making it the nation's official summer capital. His report was cited by Rhode Island leaders after World War II when they petitioned the United Nations to establish its permanent headquarters in the City by the Sea.

The U.N. took its business elsewhere, but others heeded Huntington's advice. Despite the fact that "variability" is cited as the state's chief weather characteristic, temperatures around the Bay are so equitable that the area supports several thriving vineyards, including Sakonnet, the largest winery in New England. The moderate micro-climate lends the grapevines a long, slow growing season. As Sakonnet's owner says, "All great vineyards are near water."

Of course the Bay is occasionally less than benign. At least three times in recorded history it has served as a funnel for floodwaters that have pummeled Providence to bits: the Great Gale of 1815 and the Hurricane of 1938 and of

1954 (a concrete hurricane barrier now protects Providence). The '38 hurricane was the worst disaster ever to hit the Narragansett Bay area, with winds clocked at 120 miles per hour and 311 dead when it was over. Homes demolished on the western shore were carried clear across the Bay to wash up on eastern beaches.

BLAME IT ON THE ICE AGE

Like many things, responsibility for Narragansett Bay's existence may be pinned on the last great Ice Age — or rather upon its demise. About 250 million years ago a chain of high mountains rose along what is now the southern expanse of the Bay. By the time the glaciers arrived at the beginning of the Pleistocene era, some 600,000 years ago, the region had eroded to a topography of rolling hills. About the time the glaciers retreated, the whole region sank, creating the basin that would become Narragansett Bay; the highest peaks became the islands. Between 8000 and 6000 B.C. the ice that remained began to melt, causing sea level to rise as much as 50 feet and inundating the sunken basin and its extensions, which today include the saltwater bodies of Greenwich Bay in the west, Mount Hope Bay in the east, and the Providence River estuary. By 2000 B.C. the geography was essentially the same as that encountered by Roger Williams and his followers when they arrived as dissidents from Massachusetts in 1636.

When the Bay was young, its shores were heavily forested and home to herds of mastodon, caribou, moose, and giant beavers. The western shore was dotted with immense boulders, unceremoniously dumped there by retreating glaciers. As the Massachusetts Bay colony governor John Winthrop noted in 1634, "The country on the west of the bay of Narragansett is all champain for many miles, but very stony and full of Indians." (Champain is flat, open country good for farming.)

SOCIAL HISTORY

ISLE OF PEACE

Winthrop's findings may have been news at the time, but Native Americans had inhabited the shores of Narragansett Bay for at least ten thousand years before he made his report. They were on hand to witness the end of the Ice Age, to hunt mastodon and harvest shellfish. Sites from the Paleo-Native American period are rare because inhabitants were few and made only seasonal encampments, fishing the coastal waters by summer and hunting interior forests by winter. Recently, however, archaeologists on Block Island unearthed the oldest year-round settlement in southern New England, dating back to 500 B.C. It was a stunning discovery which extended anthropologists' knowledge of permanent Native American villages by almost a millennium.

By the 17th century, the territory surrounding Narragansett Bay was inhabited by several tribes of the Algonquins, a network of related nations who
lived up and down the Eastern Seaboard from Canada to North Carolina. In
Rhode Island, the Narragansetts were the largest Algonquin tribe at about
7000 strong. They occupied the western shore of the Bay, and their rivals the
Wampanoags held the eastern side, including the principal islands; a third
tribe, the Nipmucks, were pawns of these two stronger groups. It was the
Wampanoags who gave the name "Aquidneck," which means "Isle of Peace,"
to the Bay's largest island, home to present-day Newport, Middletown, and
Portsmouth. Block Island, meanwhile, was the stronghold of the Manisseans,
who called their home Manisses, or "The Isle of the Little God." John Greenleaf
Whittier borrowed the name for his poem "The Palatine" about a famous
wreck off Block Island:

> Circled by waters that never freeze,
> Beaten by billow and swept by breeze
> Lieth the island of Manisees . . .

When Verrazzano arrived in 1524, searching for a passageway to China for
the king of France, it was Block Island he described as being "in the form of a
triangle, distant from the mainland ten leagues, about the bigness of the Island
of the Rhodes." Verrazzano dubbed it Luisa after the queen mother of France.
Great confusion followed. In 1614 Dutch navigator Adriaen Block renamed it
"Adriaen's Eyland," though it was his surname that eventually stuck. Later
still, Roger Williams and his cohorts mistakenly thought it was Aquidneck that
Verrazzano had been comparing to Rhodes. And so Aquidneck duly became
Rhode Island, until the name outgrew the 75-square mile island and took over
the whole state, the official title of which is Rhode Island and Providence Plan-
tations. Today the Isle of Peace is once again known as Aquidneck.

Verrazzano was a name-giver with a sense of humor. Before leaving Narragansett Bay he named the Dumpling Rocks off the Jamestown coast "Petra
Viva" after the breasts of the wife of a banker who helped finance his trip.
Whether or not Verrazzano was the first European to comb the Bay is an open
question; he was certainly the first to leave a record of his findings. Portuguese
navigator Miguel Corte-Real, who left Lisbon in 1502 never to return, may
have been the one to carve his name, the Portuguese coat of arms, and the date
1511 on a sandstone boulder (the Dighton Writing-Rock) in the Taunton River,
which flows into an eastern arm of the Bay. Historians are split on the authen-
ticity of the inscription, though the legend of a "Viking Tower" in Newport —
once thought to have been built by Norse explorers — has been once and for
all debunked (the tower is actually the foundation of a colonial windmill, built
c. 1670). Whether or not the Vikings sailed their longboats into Narragansett
Bay will remain forever a mystery.

The "Viking Tower" in Touro Park in Newport. Legend had it that this massive structure was constructed by Vikings in the 11th century, but the real story is that English colonists built it around 1600.

Craig Hammell

EARLY SETTLERS, EARLY TROUBLES

Roger Williams founded Providence in 1636. While the Puritans in Massachusetts Bay may be famous for having sought religious freedom, once they got it they applied it only to themselves. Williams was more inclusive — for which he was politely asked to leave — and opened his settlement to one and all, in the process securing the trust of Native Americans whose right to the land he recognized over that of the King of England. Scorn followed (remember Cotton Mather's "sewer of New England" remark), but so did a host of fellow nonconformists eager to establish communities of their own.

Two of these were Anne and William Hutchinson, who founded Portsmouth on the northern tip of Aquidneck in 1638. Anne was the first woman to found a town in North America; her party's Portsmouth Contract also called for the first truly democratic form of government in the world.

The Hutchinsons' wealthiest follower was William Coddington, who moved on to establish Newport in 1639. Coddington tried to prevent Aquidneck and neighboring Conanicut from merging with Williams's Providence Plantations — it was to be his feudal realm — but was thwarted by Williams and Dr. John Clarke, a physician from Newport. It was Clarke who wangled Rhode Island's famous royal charter from King Charles II. The charter secured "full liberty in religious concernments" and gave Rhode Island the greatest degree of self-government in the colonies. This document was so ahead of its time that it lasted until 1843, long after other states had drafted new constitutions.

Other pioneers arrived. Betty Pabodie, daughter of pilgrims Priscilla Mullens and John Alden, and the first white woman born in New England, settled in the Sakonnet region, also known as S'cunnet, Seaconnet, and Saykonate — all derived from the Sogkonate tribe, whose name means "haunt of the wild goose." At the time of her death in 1717, at 92, she had 82 grandchildren and 556 great-grandchildren (her tombstone is in the Commons Burial Ground in

Little Compton). Block Island was purchased in 1660 by 16 families who moved there a year later; their descendants are still well represented in the island's current telephone directory.

On the western side of the Bay, initial trading posts soon evolved into a plantation system of rambling, prosperous estates, much like those in the South, complete with slaves as well. (The oldest of these, Cocumscussoc in Wickford — helpfully called Smith's Castle — was destroyed in King Philip's War, but was rebuilt in 1678 and is now open to the public.) Four decades of living cheek-by-jowl with white settlers accomplished what centuries never could: it united the Wampanoags and Narragansetts, in this case against the English. The result was King Philip's War (1675-76), a brutal, guerrilla-style conflict in which over 600 colonists and several thousand Native Americans died. After Wampanoag chief King Philip was killed, what few natives remained joined together under the aggregate name Narragansett.

A GOLDEN AGE, SLIGHTLY TARNISHED

Providence was burned to the ground in King Philip's War. Roger Williams, then an old man, watched the town burn; the Narragansetts spared his house out of respect. Newport remained unscathed, poised to enter its most successful century.

By 1730 Newport was the fifth largest and wealthiest city in America, preceded only by New York, Boston, Philadelphia, and Charleston. Shipping and commerce were the cornerstone of its economy, the most lucrative aspect of which was the infamous triangle trade: rum distilled in Rhode Island was exchanged for slaves in Africa who were sold to West Indian sugar planters who paid in molasses to make rum. From a colony founded on principles of freedom and tolerance, Rhode Island became the foremost conveyor of slaves to the New World, with the city of Newport leading the way. Simeon Potter of nearby Bristol swore he would "plough the sea into pea-porridge" to make money, and many nearly did. Godfrey Malbone of Newport became so wealthy he threw feasts for returning sea captains and then let them break all the china and crystal on the table. Aaron Lopez of Newport, James De Wolf of Bristol, and John Brown of Providence all reaped millions in the slave trade, pumping some of their money into the glorious architecture that even today sets these towns apart; Bristol's town plan is even accredited to Sir Christopher Wren.

Newport and Providence both claim to have more structures intact from the colonial era than any other city in the country (actually Providence has more intact colonial structures, but Newport has more outright). According to historian William McLoughlin, "Only Boston equaled the stylish grace and urban sophistication of Newport in the decades prior to the Revolution." Some civic and ecclesiastical standouts in Newport's Historic District include Trinity Church (1725-26), another Wren design; the Colony House (1739), site of Rhode Island's annual General Assembly meeting until Providence became

Courtesy Saint Louis Art Museum

Rhode Island sea captains live it up in Surinam in an 18th-century painting.

the state's only capital in 1900; the Redwood Library (1748-50), which is the oldest in the country to remain in its original building; Brick Market (1762) built at the head of 17th-century Long Wharf; and Touro Synagogue (1763). Although it closed in 1791, the synagogue reopened for regular services in 1883, and has been holding them ever since.

Newport's most illustrious visitor from the early part of this period was Irish clergyman, essayist, and philosopher George Berkeley, who had the following to say about Aquidneck and his host city:

> The climate is like that of Italy north of Rome. . . . The land is pleasantly diversified with hills, vales, and rising grounds. Here are also some amusing rocky scenes. There are not wanting several fine rivulets and groves. The sea, too, mixed with capes and adjacent islands, makes very delightful prospects. . . . The town is prettily built, contains about five thousand souls, and hath a very fine harbour. The people are industrious, and though less orthodox, I cannot say have less virtue . . . than those I left in Europe. They are indeed a strange medley of different persuasions, which nevertheless all agree in one point, viz. that the Church of England is the second best.
>
> — Letter to Lord Percival, 1729

FIRST IN WAR, LAST IN PEACE

Rhode Island's tradition of dissent and wariness of external authority — codified in its liberal charter — gave it the most to fear from a meddlesome central government, whether in London or in Washington. One result was that on May 4, 1776, Rhode Island became the first colony to renounce the crown; another was that on May 29, 1790, it became the last state to ratify the Constitution, of which Rhode Islanders were deeply suspicious. The following poem by a Connecticut author refers to the state's ratification stalling:

> Hail, realm of rogues, renowned for fraud and guile,
> All hail, the knaveries of yon little isle . . .
> Look through the state, the unhallowed ground appears
> A nest of dragons and a cave for bears . . .
> The wiser race, the snare of law to shun,
> Like Lot from Sodom, from Rhode Island run.

During the War of Independence, the town of Portsmouth put up the first black regiment ever to fight under the American flag. Members took part in the Battle of Rhode Island in August 1778. In 1784, the state legislature passed an emancipation statute freeing all children born of slave mothers, and in 1787 anti-slavery forces, led by John Brown's Quaker brother Moses, succeeded in prohibiting Rhode Islanders from participating in the slave trade.

The Battle of Rhode Island had come at the end of a long siege designed to pry the British out of Newport, which they had occupied since 1776. The city's exposed position, combined with the loyalist leanings of many prominent Newporters, had made it a sitting duck. The Redcoats didn't budge, but the battle marked the first joint expedition of American and French forces. When the British voluntarily gave up the city in 1779, the French made Newport their home base. All of this upheaval did nothing for Newport. In fact, it never truly recovered from the Revolution, and the 19th century saw the ascendancy of Providence as Rhode Island's chief city.

OF CHICKENS AND COSMOPOLITES

The first three-quarters of the 19th century were fairly quiet for Newport and the southern Narragansett Bay towns; as for Block Island, it had been in its own special cocoon since 1661. The area remained essentially rural and agrarian. While northern Rhode Island, Providence especially, was becoming urbanized and industrialized, with an influx of new immigrants to work the growing cotton, wool, and metal industries, the big event for the Narragansett Bay area was the breeding of the Rhode Island Red chicken. Between 1854 and 1896 a Little Compton farmer, William Tripp, worked with scientists and other area farmers to cross-breed the revolutionary fowl; it even has a monument, in the village of Adamsville.

The town of Bristol, burned by the British in 1775, had rebounded by 1820. The prosperity of the town was linked to that of the De Wolfs — the wealth of both can be gauged from Linden Place, George De Wolf's elaborate mansion at 500 Hope Street. But De Wolf over-speculated and in 1825 his financial empire

During the Revolutionary War, British General Prescott was captured here by American forces. It's been called Prescott Farm ever since.

Craig Hammell

collapsed. He and his family skipped town literally under cover of darkness for their Cuban estate, leaving Bristol reeling. Virtually the entire town went bankrupt overnight, and like Newport, never fully recovered.

While the western Bay communities of Narragansett and North Kingstown remained ensconced in the rural plantation system that encompassed much of "South County" (Rhode Island's southwesternmost county, officially called Washington), "real" plantation owners from the antebellum South were already arriving in Newport for "the season." As early as 1784 a group of planters from Charleston had begun to summer in the City by the Sea, fleeing Southern heat and malaria; by 1830 wealthy families from Virginia and South Carolina were returning year after year to spend the summer on rented farms or in big new boarding houses. Ironically, one of the most luxurious of these latter was the Sea Girt House, built in 1855 by George T. Downing, a distinguished black businessman who almost single-handedly persuaded the Rhode Island legislature to outlaw racial segregation in public schools (1866).

During the Civil War, the U.S. Navy transferred its academy from Annapolis to Newport; the Academy returned south after the hostilities were over, but Newport was compensated by being chosen as home to the prestigious Naval War College in 1884. Newport remains the Navy's premier educational center, with adjuncts to the War College such as the Naval Justice School having been added over the years.

Not surprisingly, the Southerners didn't return to summer in Newport after the Civil War. They were replaced in the 1840s by a band of "slightly disenchanted cosmopolites," in the words of Henry James. These were the people Newporters dubbed "the nice millionaires." Luminaries like James, Edith Wharton, Henry Wadsworth Longfellow, Oliver Wendell Holmes, John Singer Sargent, and Julia Ward Howe headed a group of Boston artists and intellectuals who descended for the summer to think deeply beside the sea. But their holiday court wasn't in session long: soon the New York crowd began to arrive and the Brahmins beat a quick retreat. Of the reasons for their departure, Edith Wharton simply said, "I did not care for watering-place mundanities."

THE PLAYGROUND OF THE GREAT ONES OF THE EARTH

A void Newport like the plague until you are certain you will be acceptable there. If you don't it will be your Waterloo."

By the time Harry Lehr uttered this advice to would-be social climbers, Newport had already become what William McLoughlin called "the most palatial, extravagant, and expensive summer resort the world had seen since the days of the Roman Empire." Credit for transplanting New York society to Newport for the summer generally goes to Samuel Ward McAllister, known behind his back as "Mr. Make-a-lister." McAllister is the one who came up with the term "The Four Hundred," referring to the number of people in New York worth knowing. There were, according to his calculations, "about four hundred people in fashionable New York Society. If you go outside that number you strike people who are either not at ease in a ballroom or make other people not at ease."

The real arbiters of this crowd were women. Shut out of the business world in which their husbands were kings (or robber barons to the press), wealthy wives set themselves up as queens in a seaside court of their own devising. The rules of entry were stringent and byzantine. According to one socialite, "Newport was the very Holy of Holies, the playground of the great ones of the earth from which all intruders were ruthlessly excluded by a set of cast-iron rules." If you got in at all it usually took at least two seasons. Neophytes were advised to spend a summer at Bar Harbor first, honing their skills. Once in town, however, there was protocol to learn: don't build a "cottage" immediately, rent first; never out-jewel or out-dress your hostess; never actually enter the home of a lady upon whom you've called — just leave your card. Above all, try to be as idle as possible in the city where, according to Oscar Wilde, "idleness ranks among the virtues."

However frivolous, such a lifestyle required an immense amount of managerial skill. Again in McLoughlin's words, these women "were not brainless big-spenders, but talented, shrewd, and forceful administrators." To live out a life of "conspicuous consumption" — a term Thorstein Veblen coined in his 1899 work *The Theory of the Leisure Class* — one needed vast amounts of capital and the courage to spend it. The average "cottage," which in truth was more like a private resort hotel, had between fifty to seventy rooms and up to one hundred servants — with twice that number hired for special occasions. Ten-course dinners with solid gold service were held nightly (unimaginably consumed by people in corsets); one ball could cost as much as $200,000 — and that was when money was worth more; one 1890 dollar equals one hundred dollars today.

All of this took stamina as well. Bessie Drexel, who was unhappily married to the court jester of Newport society, Harry Lehr, wrote in her autobiography *King Lehr and the Gilded Age*, "Every summer Harry and I went to Newport like everyone else in our world, for in those days so much prestige was attached to spending July and August at the most exclusive resort in America that to have neglected to do so would have exposed a definite gap in one's social armor." Some were better at the game than others. Some were terrifying. Alice "of the Breakers" Vanderbilt used to don immaculate white gloves every morning and run her fingers over the tops of picture frames and stair railings. Heads rolled if they came away less than white. Alice had her kinder and gentler moments as well. In the middle of dinner she once ordered a pair of scissors and cut off a third of her pearls, then worth $200,000. She handed them to her pearl-less daughter-in-law, mother of "Little Gloria," and said, Here, take them. All Vanderbilt women have pearls."

The "Great Triumvirate" of women who ruled Newport society in the 1890s were Alva Vanderbilt Belmont, Tessie Oelrichs, and Mamie Fish. (Corresponding mansions include Marble House and Belcourt Castle for Alva, Rosecliff for Tessie, and Crossways for Mamie). Tessie's greatest coup was simply to get to Newport at all. From birth in a mining camp — her father unearthed the Comstock Lode — she wound up not only on Bellevue Avenue (*the* Newport address), but in Rosecliff, arguably the most elegant mansion of all. Mamie was the best party-giver of the lot. It was she, with encouragement from Harry

In their finery: Miss Minnie Stevens, later Lady Paget, and Perry Belmont, who built Belcourt Castle on Bellevue Avenue in Newport, outfitted for a Gilded Age costume ball. (Both photos Courtesy Newport Historical Society)

Lehr, who threw the "Dogs Dinner," to which one hundred society dogs were invited to dine on stewed liver, rice, and fricassee of bones. News of this hit the papers during the country-wide recession of the mid-1890s — needless to say it did not go down well on editorial pages.

Alva's greatest achievement came in marriage-brokering. That many dabbled in this pastime is evident from the spreadsheets: by 1909 five hundred American heiresses were married to titled Europeans (the chief catch) with dowries totaling $220 million. But Alva engineered society's greatest coup, persuading the Duke of Marlborough to marry her daughter Consuela in 1895 for a price of $10 million (it hardly matters that the marriage didn't last). Some men brokered for themselves, with less efficiency. John Jacob Astor VI finally let the courts decide to whom he was legally married (since there were so many contenders), but the prize goes to William Budlong, who divorced a total of 21 wives.

Newport men were decidedly less flamboyant than Newport women. Often they came only on the weekends, and then tended to be uncomfortable and ill-at-ease at teas and dinner parties. One notable exception was James Gordon Bennett, the New York publisher who famously sent Stanley to Africa to find Livingstone. Bennett not only had a yacht equipped with a full Turkish bath and a miniature dairy, and another bedecked with a full-size pipe organ, but used to drive his coach stark naked at midnight through the streets of Newport — "to breathe," he said. Bennett was also the driving force behind the Newport Casino, which he commissioned Stanford White to design in 1879. Then the first country club in America, the Casino was the original home of the U.S. Lawn Tennis Tournament and today houses the Tennis Hall of Fame.

In his book *The Barons of Newport*, Terence Gavan suggests that the excesses of the summer crowd stemmed from their "collective insecurities" in having become too rich too fast. There was a rush to create an aura of refinement and good taste with money that hadn't quite "cooled off," which is why Newport, with its understated colonial elegance and patrician architecture, became the resort of choice. More often than not this rush took the form of one-upmanship in jewels, yachts, clothes, and coaches, but more than anything else, in houses. The lasting legacy of the Great Ones of the Earth are their "cottages" on Bellevue Avenue and Ochre Point Road (many of these back up to the famous Cliff Walk), and Ocean Drive. The mansions are still, to use McLoughlin's term, "wondrous to behold," and thanks to organizations like the Preservation Society of Newport and Doris Duke's Newport Restoration Foundation, many are now restored and open for tours. Most are copies of Italian palazzos, Elizabethan country houses, French chateaux, and whatever else looked good and inspired awe.

Fittingly, when the cameras rolled on *The Great Gatsby* in 1973 (starring Robert Redford and Mia Farrow), they did so at Rosecliff, a copy of the Grand Trianon built for Louis XIV at Versailles. It's a bewildering and appropriately ironic legacy: a palace passed from the Sun King to a miner's daughter, rebuilt in an exclusive resort that was once the leading city in the most radically egalitarian of all thirteen original colonies; film site of Fitzgerald's great American myth, and today what Henry James called a white elephant, a tourist attraction. For little though they knew it at the time, Gilded Agers were ushering in what was to become a staple of Rhode Island's economy in the 20th century: tourism.

> What an idea . . . to have seen this miniature spot of earth, where the sea-nymphs on the carved sands . . . chanted back to the shepherds, as a mere breeding-ground for white elephants! They look queer and conscious and lumpish — some of them, as with an air of the brandished proboscis, really grotesque — while their averted owners, roused from a witless dream, wonder what in the world is to be done with them. The answer to which, I think, can only be that there is absolutely nothing to be done; nothing but to let them stand there always, vast and blank, for reminder . . . of the peculiarly awkward vengeances of affronted proportion and discretion.
>
> — Henry James, *The American Scene*, 1907

AMERICA'S FIRST RESORT

One of Rhode Island's nicknames for itself is "America's First Resort." While its northern cities were becoming rich on the fruits of industry, the towns along Narragansett Bay and the south coast were capitalizing on the latest popular fashion: the summer vacation. What began as a trend among the elite took hold in all strata of society, and Rhode Island was one of the first states to respond by offering a niche for just about everyone. The general rule was that the upper Bay, around Providence, was the in-state playground (more downscale), and the lower Bay the out-of-state playground (more upscale). The following thumbnail histories of how tourism has shaped or bypassed the towns covered in The Newport and Narragansett Bay Book will also give an overview of their character today.

A JOURNEY AROUND THE BAY

WEST BAY

In addition to Block Island, **Narragansett Pier** was Newport's only serious rival as a Gilded Age resort. It even had its own Stanford White-designed casino, built in 1886 but destroyed by fire in 1900. Today only the casino's decorative towers are still standing astride Ocean Road as a memorial to swankiness past. "Narragansett Pier" is really the oceanside village center of the

Courtesy Rhode Island Historical Society

The famous Narragansett Casino was a landmark on the coast at Narragansett Pier for only fourteen years: it burned down in 1900. Today only The Towers, on the left, remain.

sprawling municipality of Narragansett, which also includes the commercial fishing villages of **Point Judith** and **Galilee** (the Block Island ferry departs from the latter).

To the north, the village of **Wickford** in North Kingstown maintains an elegant little harbor and fine shops, also a legacy of popularity with a wealthy Gilded Age crowd, though sportier and less ostentatious. **East Greenwich** was never developed as a resort, and retains the quiet air of a fine old country seat. Like Wickford, it is full of 18th- and 19th-century homes, kept quietly in decent shape over the years rather than lavishly and recently restored.

The village of **Jamestown** on Conanicut Island has come to describe the whole place — the island is just "Jamestown" these days. While the Astors and the Vanderbilts were living it up in Newport, Jamestown was popular with a fashionable but "quietly rich" crowd who wanted to get away from it all. Their modest, mostly Shingle style estates cluster on Beaver Tail, the island's southern peninsula. Much of Jamestown is still rural and undeveloped — a small, well-kept secret between two big bridges (the Newport Bridge to the east and the Jamestown-Verrazzano Bridge to the west).

EAST BAY

The East Bay towns of Bristol and Warren were generally immune to the turn-of-the-century resort fever. **Bristol** did get one mansion erected by a renegade millionaire escaped from Newport: the elegant Blithewold, built by Augustus Van Wickle in 1908 on 33 acres now maintained as a park and arboretum. It was Bristol's good luck to be home to the Haffenreffer family, who donated 500 acres known as Mount Hope to Brown University (site of the Haffenreffer Museum of Anthropology) and thus spared the town further development. Mount Hope is the anglicized version of "Montaup," the Wampanoags' name for this land.

It has been said, accurately, "He who would live in a dream of fair houses should go to Bristol and pitch his tent there." These fair houses have always been occupied year-round, so over the years there was virtually no room in town for summer people to pitch their tents. They did come, however, from 1863 to 1946, to commission yachts from the world-famous Herreshoff Boatyard. Herreshoff-designed yachts dominated America's Cup competition in the days when contenders where enormous racing machines up to 144 feet long and sailed by 66-man crews.

Warren has always been a little overshadowed by its somewhat fancier southern neighbor. The homes are slightly more modest if just as old (federal-style clapboards versus magnificent Greek Revival temples), and are often hidden beneath asphalt shingles and aluminum siding. But Warren still offers something that few other Bay towns retain — the charm of discovery. An evening stroll on Water Street in summer is akin to putting your guidebook away in a European capital and wandering into an uncharted neighborhood. It's where the locals go and where no one cares that the sidewalk café is just a few blocks down from the seafood plant. (And many of the townspeople still speak some Portuguese — from the 1850s throughout the early 20th century, large numbers of Portuguese and Italian immigrants settled in both Warren and Bristol.)

AQUIDNECK

Except for strip-like stretches along Aquidneck's two north-south axes (routes 138 and 114), much of **Portsmouth** and **Middletown** still offers a quiet contrast to the exuberance of Newport. In fact, these two northern communities are hardly towns, with their stretches of farmland haphazardly ringed by stone walls — protected by the National Trust — which arch over the island and meander down to both eastern and western shores. Those who built country estates here hid them at the end of narrow lanes (one such is Green Animals, which boasts perhaps the best topiary gardens in the country). Since the Gilded Age, upper Aquidneck seems to have taken on the role of foil to Newport, a necessary haven of peace and quiet and potato and tree farms after a day at a Newport mansion.

Quietest of all are the inner Bay islands of Hog and Prudence, administered by the town of Portsmouth. **Hog**, one-and-a-half square miles and less than two miles from Bristol harbor, has only a seasonal ferry and its 200 summer residents have no public electricity; **Prudence**, much bigger at about five square miles with a year-round ferry from Bristol (only a twenty-minute ride), still has no hotel and just one general store. Prudence was a thriving farming community before the Revolution, but was burned by the British in the war;

like Bristol and Newport it never really recovered. Today the island is full of deer and of abandoned stone walls making a latticework through the woods that have overgrown tilled land.

Meanwhile, down at Aquidneck's southern tip, after a half-century of relative quiet, **Newport** is back in full swing. It is a more balanced town now than it was during the Gilded Age. In addition to Bellevue Avenue, the Cliff Walk and, of course, the mansions — six of which are operated by the Newport Preservation Society — the old colonial city has come back into its own. In the Point Section near Newport Bridge, and between Bellevue Avenue and historic Thames Street (the "th" is pronounced and rhymes with "games" — not like the London river) are a host of wonderfully restored 18th-century clapboard homes. Beginning in 1962, the Redevelopment Agency of Newport took on the project of reclaiming Thames Street (just a block up from the Harbor) and the wharf area, concentrating on 17th-century Long Wharf and the 18th-century Brick Market building. The agency also added a new street, America's Cup Avenue, and today the whole Harbor area bustles with shops and chic restaurants, bars, marinas, and outdoor festivals. Moored offshore are the magnificent yachts and sailboats you'd expect to find in America's preeminent sailing city.

SAKONNET

The fact that Rhode Island is the smallest and second most densely populated state in the union only makes the Sakonnet area more remarkable. There are no pockets of strip malls in **Tiverton** or Little Compton, no supermarkets or big fancy restaurants, no movie theaters or convenience stores, even. This thin peel of land between the eastern arm of the Bay and the Massachusetts border was deeded to Rhode Island in 1747 (along with Warren and Bristol) as part of a land settlement with Massachusetts Bay. It's an area blessed by a rich partnership between farmlands and the sea, and it's not much of an exaggeration to say that it probably doesn't look much different than it did when Tiverton and Little Compton first became part of Rhode Island over 200 years ago.

Little Compton has had its own summer colony for ages, but it was never part of the resort network. Today's "summer people" are more on the order of the southern families who first came to Newport in the late 18th and early 19th centuries — quiet country-lovers who rent or own old colonial farmhouses. A clue to both the charm and aloofness of this area is that its best beach, Goosewing, not only has no parking but no access by car. Little Compton's historic village center, called The Commons, is the loveliest in the state.

BLOCK ISLAND

Block Island — former home of the Manisseeans' "little god," nicknamed "the stumbling block" by sailors — is just three miles wide by seven miles long, ten miles off the coast of Point Judith and marooned in the open ocean. It

A 19th-century fishing fleet on Block Island.

Courtesy Block Island Historical Society

boasts Mohegan Bluffs, claimed to be the highest sea cliffs in New England, and a distinctly Old World feel, as if the island just recently broke off the Irish coast and floated to this side of the Atlantic.

Block first emerged from its two-century cocoon in the 1870s, when islanders finally persuaded the government to build a breakwater now known as Old Harbor; before that, no natural harbor existed. The project effectively issued an invitation for "off-islanders" to come and visit.

And they did. By 1900, Block Island was in full swing as an elite resort, with thirty hotels and over two thousand summer visitors a day. Families interested in sporty pursuits like sailing and fishing and "taking the waters" at the Spring House, rather than in conspicuous consumption, came here instead of Newport. More than any other resort in the state, Block Island epitomized a kind of

A Victorian beach party on Block Island.

Courtesy Block Island Historical Society

*The Spring House Hotel in
the late 19th century.*

Courtesy Block Island Historical Society

national romance with the past that attended the 1876 Centennial. People
bewildered by incomprehensible new technologies and rapidly changing cities
sought places that filtered out modern life and preserved "the good old days."
Thanks to its isolation, Block Island was such a place par excellence.

The result was a four-decade boom of houses and hotels of shingle and clapboard around Old and New Harbor, bedecked with mansard roofs, wraparound porches, and gingerbread trim. After the World War I, however, Block
Island fell into a Sleeping Beauty-like phase from which it didn't awaken until
the 1970s. During that time, the island was decimated by the 1938 hurricane,
after which virtually all its cultivated fields were left to overgrowths of wild
bayberry, exactly as they remain today. When Block Island awoke, visitors
were again treated to a rare glimpse of the past, this time as an archive of Victorian architecture perfectly preserved in rambling hotels and the shingled tur-
rets of beach cottages.

Today Block is once again a hopping place to be, with visitors in pursuit of a
latter-day version of the nostalgia our ancestors sought a century ago. Thanks
to a recent zoning law designed to protect the island's open space, new construction is limited to sizable lots, on which big "post-modern" beach houses
are being built — our legacy to the next century. Most promising, however, is
that Block Island was named by the Nature Conservancy as one of the Western
Hemisphere's "Twelve Last Great Places," an honor it shares with such glamorous locales as the Amazon Rain Forest. Not bad for a little island off the lit-
tlest state.

CHAPTER TWO
Between the Bridges
TRANSPORTATION

Think of Narragansett Bay and its islands as a patchwork quilt, green and blue, held together by steel and concrete threads in the form of bridges. Think of the ferries as needles having to re-sew perpetually split seams, and you should have a good understanding (and appreciation) of the Bay and its transportation systems.

Over the years the best way to get around Narragansett Bay and Block Island Sound has been, of course, by boat. The waters have accommodated commuters, in everything from canoes, a form favored by both

Craig Hammell

Masts and cables — Newport Harbor and the Newport Bridge.

Native Americans and early settlers — the latter used them to commute to what amounted to 17th-century business meetings — to the Fall River steamships that carried businessmen to and from Newport when "the season" was in swing. Ships of trade — on which many a passenger hitched a ride — have plied the Bay as well, most romantically the great, square-rigged China clippers of the 19th century.

Ever since the commodores of the Gilded Age made Newport the yachting capital of the world, most of the craft afloat on the Bay have been pleasure boats participating in the scores of races and regattas held throughout the summer.

For the boatless, the Bay can be bit trickier to navigate. To get from Narragansett Pier to Sakonnet Point in Little Compton, for example, a distance of only 12 miles, you must cross the Jamestown-Verrazzano Bridge, traverse

Conanicut Island, cross the Newport Bridge, drive the length of Aquidneck, cross the Sakonnet Bridge, then drive the length of Rhode Island's eastern shore, finally arriving in Little Compton about an hour later. It seems easier to swim, but then you'd miss out on the rolling landscape, historic homes, pastures, roadside vegetable stands, and the classic Bay-side seafood places that make the landward journey such a pleasure.

GETTING TO THE NARRAGANSETT BAY AREA

BY CAR

From South and West (New Jersey, New York, Connecticut): Take I-95 to RI exit 3; pick up Rte. 138 E. to Jamestown Bridge, cross Conanicut Island and continue to Newport (still on 138) via the Newport Bridge (toll $2.00).

From North (through Providence): Get to Newport by heading down either the eastern or western sides of Narragansett Bay. The eastern route is slightly faster.

Eastern route: Take I-95 to I-195 E. into Massachusetts; at MA exit 2 follow Rte. 136 S., which will lead you back into Rhode Island and eventually to the Mt. Hope Bridge (toll 30¢; before reaching the bridge, if you wish to drive through the charming town of Bristol simply take any right-hand turn off 136 after you cross the Warren/Bristol line; any of these turns will lead to T-junctions on Rte. 114; turn left; 114 parallels 136 and also brings you to the Mt. Hope Bridge).

Once on Aquidneck continue on either Rte. 114 or 138 S. to Newport (138 has less traffic; take it to a left turn onto 138A, also known as Aquidneck Avenue; follow this until it becomes Memorial Drive at the Newport/Middletown line. Easton Beach will be on your left. At the top of the hill Memorial intersects Bellevue Avenue; the mansions are to the left). A minor alternative is to remain on I-195 until MA exit 6, where you can take Rte. 24 S. across the Sakonnet River and pick up 138 or 114 once on Aquidneck. Some say this is faster.

Western route: Take I-95 S. from Providence to exit 9 where the highway splits; bear left onto Rte. 4 S. which feeds directly into Rte. 1 S. Take 138 E. to the Jamestown Bridge and across Conanicut Island, over the Newport Bridge (toll $2.00) to Newport. If you wish to head south to Narragansett instead of east to Newport, continue on Rte. 1 to Bridgetown Road which leads to Scenic Rte. 1A S. This will take you directly to Narragansett Pier.

From North and East (through Boston and Fall River): From the Boston area follow Rte. 24 S. through Fall River, over the Sakonnet River bridge (at which point you'll be in Rhode Island), and onto Aquidneck. Then see *Eastern route* directions under **From the North** beginning at "Once on Aquidneck. . . ." If you're arriving from the east take I-195 W. until MA exit 6, which puts you onto Rte. 24 S.

BY BUS

Rhode Island Public Transit Authority (RIPTA) runs several direct buses between Providence and Newport from 5:30am to 11:05pm daily. Call 781-9400 (in Providence), 847-0209 (in Newport) or 800-662-5088 for schedule information and other destinations throughout the Narragansett Bay area.

RIPTA arrives in Newport at the Gateway Convention & Visitors' Bureau at 23 America's Cup Avenue, as does Bonanza Bus Lines (846-1820 in Newport, 751-8800 in Providence, or 800-556-3815). Bonanza has direct daily service to or from Boston and connections to and from all points in New England (including Cape Cod) and New York City.

BY PLANE

To travel to the Narragansett Bay area by plane, the best bet is to fly into T.F. Green State Airport in Warwick, Rhode Island (Post Rd./Rte. 1, 737-4000). It's small, uncrowded, efficient, has inexpensive, ample parking (but, alas, only one parking lot toll gate — sometimes you have to wait 10 minutes or so to pay and get out), and best of all, when you leave the airport you don't sit in traffic but have immediate access onto a traffic-free stretch of I-95. The other option for arriving on a regularly scheduled flight is to fly into Logan Airport (617-542-6700) in Boston, which is and has none of the above, and after leaving Logan you may sit in traffic in the Sumner Tunnel. Then there's the hour drive just to get from Boston to Providence.

The following airlines serve T.F. Green:

American (800-433-7300)

American Eagle (800-433-7300)

Business Express (800-345-3400)

Continental (800-525-0280)

Delta (800-221-1212)

Northwest (800-225-2525)

USAir (274-5600)

US Air Express (274-5600)

United (800-241-6522)

Airport transfer services: The only scheduled limousine shuttle service between T.F. Green and Newport is run by *Cozy Cab* (846-2500/1500), although both *Newport Scenic Tours* (849-8670) and *Viking Tours & Transportation* (847-6921) offer airport transfer service to Newport as well. For group travel to and from the airport try *Laidlaw Transit, Inc.* (245-1100, 800-782-4065) for inexpensive group rates. The airport is about 40 minutes from Newport by car.

Rental car companies at T.F. Green Airport include the following:

Alamo (800-327-9633)

Avis (736-7500)

Budget (739-0487)

Hertz (738-7500)

National (737-4800; office is across the street, with shuttle service to/from the terminal)

Thrifty (732-2000)

Sears (739-8908)

United (732-6180; office is across the street, with shuttle service to/from the terminal)

There are several other small, state-run airports throughout Rhode Island. There are no scheduled flights arriving at the **Newport State Airport** in Middletown (846-2200), but it does serve charters and private aircraft. The **Quonset State Airport** in North Kingstown (294-4504) also serves some corporate and private planes, though principally naval craft. See the section on Block Island transportation below for information about flights to and from the island.

BY TRAIN

There are three **Amtrak** (800-872-7245) stations in Rhode Island: Westerly, Kingston (the best bet for those en route to Newport) and Providence. Newport-based *Cozy Cab, Newport Scenic Tours,* and *Viking Tours & Transportation* (see the By Plane section above, airport transfer services, for telephone numbers) all provide limousine service to and from Kingston and Providence stations. RIPTA also runs regularly scheduled buses from Kingston to Newport. See information in By Bus above.

The docks of Galilee in Narragansett, home to Rhode Island's commercial fishing fleet.

Craig Hammell

NARRAGANSETT BAY ACCESS

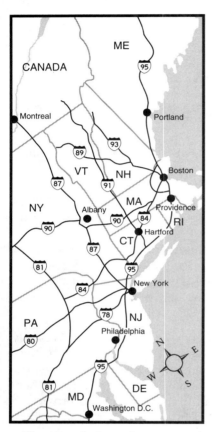

The chart below gives approximate miles and driving times from the following cities to Newport:

City	Time	Miles
Albany	3.5 hours	185
Boston	1.25 hours	65
Hartford	1.5 hours	85
Hyannis	2 hours	105
Montreal	7 hours	365
New York	3.5 hours	175
Philadelphia	5 hours	270
Portland	3 hours	175
Providence	45 minutes	35
Washington, D.C.	7.5 hours	400

GETTING AROUND NARRAGANSETT BAY

BY CAR & PARKING

There's no way around it: the car, for all its faults, is the best non-aquatic way to explore the Narragansett Bay area. However, eventually you have to park the car somewhere. In Newport, that can be a problem.

Seasoned travelers who claim that Newport is one of their favorite places on earth nevertheless single out parking as the city's chief hitch for visitors. The Visitors' Bureau recommends (naturally) the lot directly behind their Newport Gateway center at 23 America's Cup Avenue, which has a capacity of 1000+ cars. All-day parking costs only $8, but it's a substantial hike from here to the Cliff Walk. There are several wharf lots nearby in the heart of the Thames Street and Newport Harbor shopping district, but these are smaller and fill up fast; the same goes for the lot in front of the Newport Creamery on Bellevue Avenue, directly opposite the Tennis Hall of Fame (it's great for mansion touring, if you can get in).

Be careful parking on the street: many areas require a residential permit and others are limited to one or two hours, all strictly enforced. That said, here's a tip as to the best parking place in town. Spring Street is parallel to and runs between Thames and Bellevue; it's also one-way in a northward direction. Drive south on Bellevue and turn right on any through street after The Elms mansion, then take the first right onto Spring. In the morning there is ample street parking here without any restrictions. Not only is it equidistant to the Cliff Walk and Newport Harbor, but the walk to the latter is delightful: you can set out down Spring, which is lined with 18th- and 19th-century clapboard homes (the side streets too), and return along lower Thames, which is full of funky shops and fine restaurants that many tourists miss.

Another tip: keep calm if you get lost in the Sakonnet region. The town of Little Compton seems to have an aversion to road signs, but the area is so beautiful that it's fun to prowl a little bit even if you don't know where you're going.

For additional advice on getting around the Bay on land, or for roadside assistance, try **AAA** offices in the following towns:

- **Middletown** (841-5000)
- **Narragansett** (789-3000)
- **Providence** (272-6353)
- **Warwick** (732-5100)

BY FERRY

Ferries to **Prudence and Hog islands** leave from Church Street Wharf in Bristol. Call 253-9808 for schedule information. The Prudence crossing takes 20 minutes; ferries run year-round to and from the village of Homestead on the island. On select days in season the ferry makes stops at Hog Island as well; the crossing to Hog takes 10 minutes.

The famed Jamestown Ferry was retired in 1969, but in the summer of 1993, ferry service between **Jamestown and Newport** was revived by industrious Jamestown resident and college student Paul Sprague. His 28-foot wooden boat makes hourly crossings beginning at 8am daily (in summer only), and is a great way to escape sitting in traffic on the bridge.

Narragansett Bay Bridges

Scenario: two figures walking along the beach. The outline of a bridge looms in the distance, hazy across the water. One bends to ask the other something. A romantic moment? Possibly, but more probably the question was, "Now, which one is that?"

This refrain — Which bridge did you say that was? — can be heard up and down Narragansett Bay. Bridges make the Bay a network of fascinating, related, and diverse components. But with four principal bridges, telling them apart can sometimes be difficult. Here's a short guide:

The Newport Bridge connects Newport (the southwestern peninsula of Aquidneck) with the eastern shore of Jamestown. It is just over 2 miles long and is considered "Narragansett Bay's most spectacular man-made sight." When the bridge was opened in June, 1969, it retired the Jamestown Ferry, which had provided the oldest continuous ferry service in the country. The same family (the Carrs) had participated in the running of the ferry for almost 300 years. The real name of the Newport Bridge (a great trivia question) is the Claiborne Pell Bridge; 1,441,200 vehicles crossed its span during July and August, 1993.

The Jamestown-Verrazzano Bridge connects the western shore of Jamestown to the eastern shore of the Rhode Island mainland, about 3 miles south of Wickford. This brand new bridge, which has a span of about 650 feet, opened in 1992. It replaced the Jamestown Bridge which had been built in 1940 (Rhode Islanders call the new one the Jamestown Bridge, too). Ask locals about the near mythical snafu over how long it took to build the J-V Bridge — it's a typical Rhode Island saga.

The Mount Hope Bridge connects the Rhode Island mainland at the Bristol peninsula to the northern tip of Aquidneck. The precipitous Mount Hope Bridge was built in 1929, replacing a ferry that had run between Bristol and Portsmouth since 1698. At the time, its main span of 1200 feet made it the eighth largest suspension bridge in the world (and also the first ever to be painted — it's green). In 1930 the bridge received an American Institute of Steel Construction Award as the most beautiful bridge in its class. Note the wonderful gas-lamp-style streetlights.

The Sakonnet Bridge connects the northeastern tip of Aquidneck (an area called The Hummocks in Portsmouth) to the town of Tiverton on the easternmost strip of Rhode Island. The bridge, built in 1956, is short, but has a much longer history. Three previous drawbridges existed in its place between 1794 and 1957, all called Stone Bridge. The stretch of the Sakonnet River they spanned has always been known as Howland's Ferry, in honor of the previous form of river crossing.

The **Oldport Marine Harbor Ferry** (847-9190) plies Newport Harbor daily from 10am–8pm, with stops at Goat Island, Fort Adams, the Ida Lewis Yacht Club, and other locations.

BY PRIVATE BOAT

For information on state guest moorings and rental slips, see the listings in the Marina section in the *Recreation* chapter, under Sailing and Boating.

BLOCK ISLAND

Oxen teams at Old Harbor, Block Island.

Courtesy Block Island Historical Society

BY FERRY

There are several options for arriving on Block by ferry. Between them they present a fair range of embarkation ports and travel times.

Interstate Navigation Company (in New London, Connecticut 203-442-7891/9553; in Galilee, Rhode Island 783-4613) Runs seasonal ferries from Providence (4 hours), Newport (2 hours), and New London (2 hours), plus a year-round boat from Galilee State Pier (1 hour, 10 minutes). Cars are allowed only on the Galilee and New London boats, and reservations are absolutely necessary. All ferries arrive/depart Old Harbor, Block Island.

Jigger III (in New York 516-668-2214) Runs seasonal service mid-June–Sept. The boat leaves Montauk Point, Long Island at 9:30am daily, and returns from New Harbor, Block Island at 4:30pm. Crossing time is 2 hours.

Viking Fleet (in New York 516-668-5709) Seasonal daily service from June–Labor Day, weekend service from Apr.–June and Sept.–Oct. Boats leave Montauk Point at 9am and arrive 2 hours later in New Harbor, Block Island; leave New Harbor at 4:30pm.

Note that the Montauk ferries are for passengers only (no cars), though they do accept bicycles.

For passengers arriving at T.F. Green State Airport bound for the Galilee ferry, there are daily Rhode Island Public Transit Authority (RIPTA) buses from the airport to the Galilee dock; all require one transfer at Wakefield. The same goes for ferry-bound folk arriving on Amtrak at the Kingston station. Call RIPTA at 781-9400 in Providence or 800-662-5088 for schedule information.

Private Chauffeur Service (783-9369) also offers transportation to the Galilee dock.

BY CAR TO THE GALILEE FERRY

Coming from the north or south it's about a 30 minute drive from I-95 to the Block Island boat at Galilee. Be sure to arrive *at least* half an hour before departure time: there is often a line at both the parking lot (across the street from the dock) and the ticket window. If seasickness depends on where you sit on the ferry, arrive an hour in advance to get choice locations.

From the North: I-95 S. splits at RI exit 9; bear to the left onto Rte. 4 S. which leads directly into Rte. 1 S.; from there take exit for Rte. 108 S.; continue approximately 3 miles to the right-hand turn for the Block Island Ferry.

From the South: Take CT exit 92 from I-95 and bear right onto Rte. 2 (N. Stonington Road); take right-hand turn onto Rte. 78; at end of 78 take left onto Rte. 1 N. and continue until exit for Rte. 108 S.; continue 3 miles to the right-hand turn for the Block Island Ferry.

BY PRIVATE BOAT

For public docking facilities on Block Island, see Marinas in the Recreation chapter, under Sailing and Boating.

BY PLANE

There are regularly scheduled flights between Block Island and Westerly, Rhode Island, as well as Groton, Connecticut.

Action Airlines has both scheduled and charter service year-round to Block from the Groton/New London area. Call 203-448-1646 or 800-243-8623 for information.

New England Airlines (596-2460 in Westerly, 466-5881 on Block Island, or 800-243-2460) flies hourly to Block Island from the **Westerly State Airport** (596-2357/6312).

Charter service only is provided by **Long Island Airways** (516-537-1010) between Block and East Hampton, Long Island.

For information on flights and weather conditions contact the **Block Island State Airport** at 466-5511.

ONCE ON BLOCK ISLAND

At first it may seem like an inconvenience, but believe me, you'll soon be glad there are virtually no cars for rent on Block Island. It's too small and too full of people (and of rare species unique to the island like the small, furry creature called the Block Island vole) to warrant a lot of cars and exhaust fumes. Islanders complain that motor traffic is dangerous and frightens the wildlife, and they're probably right. By far the best way to see Block Island is by bike or on foot. Sure, some of the hills are tough, but the pleasures of smelling and hearing the island, as opposed to catching a quick glimpse of it, far outweigh the extra exertion.

True to Block's nickname "The Bermuda of the North," there are mopeds available for rent as well as bikes and taxis. For bike, moped, and water sport rentals see Chapter Six, *Recreation*.

For taxi service on Block Island, try **Cathy Payne** (466-5572), **The Colonel** (466-2235), **Lady Bird Taxi** (782-5796–mobile phone), **Minute Man Taxi** (466-3131), **OJ's Taxi** (466-2872; 782-5826–mobile phone), **Sam's Van** (466-2585; 782-5661–mobile phone), **Swamp Fox** (466-2431), **Uncle Tim's** (466-5060), or **Wolfie's Taxi** (466-5550). There are always a small pack of cabs awaiting scheduled ferry arrivals.

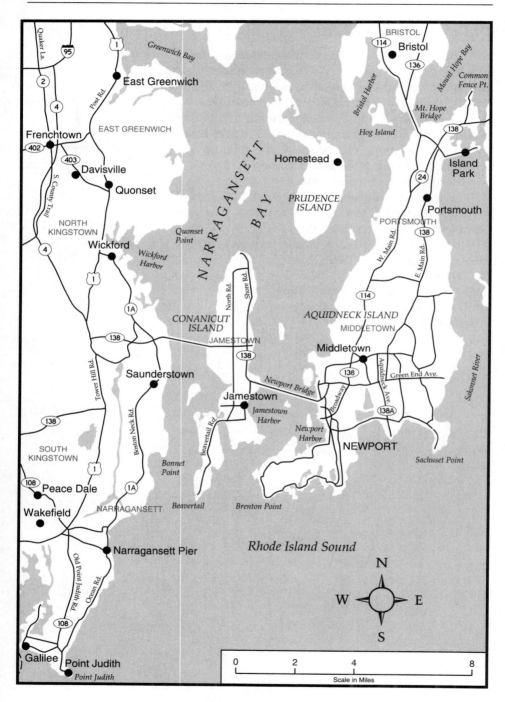

West Bay and Aquidneck

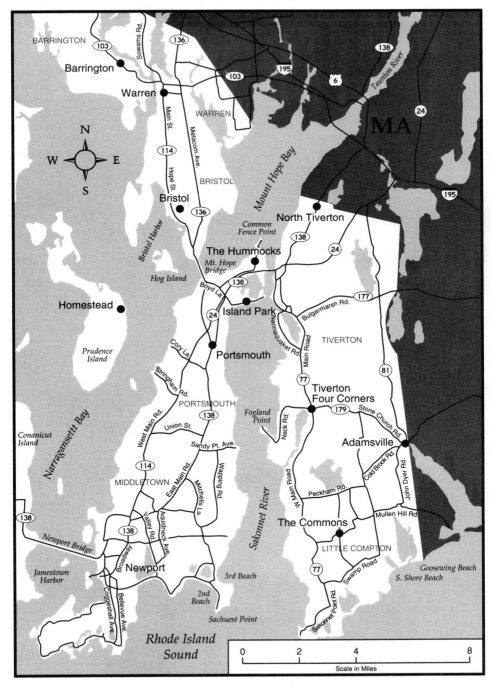

East Bay and Sakonnet

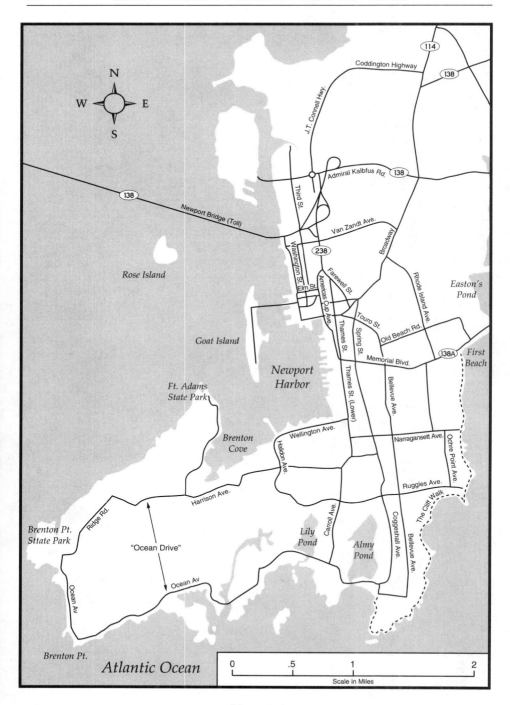

Newport

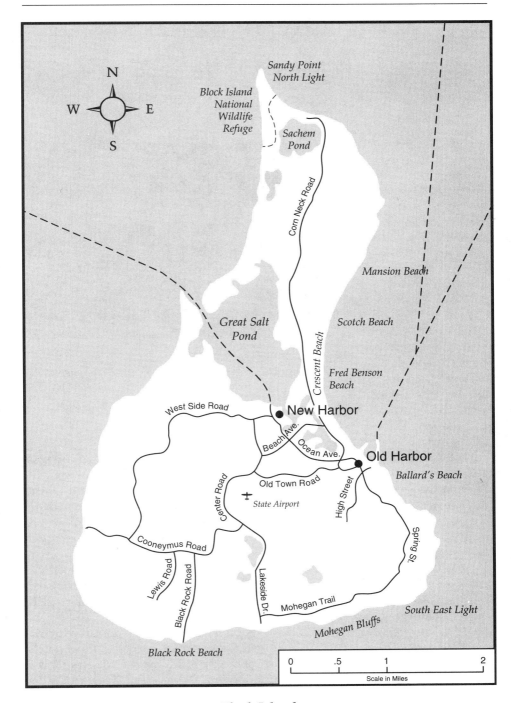

Block Island

CHAPTER THREE
Sleeping by the Sea
LODGING

In 1945, Newport submitted a proposal to the United Nations that it set up headquarters in the City by the Sea. The report boasted that Newport had seven resort hotels. Times have changed. Newport now has more "Bed & Breakfast" establishments than any other city in the country. San Francisco, a much bigger place, comes in second.

Why? It comes down to an intersection of architecture and culture and the sea. The city is brimming with substantial old homes, from early colonials to late 19th-century Queen Anne cottages.

Craig Hammell

There are few better places for rocking chairs and contemplation than an open porch overlooking the sea — especially at the Surf Hotel on Block Island.

These homes suit the mood of a city that offers music festivals, yachting regattas, and tennis and polo championships as its seasonal entertainment, not to mention a stunning coastline, alternately rugged and sandy. Homeowners are happy to open up a room or two for enthusiasts of these pastimes, and just as happy to reclaim their territory come winter — though many B&Bs are open year-round.

Which brings up an issue. "Bed & Breakfast" in this book refers to European-style lodging in a home — in other words, the home came first, the business came later. Many larger inns call themselves B&Bs, but when an establishment is really an inn, it's listed here as such.

Given the overwhelming number of good lodgings in Newport, the following list has had to be selective: it offers a cross-section of B&Bs, inns, hotels, and some good motels, with a a range of prices, locations, and decors. This is also the case for the other towns around the Bay. While lodging is scarce in the Sakonnet region, there are more options in the East Bay and even more in the West, Narragansett in particular (another haven of late 19th-century seaside architecture). Block Island, however, offers an architectural feast of big old Victorian hotels, built c. 1870–1910, when the island enjoyed its first heyday as a seaside resort. These old inns have huge wraparound porches ideal for sitting in a rocking chair and watching the ocean for hours.

LODGING NOTES

Tax. Most prices are quoted without the 7% Rhode Island sales tax; to that add another 5% room (also called bed) tax. If the full 12% tax is included in the price, this is noted.

Parking. When making a reservation in Newport always ask about free off-street parking.

Minimum stay. Most establishments, large and small, have minimum stay requirements (though they tend to be flexible if it's been raining all summer). Check first; it's usually two nights in season, three on holiday or festival weekends.

Deposit/Cancellation. Requirements vary, but most places ask for payment of at least one night's stay in advance. If you book through a reservation service, you can usually reserve by putting the first night on a credit card, and pay the rest by cash or check to the owner when you arrive.

Handicap access. This chapter's assessment of what is and is not accessible at each lodging is more casual than recently established government regulations — which few inns, especially those in old houses, can meet. Be sure to ask about your specific requirements.

When to book. It's always a good idea to reserve early, particularly for Block Island: holidays, such as the 4th of July, are often fully booked by January. Start planning early.

Prices. All rates listed are based on one night, double occupancy (most rooms are doubles), and reflect high season prices (generally from Memorial to Labor Day). Off-season rates are substantially lower. In the few cases that breakfast is not included, this is noted.

Refunds. Make a point of asking about refund policies due to weather; for example, for Block Island, many inns expect guests to reach the island by ferry if flights are canceled (and vice versa).

Reservation Services. The following services are free to folks trying to hunt down a room in Newport or other destinations in the Bay area. They represent scores of wonderful small B&Bs that deal exclusively through the service (and therefore are not included here), as well as many that are in these listings. (A reservation service that will cover as many as 30 small B&Bs is in the works for Block Island).

Anna's Victorian Connection (846-2489; 5 Fowler Ave., Newport 02840) Predominately Newport.

Bed & Breakfast, Newport (846-5408; 33 Russell Ave., Newport 02840) Deals mainly with Newport but covers most of Aquidneck as well. Many small, exclusive B&Bs not listed elsewhere.

Bed & Breakfast of Rhode Island (849-1298; PO Box 3291, Newport 02840) Covers the entire state.

Block Island Chamber of Commerce (466-2982; Drawer D, Block Island 02807) Ask for Alva; she knows.

Narragansett Chamber of Commerce (783-7121; The Towers, Ocean Rd., Narragansett 02882).

Taylor-Made Reservations of Newport (848-0300; 800-848-8848; 16 Mary St., Newport 02840) Lodging and concierge service (for restaurants, mansions, etc.) for Newport, the rest of Aquidneck, and Block Island. Handles mainly larger B&Bs, inns, hotels, and time-shares.

Lodging Price Code

Inexpensive	Under $50
Moderate	$50 to $100
Expensive	$100 to $180
Very Expensive	Over $180

Credit Cards

AE — American Express
CB — Carte Blanche
D — Discover
DC — Diners Club
MC — MasterCard
V — Visa

WEST BAY

Jamestown

BAY VOYAGE INN
Manager: John Ludwick.
847-9780; 800-225-3522.
150 Conanicus Ave.,
Jamestown 02840.
Open: Year-round.
Price: Moderate to Very
Expensive.
Credit Cards: AE, DC, MC,
V.
Smoking: Yes.
Handicap Access: Yes.

The name "Bay Voyage" literally describes the history of this Shingle style beach "cottage," which was hauled across the Bay by steamer from Middletown in 1889 (the owner thought James-town more exclusive). Today its one-bedroom suites are appointed with colonial-style furniture, TVs, telephones, and kitchenettes with microwaves and coffee makers. Bay-view rooms have a small balcony and a magnificent view. Continental breakfast is served in the dining room, which is

The Bay Voyage Inn in Jamestown was originally built in Middletown and barged across the Bay — hence the name.

Craig Hammell

Note: No pets.
Special Features: Outdoor pool, exercise room, Jacuzzi.

JAMESTOWN B&B
Owner: Mary Murphy.
423-1338.
59 Walcott Ave., Jamestown 02835 (no sign).
Open: Year-round.
Price: Moderate.
Credit Cards: None.
Smoking: Not encouraged.
Handicap Access: No.
Note: No pets.

LIONEL CHAMPLIN HOUSE
Owners: Joyce & Dick Allphin.
423-2782.
20 Lincoln St., Jamestown 02835.
Open: Year-round.
Price: Moderate.
Credit Cards: None.
Smoking: On porch only.
Handicap Access: No.
Note: No pets.

open to the public for dinner and sumptuous Sunday brunch. Ask about the "buy-back" token policy for the otherwise expensive ($2 each way) Newport Bridge.

Mary's home near Jamestown village is comfortable and spacious, with three second-floor guest rooms (there's a choice of queen, full, or twin beds) — nothing fancy, but attractive, airy, and very clean. Guests are welcome to use a first-floor TV room and deck out back. Best of all, Mary cooks up a full breakfast including those famous Rhode Island jonnycakes. A quiet, economical base for touring Newport.

This fully renovated Victorian is strong on creature comforts, such as plush, wall-to-wall carpeting, big, comfy beds with fluffy pillows, and individual thermostat controls in each of the five guest rooms, all of which have private bath. The decor is bright and cheerful, with light woods and pastels. From the Captain's Room on the third floor, you can watch the yachts sail across Newport Harbor. The Allphins cook up a delicious full breakfast, served at individual tables in their warm, cozy breakfast room — look forward to a gourmet concoction.

Narragansett

DUTCH INN
Owner: Brad Bernardo.
789-9341; 800-388-2446.
Great Island Rd., Narra-
    gansett/Galilee 02882.
Open: Year-round.
Price: Expensive.
Credit Cards: AE, D, DC,
    MC, V.
Smoking: Non-smoking
    rooms available.
Handicap Access: Yes.
Note: No pets.
Special Features: Indoor
    pool, sauna, exercise
    room.

The Dutch Inn would be merely a fine, upstanding, ordinary motel — except that it's directly
opposite the Block Island ferry dock. This makes it
essential, especially if you've missed the last boat.
The restaurant has entertainment on weekends
(week nights in season), and the rooms have cable
TV. No breakfast, but they do have some nice par-
rots in the lobby.

HISTORIC HOME B&B
Owners: Nancy & Steven
    Richards.
789-7746.
144 Gibson Ave., Narra-
    gansett Pier 02882 (no
    sign).
Open: Year-round.
Price: Moderate to Expen-
    sive.
Credit Cards: None.
Smoking: No.
Handicap Access: No.
Note: No pets, or children
    under 12.

Lined up as if for roll call along Gibson Avenue
are some of Narragansett's loveliest old beach
"cottages." Just before the street dead-ends, at the
left through a gap in high hedges is the loveliest
house of all: a gabled stone cottage built in 1884.
Secluded and veiled in ivy, it looks like a modest
English manor. The interior retains an atmosphere
of gracious calm. On hot afternoons the rooms are
coolly shaded by old trees, and show their age hon-
estly and charmingly by way of free-standing radi-
ators, worn Oriental rugs, immense closets, and
bathrooms with claw-foot tubs (no showers; choose
either shared or private bath). All four guest rooms
have working fireplaces and all include compli-
mentary decanters of sherry. Furnishings reflect the casual, seaside air — old
and charming but not imposing. There's also a newly renovated two-room
suite. Work off the full breakfast by strolling through the formal gardens, over
the immense lawn, and along a wooded path down to the beach.

MON REVE
Owners: Eva & Jim Doran.
783-2846.
41 Gibson Ave., Narra-
    gansett Pier 02882.
Open: Year-round.
Price: Moderate.
Credit Cards: None.

Mon Reve is the epitome of a Victorian beach
cottage (built c. 1890). High Victoriana reigns
in the living room, with a wonderfully crowded
selection of paintings. Usually only four guests are
accepted at a time (though the house will take
more), and are given their pick of second- and
third-floor rooms — decorated in a "country Victo-

Smoking: In living room
   only.
Handicap Access: No.
Note: No pets.

rian" style — with private bath. Limiting the number of guests means that Eva can fuss over them,
and serve up a delicious full breakfast.

MURPHY'S B&B
Owners: Martha & Kevin
   Murphy.
789-1824.
43 South Pier Road, Narra-
   gansett Pier 02882.
Open: May–Oct., weekends
   off-season.
Price: Moderate.
Credit Cards: None.
Smoking: Porch only.
Handicap Access: No.
Note: No pets, or children
   under 8.

Martha Murphy is the author of *The Bed and Breakfast Cookbook*, and her full breakfasts show her expertise. She's also a seasoned traveler, and her B&B is well appointed to suit visitors' needs. Guests have the first-floor living room to themselves, including use of the big fieldstone fireplace. The second floor is reserved for the family, with guest rooms on either side of the spacious third-floor landing, insuring privacy for all. One room has a queen-size bed, the other twins; both have sunlight, private baths, walk-in closets, and cupboard TVs. The larger room has a view of the ocean, just a block away. This 1894 "cottage" is simply but elegantly appointed throughout, with a mix of comfy furniture, antiques, and marine art. From the hanging baskets on the front porch to Martha's map with pins marking guests' hometowns, it's a special place.

THE 1900 HOUSE B&B
Owners: Bill & Sandra
   Panzeri.
789-7971.
59 Kingstown Rd., Narra-
   gansett Pier 02882.
Open: Year-round.
Price: Moderate.
Credit Cards: None.
Smoking: On porch only.
Handicap Access: No.
Note: No pets, children not
   encouraged.
Special Features: Gift cer-
   tificates available.

When a guest book indicates lots of return business, the owners are obviously doing something right. In this case, Bill and Sandy are being themselves: kind, friendly, and fun. Their wonderful home, with a lavender front door and pretty garden, is on a quiet side street. Of three guest rooms, one has a private bath, the others share. Each room is unique, but all include country antiques, wooden bed frames, thick Oriental rugs, and best of all, small special touches (such as the marriage certificate of the original owners). A full breakfast is served in the dining room.

THE OLD CLERK HOUSE
Owner: Patricia Watkins.
783-8008.
49 Narragansett Ave., Narragansett Pier 02882.
Open: Year-round.
Price: Moderate.

Patricia is from Wales and now runs a graceful, British-style B&B in the heart of Narragansett Pier. The front walkway of this century-old home is draped with roses. Inside, the charming front parlor (reserved for guests) is filled with family heirlooms and antiques, including a splendid

Credit Cards: None.
Smoking: No.
Handicap Access: No.
Note: No children or pets.

STONE LEA B&B
Owners: Carol & Ernie
 Cormier.
783-9546.
40 Newton Ave., Narra-
 gansett Pier 02882-1368.
Open: Year-round.
Price: Moderate.
Credit Cards: MC, V (5%
 processing fee).
Smoking: No.
Handicap Access: No.
Note: No pets, or children
 under 10.
Special Features: Gift cer-
 tificates available.

TOTUS TUUS
Owners: Chris & Diane
 Wilkens.
789-4785.
67 Narragansett Ave., Nar-
 ragansett Pier 02882 (no
 sign).
Open: May–Sept.
Price: Moderate.
Credit Cards: None.
Smoking: Permitted.
Handicap Access: No.
Note: No pets.

THE VILLAGE INN
Manager: Pi Patel.
783-6767.
1 Beach St., Narragansett
 Pier 02882.
Open: Year-round.
Price: Expensive.

grandfather clock made in 1775. The two bedrooms (choose between twin, double, or king) have private bath, TV, and air conditioning; a VCR, stereo, and fridge are also available. French doors open off the parlor onto a bright, plant-filled sun room, where a three-course breakfast is served on crystal and china. A warm, welcoming, gracious spot.

McKim, Mead, and White (who designed the Newport Casino and Rosecliff, among other landmarks), built this magisterial, Shingle style cottage around 1884. It sits just south of Narragansett Pier village, alone on a bluff overlooking the ocean. The views are stupendous — the back porch is named the "Do Nothing Room," since you can't do anything but stare at the sea. The common areas are paneled and stately, with a library, billiards table, TV, and player piano — a contrast to the rather matter-of-fact breakfast area. The four guest rooms are spacious, with private bath and brass beds; one has a fireplace. A full breakfast is served in the morning. (Note: the house is being sold but will continue as a B&B.)

Totus Tuus is Latin for "totally yours," and that's just what this over-the-garage apartment is. With a queen-size bedroom, living-cum-dining room that can sleep two, a small kitchen (with microwave), TV, and full bath, plus private deck and entrance, this is the place of choice for young families. Chris and Diane have lots of children of their own and welcome playmates of all ages (Diane has a full supply of toys and kid gear she's happy to loan). The apartment is light and airy, decorated in child-proof contemporary. The kitchen is stocked with fixings for a make-your-own continental breakfast.

You can't miss this one: it's the big weathered-shingle complex in Pier Marketplace, a sprawling shopping center across from Narragansett Pier Beach. If you value convenience over charm, stay here. There are two restaurants on the premises (breakfast isn't included), plus an indoor pool and

Credit Cards: AE, CB, D, DC, MC, V.
Smoking: Non-smoking rooms available.
Handicap Access: Several rooms.
Note: No pets.

WHITE ROSE B&B
Owner: Pat & Sylvan Vaicaitis.
789-0181.
22 Cedar St., Narragansett Pier 02882.
Open: Year-round.
Price: Moderate.
Credit Cards: None.
Smoking: No.
Handicap Access: No.
Note: No pets, or children under 6.
Special Features: Private charters available on the sloop *White Rose*.

North Kingstown

JOHN UPDIKE HOUSE
Owners: Mary Anne & Bill Sabo.
294-4905.
19 Pleasant St., North Kingstown/Wickford 02852 (no sign).
Open: Year-round.
Price: Moderate.
Credit Cards: None.
Smoking: On deck only.
Handicap Access: No.
Note: No pets.
Special Features: Private sandy beach.

MEADOWLAND B&B
Owner: Linda Iavarone.
294-4168.
765 Old Baptist Rd., North Kingstown 02852.

Jacuzzi. Each of the 58 rooms has air conditioning, TV, and telephone, and is decorated in "American motel" style. For a water view request the third floor; first-floor verandas feature the parking lot more than the ocean. Kids under 12 stay free.

"Casual but elegant" fits the White Rose perfectly. Just a block from the beach, this big, airy Victorian has taken on the sporty and relaxed attitude of its owners. Big shade trees keep it cool; white roses twine around the back porch. The four guest rooms share two baths and are decorated in a simple, unfussy style: brass beds, hardwood floors, lace curtains, floral wallpaper. There's an upstairs sitting room with a TV and fridge stocked with complimentary beer and wine. A baby grand is in the front hallway. Croquet, horseshoes, darts, bikes, bocce, and gear for diving and fishing are also available.

Built in 1745, the Updike House is the second oldest in Wickford. On a quiet side street, this sturdy old Georgian backs up to the waterfront, with private beach at the end of a manicured lawn. The arrangements are conveniently flexible: rent the second floor as an apartment, or each of the two bedrooms individually (shared bath; both have fireplaces). The comfortable common room (with TV) in between is dominated by an even larger fireplace. $15 extra adds full use of the adjoining kitchen, with a washer and dryer and separate phone. Best of all is the second-floor deck which runs the full length of the house and overlooks Wickford Harbor. A "continental-plus" breakfast is served (even if you've rented the kitchen).

The "country seat" counterpart to the B&Bs in Wickford village, Meadowland is set on a quiet half-acre of what used to be a celery farm. The homestead, once a house of ill-repute, was built in 1835 and has a mansard roof and distinctive pink

Open: Year-round.
Price: Moderate.
Credit Cards: None.
Smoking: No.
Handicap Access: No.
Note: No pets.
Special Features: "Bed,
   Breakfast and Boat"
   package; gift certificates.

MONTE VISTA MOTOR INN

Manager: William Ala-
   monte.
884-8000; 800-524-8001.
7075 Post Rd., North
   Kingstown 02852.
Open: Year-round.
Price: Moderate.
Credit Cards: AE, CB, D,
   DC, MC, V.
Smoking: Yes.
Handicap Access: Yes.
Note: No pets.

THE MORANS' B&B

Owners: Grace & Ed
   Moran.
294-3497.
130 West Main St., North
   Kingstown/Wickford
   02852.
Open: Year-round.
Price: Moderate.
Credit Cards: None.
Smoking: In front parlor
   only.
Handicap Access: No.

THE 1773 NARRA-GANSETT HOUSE

Owners: Joyce & Paul Dod-
   son.
294-3593.
71 Main St., North
   Kingstown/Wickford
   02852 (no sign).
Open: Year-round.

and blue trim. Linda's living room is a pink-carpeted Victorian haven, with a working fireplace (and TV) that guests love to use. The six bedrooms with shared bath are all sunny, cheerful, and unique. There's a romantic "honeymoon suite" on the third floor. A full candlelight breakfast is served every morning in the dining room. The "Bed, Breakfast and Boat" package features a cruise on the 46-foot yacht *Morning Star*.

If you're looking for a motel, this Best Western-run motor inn is the pick of a group of them that cluster on Rte. 1 near Wickford. Benefits include a pool screened from the road by flowering hedges, complimentary breakfast, 49 clean units with cable TV, and Rachel's Restaurant, open for all meals. Also close to the Red Rooster Tavern.

Nothing fancy" is what Grace and Ed say of their traditional B&B in a lovely yellow '30s-era cottage on the edge of Wickford village. The two second-floor, air-conditioned guest rooms are homey and comfortable, one with a queen-size bed, the other twins, and the shared bath between them is spotlessly clean. Each morning at 8:30 Grace serves breakfast on the order of pancakes or eggs with home-baked muffins in her cozy dining room. The front porch, decorated with hanging flower baskets, is an inviting place to sit and watch Wickford go by.

With buildings like this one, Main Street in Wickford looks like it's under an 18th-century spell. Built as a tavern with 10 working fireplaces, this B&B was restored five years ago by Joyce and Paul themselves (flood waters had reached the second floor in the 1938 hurricane), and now it's an elegant showplace. A guest apartment has a private entrance, living/dining area,

Price: Moderate to Expensive.
Credit Cards: None.
Smoking: Absolutely not.
Handicap Access: No.
Note: No pets, or children under 10.

full kitchen and bath, and queen-size bedroom. An adjoining single room — simply but gracefully furnished, with a small fireplace — is also available. A full breakfast on antique china is served in the fabulous dining room or out on the garden terrace. Daily housekeeping plus a nightly turn-down service is also offered. The artwork in the apartment is on loan from local shops, and is for sale.

EAST BAY

Bristol

Built c. 1694, the Joseph Reynolds House in Bristol is the oldest three-story home in New England. Lafayette used it as his headquarters during the Revolutionary War.

Craig Hammell

JOSEPH REYNOLDS HOUSE B&B
Owners: The Andersons.
254-0230.
956 Hope St., Bristol 02809.
Open: Year-round.
Price: Moderate.
Credit Cards: None.
Smoking: No.
Handicap Access: No.
Note: Pets welcome, no children under 12.

The Joseph Reynolds House is the oldest three-story home in New England, as a glance at the superb hearth paneling in the parlor will prove: the lines run charmingly askew in all directions. The National Register plaque says the house was built in 1698, but Wendy recently discovered letters — preserved in the Reynolds family archive in England — that indicate it went up between 1693 and 1695. Plans are underway for a 300th anniversary celebration. Lafayette slept here (he was only 21 at the time, and was mistaken for a servant), and so can you, in one of four comfortable, shared-bath rooms; several suites are also available. Antiques make up the furnishings, but they're of the sturdy, rather than delicate, variety. A full breakfast is served in the kitchen. A friendly Lab-mix pup is on hand as well.

KING PHILIP INN
Manager: Lisette Correia.
253-7600.
400 Metacom Ave., Bristol
02809.
Open: Year-round.
Price: Moderate.
Credit Cards: AE, D, DC,
MC, V.
Smoking: Non-smoking
rooms available.
Handicap Access: One
room.
Note: No pets.

This high-rise on Rte. 136 near the Mt. Hope Bridge doesn't have much to recommend it from the outside, but the rooms are very nice. The furnishings are more attractive than the usual motel style, and include TV and VCR. Breakfast doesn't come with the room, but the King Philip Restaurant serves all meals. (The inn was named for a Wampanoag chief who led an ill-fated revolt against the English in 1675.)

ROCKWELL HOUSE INN
Owners: Debra & Steve
Krohn.
253-0040.
610 Hope St., Bristol 02809.
Open: Year-round.
Price: Moderate.
Credit Cards: AE, MC, V.
Smoking: No.
Handicap Access: Yes.
Note: No pets, or children
under 12.

The four guest rooms at the Rockwell, all with private bath, two with gas-log fireplaces, are decorated in colonial high style with antiques that are rich and dignified yet still comfortable. Each room has terrycloth robes and can offer a nightly turn-down service. The full breakfast features Debra's "famous homemade granola," and a hot entrée on the order of cheese-stuffed French toast. In winter, breakfast is served by candlelight in the dining room, in summer on the rear porch or court-yard. Afternoon tea is served between 4 and 5pm. Guests are welcome to watch TV in the magnificent front parlor where Debra also offers sherry in the evening.

WILLIAM'S GRANT INN
Owners: Mike & Mary
Rose.
253-4222
154 High St., Bristol 02809.
Open: Year-round.
Price: Moderate.
Credit Cards: AE, CB, D,
DC, MC, V.
Smoking: On back porch.
Handicap Access: No.
Note: No pets, or children
under 12.

The artistic talents of family and friends — a mural of Bristol Harbor graces the entrance hall — and the many wonderful heirlooms here have created a warm and original atmosphere. The three bedrooms on the first floor have private baths, the two on the second-floor share; all have fireplaces and a journal in which to share thoughts with other guests. The "Middleburg Virginia Room" has walls hand-rubbed with rich, golden paint and trim of deep plum. The common room has a piano, games, and sherry. Mary serves a full breakfast, and on weekends Mike steps in to make his famous Huevos Rancheros from home-grown vegetables. A friendly, whimsical, historic gem of an inn on a quiet, stately street.

Warren

NATHANIEL PORTER INN
Owners: Viola & Robert Lynch.
245-6622.
125 Water St., Warren 02885.
Open: Year-round.
Price: Moderate.
Credit Cards: AE, D, DC, MC, V.
Smoking: Not in bedrooms.
Handicap Access: No.
Note: No pets.

Built in the 18th century by a local sea captain, the inn is deservedly on the National Register. Its three guest rooms, two with double beds, one with twins, slope whichever way their wide, listing floorboards lead them. The Early American furnishings are charming but not fancy. All rooms have air conditioning, private bath, and fireplace, and share a common sitting room. Continental breakfast is included, and the downstairs dining room — actually a number of small rooms — is one of the best (see Chapter Five, *Restaurants*).

AQUIDNECK

Middletown

ATLANTIC HOUSE B&B
Owner: John E. Flanagan.
847-7259.
37 Shore Dr., Middletown 02842.
Open: Daylight saving months.
Price: Moderate to Expensive.
Credit Cards: None.
Smoking: No.
Handicap Access: No.
Note: No pets (possible exceptions), no children.

The Atlantic House is built smack on the sea at Easton Point. Just to the north the coast curls around to form First (Easton) Beach; directly opposite the mansions line up along Newport's famous Cliff Walk. The three guest rooms aren't fancy, decorated to match the '70s style vacation architecture, but are clean and filled with the smells and sounds of the sea. One has private bath, all have TVs. John, a retired lawyer, serves a full breakfast and may even show you around his law library if you ask nicely.

THE COUNTRY GOOSE B&B
Owner: Paula Kelley.
846-6308.
563 Green End Ave., Middletown 02842.
Open: Year-round.
Price: Moderate.
Credit Cards: MC, V.
Smoking: In kitchen area only.

Green End Avenue is well named: it leads through what's left of Middletown's meadows and fields. The Country Goose, built in 1898, is the original farmhouse for the area. Though the house lacks some little touches that would otherwise make it utterly charming, it's still pleasant and private. Three second-floor bedrooms share two full baths, one downstairs; all have ceiling fans and TVs and include buffet-style continental break-

Handicap Access: No.
Note: No pets.

fast. Though not in tip-top shape, this is a nice, quiet spot, and Paula, a restaurateur in Newport, is helpful and knowledgeable about the area.

Shadows really do fall across the sweeping lawns at Finnegan's Inn at Shadow Lawn in Middletown.

Craig Hammell

**FINNEGAN'S INN AT
   SHADOW LAWN**
Manager: Sheila Finnegan.
847-0902.
120 Miantonomi Ave., Mid-
   dletown 02842.
Open: Year-round.
Price: Expensive.
Credit Cards: AE, MC, V.
Smoking: Permitted.
Handicap Access: Yes (not
   in main building).
Note: No pets.

Take the "lawn" in the name seriously: an immense expanse of grass sets off this magnificent Italianate home, built by Richard Upjohn in 1853 and now on the National Register. Despite its proximity to Newport, peace and quiet reign, especially in the eight rooms of the main house (another four are in the lodge out back), each of which includes a fireplace, private bath, small fridge, and TV. The emphasis is on comfort, so don't expect the exquisite Victorian atmosphere of the downstairs parlors in the bedrooms, though each is pleasantly and brightly decorated. Breakfast is continental style. The stained-glass windows, paneled library, tooled leather dining room walls, and shaded veranda add to the atmosphere. Tall copper beeches provide the "shadow" in Shadow Lawn.

HEDGEGATE B&B
Owners: Anna & Francis
   Parente.
846-3906; 849-4109.
65 Aquidneck Ave., Mid-
   dletown 02842.
Open: Mid-May–Columbus
   Day.
Price: Moderate.
Credit Cards: None.
Smoking: On veranda only.

Like staying at your Aunt Mary's" is how Anna describes this turn-of-the-century Dutch colonial that has been in her family for years. It has a wraparound veranda, complete with rockers, and terrific view of Easton Pond and First Beach. The snack bars and surfing shops of Aquidneck Ave. are nearby, but behind the Hedgegate's high namesake hedges you don't notice. There are six guest rooms, basic but clean, furnished with hand-me-

Handicap Access: No.
Note: No pets, or children under 12.

downs just the way beach houses used to be. The shared bath space can be tight, but there are additional facilities in a bathhouse out back. Since the owners live in an adjacent home on the property, guests have full run of the house, and receive a full, complimentary breakfast at a coffee shop down the street. There's a TV in the living room, but head to the gazebo-style "tea house" in the lovely back garden instead. The whole house is available for rent by the week.

**HOWARD JOHNSON'S
MOTOR LODGE**
Manager: Jeffrey Miller.
849-2000.
351 W. Main Rd./Rte. 114, Middletown.
Open: Year-round.
Price: Moderate to Expensive.
Credit Cards: D, DC, MC, V.
Smoking: Non-smoking rooms available.
Handicap Access: One room.
Note: Pet rooms available.
Special Features: Indoor pool and sauna; outdoor tennis courts.

Ho Jo's? Yes, Ho Jo's. There are many small, independent motels on Rte. 114 near the Newport border, but they can't offer what Howard Johnson's can for the price. There are 155 rooms to choose from, plus a studio and suites. You know they're clean, and the restaurant is open 24 hours.

LITTLE SUMIYA B&B
Owner: Mary Ellen Fatulli.
847-7859.
48 Kane Ave., Middletown 02842.
Open: Year-round.
Price: Expensive.
Credit Cards: None.
Smoking: Yes.
Handicap Access: No.
Note: Pets and children welcome!
Special Features: Pool.

Little Sumiya means "Little House on the Corner" in Japanese. This contemporary residence in a quiet neighborhood offers two second-floor guest rooms which share a separate entrance and sitting area (with small fridge and ironing board); each has private bath, A/C, fluffy robes, and cable TV. Best of all, the rooms overlook Mary Ellen's pride and joy, a heated pool set in landscaped gardens. A gazebo-like shelter at one end is laden with flowers — don't be surprised to find hummingbirds too (plus Alex, the talkative family parrot). A full breakfast is served out here in summer that includes homemade danishes and other goodies. The wet bar provides drinks after your swim. Ask Mary Ellen about picnic basket lunches.

POLLY'S PLACE B&B
Owner: Polly Canning.
847-2160.
349 Valley Rd./Rte. 214,
    Middletown 02842.
Open: Year-round.
Price: Moderate.
Credit Cards: None.
Smoking: No.
Handicap Access: No.
Note: No pets, or children
    under 12.

Out on the trellis-covered back deck gazing over a meadow of wildflowers, or in the midst of a cook-out with Polly and your friends (a sailing crew and croquet team recently established this custom), you'll feel miles from busy Newport, just over the town line. Polly has a true B&B — a home shared with guests. There are four bedrooms, two up and two down. Each pair has one bath. All are bright and very attractively furnished, with ceiling fans and a variety of bed sizes. Polly invites you to watch TV in her living room — view the Newport Mansions video before going into town. Full breakfast usually involves fresh garden vegetables and home-baked goods. There's also a fully-equipped basement apartment which rents weekly.

ROYAL PLAZA HOTEL
Manager: Joseph Collins.
846-3555; 800-825-7072.
425 East Main Rd./Rte. 138,
    Middletown 02842.
Closed: Mid-Dec.–mid-
    Mar.
Price: Moderate to Expen-
    sive.
Credit Cards: AE, D, DC,
    MC, V.
Smoking: Yes.
Handicap Access: Two
    rooms.
Note: No pets.

The Royal Plaza is an upscale motor inn with spacious, clean rooms, some with whirlpool bath. Adjoining rooms turn into suites for families. It's a great place to hold meetings — near the Newport line but outside the Newport traffic snarls. With cocktail lounge and conference rooms.

SEAVIEW INN
Owner: Rob Wray.
846-5000.
240 Aquidneck Ave., Mid-
    dletown 02842.
Open: Year-round.
Price: Moderate.
Credit Cards: AE, MC, V.
Smoking: Yes.
Handicap Access: Yes.
Note: No pets.

Don't be fooled by the Industrial Park sign — the road to the industrial complex also serves as the Seaview driveway. There's a spectacular view of Easton's Pond and the ocean from Seaview's perch — you can even see Newport's famous Cliff Walk across the way. This white clapboard motel has been recently revamped, top to bottom; all 40 rooms have a panoramic view, two double beds, TV, and telephone. Complimentary continental breakfast and bicycles come with an evening's stay.

STONEYARD B&B
Owner: Anne Cooper.
847-0494.
13 Fairview Ave., Middle-
    town 02842.

Anne Cooper lovingly renovated her 1921 bungalow on a quiet, residential street in Middletown, and lavished the same care on the separate-entrance apartment at the rear. This is a find for

Open: May–mid-Nov.
Price: Moderate to Expensive.
Credit Cards: None.*
Smoking: No.
Handicap Access: No.
Note: No children or pets.

two people: attractive, private, with full bath and small kitchen (including microwave), TV, A/C, and private patio. Anne equips the kitchen daily for a full, gourmet breakfast, including fresh home-baked goods and coffee beans. You can take your meal outside to the patio or to the gazebo in the garden, so inviting it's easy to forget Newport is around the corner. *May be reserved through **B&B Newport** on MC, V.*

WINDSONG B&B
Owners: Rose & Gilbert Bradfield.
847-5681.
87 Shore Dr., Middletown 02842.
Open: Year-round.
Price: Moderate to Expensive.
Credit Cards: None.
Smoking: On deck.
Handicap Access: Possible.
Note: No pets, children in efficiency apt. only.

The living room has a breathtaking view of the ocean and the Newport mansions across the cove (and a telescope in the living room). It's also a short walk to beaches and restaurants. One bedroom in the main section of the house has its own bath and total privacy (but no view); there's also an apartment with separate entrance and driveway, plus a loft and sliding glass doors that offer a sea view from your bed. Continental breakfast is served on the deck or in the dining room. Despite the rocky — though picturesque — coast, Rose says you can swim right in front of the house.

Newport

(There are three Admiral Inns of Newport: the Admiral Benbow, Fitzroy, and Farragut. All maintain a high standard of service though each has its own distinctive character. Space permits only two to be reviewed here; the Admiral Farragut, in a colonial home on Clarke Street, is just as pleasant.)

The Admiral Benbow is one of three admirable "Admiral" inns in Newport.

Craig Hammell

ADMIRAL BENBOW INN
Manager: Kathy Darigan.
846-4256; 800-343-2863.
91 Pelham St., Newport
    02840.
Closed: One month in winter.
Price: Moderate to Expensive.
Credit Cards: AE, DC, MC,
    V.
Smoking: Yes.
Handicap Access: No.
Note: No pets, or children
    under 12.

The Admiral Benbow occupies an imposing mid-19th-century home on quiet Pelham Street in Newport's Historic Hill district between the Harbor and Bellevue Avenue. Polished pine floorboards, tall, arched windows and a variety of antiques and colonial reproductions — in particular the handsome four-poster beds — give the 15 guest rooms a refined but easy, livable air. All have private bath. A gourmet continental breakfast is served in the common room, which is dominated by a big cast-iron stove. The TV parlor is closed after 8pm.

ADMIRAL FITZROY INN
Manager: Evelyn Ramirez.
846-4256; 800-343-2863.
398 Thames St., Newport
    02840.
Open: Year-round.
Price: Expensive.
Credit Cards: AE, CB, DC,
    MC, V.
Smoking: In rooms only,
    not in common areas.
Handicap Access: One
    room.
Note: No pets.

This former convent was moved to bustling Thames Street in 1986; now it's a fine 18-room inn (an elevator serves five floors). The atmosphere is relaxed, the furnishings pretty and appealing, including sleigh beds and lace curtains. All rooms include private bath, A/C, TV, telephone, and fridge, the latter tucked away out of sight. Two rooms have a private back deck. The bright, cheerful breakfast room, in which guests are treated to a full or continental meal, sets the tone for the rest of the inn. Despite the busy location, the rooms are quiet and the service is amiable.

**BANNISTER'S WHARF
GUEST ROOMS**
Manager: Jan Buchner.
846-4500.
Bannister's Wharf, Newport 02840.
Open: Year-round.
Price: Moderate to Expensive.
Credit Cards: AE, D, MC,
    V.
Smoking: Yes.

Arrive by boat or by car to stay in the heart of Newport's hopping wharf district. Bannister's also houses three of the best restaurants in town: the Clarke Cooke House, the Black Pearl, and Le Bistro (see *Restaurants* chapter for reviews). At the end of the pier, amid scores of fine racing and cruising yachts, is the office for Bannister's Wharf Guest Rooms. Choose from five doubles and three suites, all of which include A/C, phone, TV, fridge, and two double beds. The decor is casual, clean and attractive; all rooms have blue bedspreads, brown wicker furniture, and varnished wood trim — a very nautical look. The views are superb.

BETHSHAN B&B
Owners: Betty & Bill Smith.

Bethshan transports guests back to 1883 when it was built. The massive brick and stone Queen

846-1777.
396 Gibbs Ave., Newport 02840
Open: Year-round.
Price: Moderate to Expensive.
Credit Cards: None.
Smoking: Yes.
Handicap Access: No.
Note: No pets.

Anne is listed on the National Register, and is just off Memorial Boulevard (the Cliff Walk and First Beach are nearby). The large entrance hall is a feast of paneled wood and the two guest rooms are spacious. Both have private bath, TV, radio, phone, and (non-working) fireplace; they're not fancy, but they're comfortable and homey. Full breakfast is served in the dining room or on a pleasant back porch (with an amazing bottle collection). Note: this is a smoker's household.

BRINLEY VICTORIAN INN

Owners: John & Jennifer Sweetman.
849-7645.
23 Brinley St., Newport 02840.
Open: Year-round.
Price: Moderate to Expensive.
Credit Cards: MC, V.
Smoking: Yes.
Handicap Access: No.
Note: No pets, or children under 8.

New owners John and Jennifer recently arrived from England to make the Brinley their home. They have refurbishment plans for their 17 guest rooms (all but four with private bath), which are currently pleasant with Victorian appointments, if in need of a little cosmetic work. (Though it's in Newport, the inn has a Block Island feel — cozy, Victorian, a little musty.) Pleasant touches, such as complimentary champagne for a couple celebrating an anniversary, make the Sweetmans and their inn very likable. There's a cheerful front parlor (without a TV); note the Colonial Room at the back, dominated by a massive brick fireplace. Breakfast is continental style.

BLUESTONE B&B

Owners: Cindy & Roger Roberts.
846-5408.
33 Russell Ave., Newport 02840.
Open: Year-round.
Price: Moderate.
Credit Cards: D, MC, V; no personal checks.
Smoking: Outside only.
Handicap Access: No.
Note: No pets.

A quiet, residential spot on the outskirts of town, yet within walking distance to Bellevue and the Harbor, the Bluestone is moderate in price, air conditioned, furnished in a country Victorian style, friendly, and offers a full breakfast — in other words, the perfect small B&B. Cindy and Roger are good cooks, and ideal hosts: they have been known to lend ties to guests who needed them for restaurant-going. As small B&Bs go (two rooms only) the Bluestone is a charmer. Cindy also operates the comprehensive reservation service Bed & Breakfast, Newport.

THE BURBANK ROSE B&B

Owners: Bonnie & John McNeely.
849-9457.

The Burbank Rose was named for American horticulturist Luther Burbank, who developed a miniature, thornless rose. He'd doubtless be pleased to stay in his namesake, and to be a guest

111 Memorial Blvd. West,
  Newport 02840.
Open: Year-round.
Price: Moderate.
Credit Cards: AE.
Smoking: Ask first.
Handicap Access: No.
Note: No pets.

of the charming, soft-spoken McNeelys. This 1830s Federal is above John and Bonnie's antique and collectibles shop of the same name and across the street from St. Mary's Church on Memorial Boulevard. The three guest rooms all have private baths and are decorated in a pleasant, plain style that highlights the hardwood floors and freshly painted walls. A buffet breakfast featuring John's omelettes and pancakes is set up in the salmon-pink dining room. There's also a parlor with TV, games, and telephone. One room has a fireplace and A/C, the others have window fans.

THE CLARKESTON
Owner: Rick Farrick.
849-7397.
28 Clarke St., Newport
  02840.
Open: Year-round.
Price: Moderate to Very
  Expensive.
Credit Cards: None.
Smoking: No.
Handicap Access: One
  room.
Note: No pets, check first
  about children.

The Clarkeston is a recent venture by the owner of Elm Street Inn. On the National Register as the Joseph Burrill House, it was built around 1705, and has the wide floorboards and fireplaces to prove it. Its nine rooms have been sumptuously decorated with antiques and four-poster beds, matched by modern conveniences such as air conditioning, TVs, and sound-proofing (an important feature in an old house). The private bathrooms received lavish attention: all are appointed with marble and some have Jacuzzis. Continental breakfast.

CLIFFSIDE INN
Innkeepers: Norbert &
  Annette Mede.
847-1811.
2 Seaview Ave., Newport
  02840.
Open: Year-round.
Price: Expensive to Very
  Expensive.
Credit Cards: AE, CB, D,
  DC, MC, V.
Smoking: On porch only.
Handicap Access: No.
Note: No pets, or children
  under 13.

This glorious 1880 clapboard cottage is on a one-block street that ends at the Cliff Walk — the beach and mansions are just moments away. All 12 guest rooms have private bath (some converted from tiny closets, others with big whirlpool tubs) and ceiling fans. The exceptional antique furnishings include towering, polished armoires and carved bed frames. Light, fresh-looking fabrics and linens add to the appeal, as do unique touches such as a washstand made from an old phonograph. Four rooms have working fireplaces. Full breakfast is served in a very handsome dining room. Cliffside was once the home of artist Beatrice Turner; of her 1000 self-portraits only 70 were saved after her death. A few originals and several laser copies hang throughout the inn.

CLIFFWALK MANOR
Manager: Anne Can-
  narozzi.

Cliffwalk Manor is a Newport landmark: the red-and-white mansion, built in 1855, overlooks First Beach at the corner of Memorial Boule-

847-1301.
82 Memorial Blvd., Newport 02840.
Closed: Dec.–mid-Mar.
Price: Expensive to Very Expensive.
Credit Cards: AE, CB, DC, MC, V.
Smoking: Yes.
Handicap Access: Yes.
Note: No pets.

vard and the Cliff Walk. Word around town is that the restaurant (open to the public) has seen better days, but the 24 rooms and two suites, all with private bath, remain nicely kept. They're huge, many with enormous baths and fireplaces to match, and boast period antiques and fabulous ocean views. Despite the antiques, the guest rooms have a slightly aloof, austere feel, lacking small touches that might have made them more homey. Complimentary continental breakfast served after Labor Day.

CULPEPER HOUSE B&B
Owner: Ann Wiley.
846-4011.
30 Second St., Newport 02840.
Open: Year-round.
Price: Moderate to Expensive.
Credit Cards: None.
Smoking: No.
Handicap Access: No.
Note: Call first about pets.

For a faithfully restored colonial home (c. 1771), Shaker-style decoration, original artwork, a full library with everything from cookery books to English mysteries, afternoon wine and conversation with the articulate owner, and — getting down to basics — terrific mattresses, stay at the Culpeper. When a place is frequently recommended by other innkeepers you know it's good, and that's the case here. The two guest rooms each have a private bath. In summer a full breakfast is served in the garden (with so many trees that it constitutes a bird sanctuary); in winter — when European down quilts warm the beds — a local chef prepares private dinners in the library-cum-dining room. Culpeper House is in the quiet old Point Section just one block from Newport Harbor. You'll know it by the roses out front.

DOUBLETREE NEWPORT ISLANDER HOTEL
Manager: Gary Richards.
849-2600; 800-222-TREE.
Goat Island, Newport 02840.
Open: Year-round.
Price: Expensive to Very Expensive.
Credit Cards: AE, D, DC, MC, V.
Smoking: Non-smoking rooms available.
Handicap Access: Rooms available.
Note: No pets.

The Doubletree has a prime spot all by itself on little Goat Island in Newport Harbor — drive over the causeway or take the water shuttle to Bowen's Wharf. The 253 rooms offer a choice between Harbor or Bay views: both are excellent. This big, deluxe hotel has two restaurants (see *Restaurants* for the Windward Grille), a health club, and indoor/outdoor pool. Breakfast isn't included unless you choose a B&B package.

THE 1855 MARSHALL SLOCUM GUEST HOUSE
Owner: Joan Wilson.
847-3787.
29 Kay St., Newport 02840.
Closed: Jan.–Feb.
Price: Moderate.
Credit Cards: AE, MC, V.
Smoking: Deck only.
Handicap Access: No.
Note: No pets, or children under 12.

A gracious, generously proportioned home on a shady side street off Bellevue, the Marshall Slocum has lace curtains in the windows, wicker chairs on the front porch, and a big deck out back. Tall trees keep the parlor and dining room a bit shaded, but the six guest rooms upstairs (three on each floor) are sunny and pleasant. They're furnished simply with touches befitting an old summer house, such as sturdy beds covered by handcrafted quilts. Two rooms have private half-baths, otherwise all share. A full breakfast is served in the dining room and a lobster dinner with every three-night stay. There's also a library of local movies like *The Great Gatsby.*

ELM STREET INN
Innkeeper: Rick Farrick.
849-7397.
36 Elm St., Newport 02840.
Open: Year-round.
Price: Moderate to Very Expensive.
Credit Cards: None.
Smoking: No.
Handicap Access: No.
Note: No pets, check first about children.

F our suites, all with private bath, cluster into this turn-of-the-century home on a residential street in the Point Section of town. All are comfortably and attractively furnished: antiques provide the atmosphere and air conditioners keep it cool (TVs and phone jacks are also present). The third floor suite is a secluded haven with eccentric eaves and a ladder — painted white with flower garlands along the sides — that leads through a trap door to the rooftop deck, and a view of Newport Harbor. A continental breakfast of fresh fruit and baked goods is served in the kitchen.

ELM TREE COTTAGE
Owners: Priscilla & Thomas Malone.
849-1610; 800-882-3356.
336 Gibbs Ave., Newport 02840.
Open: Year-round.
Price: Expensive to Very Expensive.
Credit Cards: MC, V.
Smoking: No.
Handicap Access: One room "handicap conscious."
Note: No pets, or children under 14.

O ne of a handful of truly top-drawer inns in town, the Elm Tree Cottage is a beautiful spot, owned and run by a friendly young couple who also design and make stained glass. The inn occupies an 1882 Shingle style mansion in a Gilded Age neighborhood north of Memorial Boulevard. Elegant and stately without being overpowering, the front parlor ends in a bay of windows overlooking Easton's Pond; a brilliantly sunny morning room and paneled pub area (BYOB) are off to one side. Five guest rooms and the Windsor suite are magnificently appointed with fine linens, French and English provincial antiques (highlights are the Louis XV beds), and special touches — note the washstand with Austrian crystal legs. All rooms have private bath and fireplaces, only one of which doesn't work. A full gourmet breakfast is served in the delightful dining room. Priscilla even rearranges all the furnishings to suite the changing seasons, and the magazines are top notch.

FLOWER GARDEN GUESTS

Owner: Marilyn Borsare.
846-3119.
1 Kyle Terrace, Newport 02840.
Open: Year-round.
Price: Moderate.
Credit Cards: None.
Smoking: Not in bedrooms.
Handicap Access: No.
Restrictions: No children or pets.

This quiet spot is only about a mile from the center of town, but it's tucked away in a residential area far from the hustle and bustle. The exterior is modest, but the interior is furnished with interesting antiques (including a collection of toys and dolls), and features a lovely garden room with wicker furniture and a wood-burning stove. There's also a back deck overlooking a well-tended garden. Guest rooms come with either shared or private bath. The continental breakfast is a generous one, with fresh fruit, egg dishes, vegetable quiche, and more. In season it's served on the deck; in winter; in the welcoming country kitchen.

FRANCIS MALBONE HOUSE

Manager: Will Dewey.
846-0392.
392 Thames St., Newport 02840.
Open: Year-round.
Price: Expensive.
Credit Cards: AE, MC, V.
Smoking: On garden terrace only.
Handicap Access: Yes.
Note: No pets, or children under 12.

Legend has it that the first home of slave trader Francis Malbone caught fire while he was hosting a dinner party. Rather than have his meal ruined, Malbone had his servants move the table to the front lawn where guests dined by the light of burning timbers. In 1760 Malbone built this house as a replacement. Each of the four common rooms and nine bedrooms is exquisitely furnished with period antiques and artwork; front rooms offer a Harbor view and rear rooms look out onto a quiet courtyard garden, where breakfast is served in season. A TV is in the library. The Counting House Suite on the first floor has its own entrance and garden exit. The Malbone House offers excellent "Rekindle the Fires" packages in winter.

HAMMETT HOUSE INN

Manager: Marianne Spaziano.
848-0593; 800-548-9417.
505 Thames St., Newport 02840.
Open: Year-round.
Price: Moderate to Expensive.

On busy lower Thames Street, the Nathan Hammett House is a three-story Georgian. Each of the five guest rooms has plush carpeting, air conditioning, private bath, cable TV, and a queen-size bed; the largest room has two beds. The gracious furnishings range from Victorian wicker to French Regency, canopy beds to floral wallpaper. Continental breakfast arrives at each guest room at

Credit Cards: AE, MC, V.
Smoking: No.
Handicap Access: No.
Note: No pets.
Special Features: Room ser-
vice available from the
509 Grille next door.

HARBORSIDE INN

Innkeeper: Ann McFarland.
846-6600.
Christie's Landing, New-
port 02840.
Open: Year-round.
Price: Expensive to Very
Expensive.
Credit Cards: AE, DC, MC,
V.
Smoking: Yes.
Handicap Access: No.
Note: No pets.

THE HOTEL VIKING

Manager: Douglas Rucker.
847-3300; 800-556-7126.
1 Bellevue Ave., Newport
02840.
Open: Year-round.
Price: Expensive.
Credit Cards: AE, D, DC,
MC, V.
Smoking: Non-smoking
rooms available.
Handicap Access: Yes.
Note: No pets.
Special Features: Banquet
facilities; pool, sauna,
whirlpool, exercise room;
excellent off-season packages.

HYDRANGEA HOUSE

Owners: Dennis Blair &
Grant Edmondson.
846-4435; 800-945-4667.
16 Bellevue Ave., Newport
02840.
Open: Year-round.
Price: Moderate to Expen-
sive.

7:30am; hinged trays are provided in the corridor
for this purpose. Some rooms have Harbor views.

The Harborside is a busy inn in the midst of the
tourist throng. It's convenient but a bit cavalier
about things and potentially noisy, though the
view is top notch. All suites are decorated in contemporary nautical style; all include TV, wet bar,
fridge, A/C, and sleeping loft. A continental breakfast and afternoon refreshments are served in the
comfortable Harbor Room.

Gilded Age summer folk built the Viking for
their guests (to get them out of the mansions,
no doubt) at Newport's most exclusive address: 1
Bellevue Ave. When it was new in 1926 the biggest,
grandest rooms faced the avenue, the smaller ones,
reserved for children and servants, overlooked
Newport Harbor. Today the hotel has been renovated to accommodate contemporary tastes, and a
motel-style west wing added. The lobby retains the
feel of a grand old hotel, but the rooms are fairly
standardized. Don't miss the Top of Newport, a
rooftop bar which is not only the highest spot in
town but the best for watching the sunset over the
Harbor. Also on the top floor are five "European-
style" rooms which share a bath — at up to $100
less per night they're a hidden treasure, but very
popular with those in the know.

Attention to detail, a flair for Victorian decoration, and creativity contribute to the appeal of
the small, owner-operated Hydrangea House.
Upstairs is the six-room inn; downstairs is the
owners' contemporary art gallery (see *Culture*, Fine
Art Galleries) where guests are served a full buffet
breakfast including items like homemade granola,

Credit Cards: MC, V.
Smoking: No.
Handicap Access: No.
Note: No pets.
Special Features: Breakfast
   in art gallery.

Venetian eggs, or raspberry pancakes. A journal in each uniquely decorated room records the impressions and recommendations of guests. In the evening the proprietors serve milk and homemade chocolate chip cookies, plus snacks on the second-floor veranda in the afternoon.

The Inn at Castle Hill offers comfort as well as majestic ocean views.

Craig Hammell

INN AT CASTLE HILL
Owner: Paul MacEnroe.
849-3800.
Ocean Drive, Newport
   02840.
Open: Year-round.
Price: Very Expensive.
Credit Cards: AE, MC, V.
Smoking: Yes.
Handicap Access: No.
Note: No pets, or children
   under 12.

This cedar-shingled mansion sits in majesty at the end of a long drive, with the mouth of Narragansett Bay as its backyard. Alexander Agassiz, a world traveler and biologist, built Castle Hill in 1874 and filled it with carved woodwork and antiques from the Far East, many of which still grace the dining rooms and sitting areas on the first floor (restaurant reviewed in Chapter Five). The 10 guest rooms, all with private bath, aren't quite as grand but each is attractively decorated and architecturally unique. No TV or telephone here — 19th-century atmosphere and glorious views of the open ocean instead.

INN AT OLD BEACH
Owners: Cyndi & Luke
   Murray.
849-3479.
19 Old Beach Rd., Newport
   02840.
Open: Year-round.
Price: Expensive.
Credit Cards: AE, MC, V.

A gem tucked into a residential Victorian neighborhood behind the northern end of Bellevue Avenue, this 1879 Gothic Revival home, lovely gardens, and gazebo are extremely neat and well-kept. The common rooms (with TV) are cozy and well-appointed — in summer they're full of fresh flowers, in winter logs burn in the fireplaces. A fabulous "Four Seasons" stained-glass window is in the

Smoking: On porches only.
Handicap Access: No.
Note: No pets, or children
under 12.

stairway. The five guest rooms have private bath and are gracefully decorated in flower motifs; one has a Victorian wood-burning stove; the others have fireplaces. There's a handy guest pantry on the second floor. Each morning Cyndi serves a generous, homemade continental breakfast; Luke manages the famous Black Pearl restaurant (see Chapter Five) so be sure to ask for dining tips. Two more guest rooms are in the Carriage House out back.

THE INNTOWNE
Owner: Carmella Gardner.
846-9200; 800-457-7803.
Thames & Mary Sts., New-
port 02840.
Open: Year-round.
Price: Expensive.
Credit Cards: AE, MC (MC
not accepted over the
phone), V.
Smoking: Yes.
Handicap Access: No.
Note: No pets.

This small, independent, midtown hotel is convenient, possibly a little noisy (in the heart of the wharf shopping area), and well-run, with 26 attractive rooms. The lobby is warm and appealing; spacious guest rooms have matching bedspreads and wallpaper, and are furnished with wicker and fine colonial reproductions. All have private bath, telephone, and A/C, and include continental breakfast served in a pleasant dining room. The lack of free parking (it's $10 per day extra) is made up for by complimentary use of the Marriott's swimming pool and health club. Don't miss the rooftop deck.

THE IVY LODGE
Owners: Maggie & Terry
Moy.
849-6865.
12 Clay St., Newport 02840.
Open: Year-round.
Price: Expensive.
Credit Cards: AE, MC, V.
Smoking: No.
Handicap Access: Possible.
Note: No pets.

Easily one of Newport's finest inns, the Ivy Lodge is in a big rambling 1886 home designed by Stanford White off Bellevue Avenue. The well-kept yard and dreamy veranda, lovely as they are, are only a prelude to the magnificent entrance hall, an extravaganza of carved English oak and diagonal staircases. Hosts Maggie and Terry are friendly and down-to-earth, and will make you feel at home in this Shingle style palace. There are eight guest rooms with private bath and A/C, all decorated with flair and elegance. 19th-century features abound — fireplaces, stained glass, and a wonderful turret — and are updated with contemporary colors and bright fabrics. The common rooms are delightful; the dining room table, where Maggie serves full breakfast (including Scotch eggs), seats 16; and guests are welcome to take a tray out to the veranda. Light refreshments are served in the afternoon.

JAILHOUSE INN
Manager: Eric Shollen-
berger.
847-4638.

It's impressive on the outside, a restored colonial jail built in 1772. Inside, the 22 rooms (with private bath, small fridge, TV, telephone, and A/C) are on the average side. Continental breakfast is

13 Marlborough St., Newport 02840.
Open: Year-round (winter weekends only).
Price: Moderate to Expensive.
Credit Cards: AE, DC, MC, V.
Smoking: Yes.
Handicap Access: One room.
Note: No pets.

LA FORGE COTTAGE
Owners: Louis & Margot Droual.
847-4400.
96 Pelham St., Newport 02840.
Open: Year-round.
Price: Moderate to Expensive.
Credit Cards: AE, D, MC, V.
Smoking: Yes.
Handicap Access: No.
Note: No pets, children welcome (cribs available).
Special Features: French and German also spoken.

LONG WHARF YACHT CHARTERS
Proprietor: Carl Bolender.
849-2210.
Long Wharf Marina/PO Box 366, Newport 02840 (also Channel 68 or 9).
Open: Apr.–Nov.
Price: Moderate .
Credit Cards: None.
Smoking: No.
Handicap Access: No.
Note: Children and pets allowed (litter boxes provided).

NEWPORT MARRIOTT
Manager: Rod Lowe.

included. The jail bars in the office and one of the rooms are original.

Since 1889 there have been only two sets of owner/innkeepers at La Forge Guest Cottage (the current house, a gabled clapboard with green awnings and window boxes on the front porch, was built in 1913). The Drouals have held up their end of the century very admirably — the house and grounds are delightfully maintained. There are eight guest rooms and four suites, all with private bath and queen beds plus TV, telephone, fridge, and A/C. Furnishings are old-fashioned but not antique, from brass beds to sturdy bedroom furniture of cherry and mahogany. The in-house French chef prepares either continental or full breakfast, which arrives at your bedside each morning via room service.

Newport is the City by the Sea, so why not sleep on a boat? "Boat and Breakfast" offers overnight accommodation on one of Carl's docked charter yachts. Guests may reserve ahead, or take a chance that one of the charters may be available. Board around 4pm, disembark at 10am. Most boats sleep six and have onboard TV and showers, but if not, facilities are available at Carl's floating office, the *Hurricane Gloria* (guarded by Brutus, a fierce-looking but gentle beast). Guests may also use the pool and health club at the Marriott next door. Continental breakfast includes coffee and danish.

This is arguably Newport's luxury hotel, with two restaurants (Café del Mare and JW's Sea-

849-1000; 800-228-9290.
25 America's Cup Ave.,
Newport 02840.
Open: Year-round.
Price: Very Expensive.
Credit Cards: AE, CB, D,
DC, MC, V.
Smoking: Non-smoking
rooms available.
Handicap Access: Rooms
available.

grill; see *Restaurants*), shops, and an impressive open atrium hung with yachting flags. There are 317 rooms, all of which offer either Harbor, Bridge, city, or atrium views. Seventh-floor rooms are the most lavish, with concierge service, an "honor bar" plus complimentary hors d'oeuvres and dessert in the common area, and private observation deck. A full health club, indoor/outdoor pool, sun deck, and racquetball courts are available to all. Special touches, including valet service and in-room irons and ironing boards, make the Marriott worth the expense.

Craig Hammell

The Melville House, on quiet Clarke Street in Newport, was built c. 1750.

THE MELVILLE HOUSE
Owners: Vincent DeRico &
David Horan.
847-0640.
39 Clarke St., Newport
02840.
Open: Year-round.
Price: Moderate to Expensive.
Credit Cards: AE, MC, V.
Smoking: No.
Handicap Access: One
room.
Note: No pets, or children
under 12.

Quiet Clarke Street is a dream: one block, one way, near the Harbor, on the Hill, and a moment's walk to a favorite restaurant (The Place at Yesterday's; see *Restaurants*). The Melville House, built c. 1750, is a winner too. The front parlor is a study in understated colonial charm, with a wonderful collection of old kitchen appliances. Of seven rooms, five have private bath. Look for gleaming hardwood floors, armoires, George Washington spreads, handsome area rugs, and lace curtains. All rooms include fluffy robes and journals. An extended continental breakfast is served during the week; a full version — featuring quiche, stuffed French toast, and jonnycakes — on weekends. Don't leave without trying Vincent's delicious homemade biscotti.

MERRITT HOUSE B&B
Owners: Angela & Joseph Vars.
847-4289.
57 Second St., Newport 02840.
Open: Year-round.
Price: Moderate.
Credit Cards: None.
Smoking: No.
Handicap Access: No.
Note: No pets, or children under 13.

Such a warm, welcoming atmosphere pervades this c. 1850 home in Newport's Point Section that hugs at check-out are not uncommon. The parlor is old-fashioned and cozy; the dining room, where full breakfast is served each morning (Angela's recipes have appeared in print), harbors a pretty collection of amethyst glass. There are two double rooms on the second floor, one with private bath; the other shares a downstairs bath with the family. Both have charming colonial furnishings, including a small library of old books. A room brimming with gifts guests have brought or sent from all over the world is the best recommendation for this relaxed, considerate B&B, named one of the 100 best in the country.

MILL STREET INN
Owner: Robert Briskin.
849-9500.
75 Mill St., Newport 02840.
Open: Year-round.
Price: Moderate to Very Expensive.
Credit Cards: AE, CB, DC, MC, V.
Smoking: Non-smoking rooms available.
Handicap Access: No.
Note: No pets.

Originally a 19th-century sawmill (where the window and door frames of many Newport homes were made), this National Register property has been converted into an all-suite hotel. The rooms are contemporary and bright, with exposed beams and brick walls. Some offer private decks overlooking Newport Harbor — just a block away — and all come with a queen bed plus queen pull-out sofa. An extensive continental breakfast and complimentary afternoon tea, served on deck in season, make this a good combination of the self-sufficiency of a time-share with the amenities of a hotel.

NEWPORT HARBOR HOTEL & MARINA
Manager: Patricia Joseph.
847-9000; out-of-state 800-955-2558.
49 America's Cup Ave., Newport.
Open: Year-round.
Price: Expensive.
Credit Cards: AE, CB, D, DC.
Smoking: Non-smoking floor.
Handicap Access: No.
Note: No pets.

Though smack in the heart of Newport's bustling Harbor area, these rooms are havens of quiet luxury, bright with sea-light off the water. Indulgences include a heated pool and sun deck overlooking the water, saunas, cabaret dinner shows, and Sunday afternoon jazz. Waverley's, the hotel restaurant, serves from morning till late at night and offers outdoor dining in season. If you arrive by water, there's also a 66-slip marina. If you like to stay where things are happening late into the night yet wake up to a peaceful marine view, this is the hotel for you.

**NEWPORT BAY CLUB
   AND HOTEL**
Manager: Heather Harhay.
849-8600.
America's Cup Ave. &
   Thames St./PO Box 1440,
   Newport.
Open: Year-round.
Price: Very Expensive.
Credit Cards: AE, CB, D,
   DC, MC, V.
Smoking: Permitted in all
   rooms.
Handicap Access: One
   room.
Note: No pets.
Special Features: Time-
   share units available.

The suites and townhouses of the Newport Bay Club and Hotel inhabit an eye-catcher of an old stone mill building right on Newport Harbor; some rooms have exposed beams. From one-bedroom suites to indulging two-room townhouses, all are decorated in subdued pastels and include kitchens and marble baths with oversized Jacuzzis. Some suites overlook the Harbor, but all offer great views of the wharf area and Thames St. hubbub. Downstairs the Perry Mill Market Place has shops, a pub, and the Thames Street Station nightclub.

PILGRIM HOUSE
Owners: Donna Messerlian,
   Pam & Bruce Bayuk.
846-0040; 800-525-8373.
123 Spring St., Newport
   02840.
Closed: 3 weeks in Jan.
Price: Moderate to Expen-
   sive.
Credit Cards: MC, V.
Smoking: On deck only.
Handicap Access: No.
Note: No pets, or children
   under 12.

Even though Spring Street is two long blocks from the water, the c. 1837 Pilgrim House has a rear deck with a drop-dead view of Newport Harbor. This is where breakfast is served in season and guests come for evening cocktails — the steeple of Trinity Church seems close enough to touch. But the deck isn't the only fine spot: each evening sherry and shortbread are served in the living room, which features a wonderful fireplace mantle the owners found during restoration. The 11 guest rooms (two share a bath, all have A/C), are equally charming, with lace curtains, antiques, and floral wallpaper. The atmosphere, like the decor, is pleasantly informal. Rooms seem quiet despite the central location.

RHODE ISLAND HOUSE
Owners: Michael Dupre &
   John Rich.
848-7787.
77 Rhode Island Ave.,
   Newport 02840.
Open: Year-round.
Price: Expensive.
Credit Cards: MC, V.
Smoking: No.
Handicap Access: No.
Note: No pets, or children
   under 14.

The aroma of fresh baking can be so enticing here it may take a few moments to notice the wonderful surroundings of this recently established inn. Michael Dupre has a reputation as one of the best young chefs in Newport, and plans to offer cooking classes as part of a winter weekend package. And his full breakfast is superb. The inn offers five guest rooms, each one with a private bath and a character all its own, achieved through satisfying combinations of prints, colors, and furnishings. Two have Jacuzzis and one a private deck overlooking the back garden. The windows throughout this venerable 1882 home are magnificent, especially in the downstairs common rooms.

**ROSE ISLAND LIGHT-
  HOUSE**
Owner: Rose Island Light
  Foundation.
847-4242.
Rose Island, Newport.
(Office: Newport Harbor
  Center, 365 Thames St.)
Open: Year-round.
Price: Moderate to Expensive.
Credit Cards: None.
Smoking: No.
Handicap Access: No.
Note: No pets.
Special Features: Gift certificates available.

Tiny Rose Island is in the middle of Narragansett Bay between Jamestown and Newport; its lighthouse, built in 1869 and just re-lit in 1993, is a mansard-roofed landmark. This is not an experience for everyone, but adventurous sorts who dream about being a lighthouse keeper will never forget an overnight stay here. Furnishings are c. 1900, with a brass bed, washstand, cast-iron stove, and player piano. There's no electricity, no shower, no TV, no running water (there *is* an ecologically sound toilet; the plumbing is clear, so you can watch it working). Overnight visitors are more volunteers than guests (expect to change the sheets in the morning), but duties are a small exchange for the natural joys of Rose Island. Explore on your own or take a guided tour; in summer sea birds and wild roses abound; in winter harbor seals take over. The 15-minute launch ride to the island is $10 round-trip per person.

**SANFORD-COVELL
  VILLA MARINA**
Owners: Ann & Richard
  Cuvelier.
847-0206.
72 Washington St., Newport 02840.
Open: Year-round.
Price: Moderate to Very
  Expensive.
Credit Cards: None.
Smoking: Discouraged and
  restricted.
Handicap Access: Possible.
Note: Pets "frowned
  upon."
Special Features: Heated
  saltwater pool.

The towering entrance hall rises 35 feet, accented with original stenciling and five kinds of woods. The National Register villa was built in 1869 in the Point Section, right on Newport Harbor, just before the frenzy of the Gilded Age, and still maintains the atmosphere of affluent relaxation of the old "beach cottages." Outside a wraparound porch overlooks not only the Harbor and Newport Bridge, but the villa's private wharf (with a restored gazebo at the end), and heated saltwater swimming pool and Jacuzzi. The six guest rooms (with both shared and private bath) include fireplaces, window seats with breeze-blown lace curtains, and floor-to-ceiling wood paneling. One room, a former nursery, has a big built-in chalkboard. Two rooms may be rented as a suite, with kitchenette and king-size Murphy bed. Complimentary sherry and port is served in the magnificent music room, which boasts original gas fixtures. Breakfast is continental style.

STELLA MARIS INN
Owners: Dorothy & Ed
  Madden.

This big, beautiful, mansard-roofed brownstone in Newport's quiet Point Section — a great place for views of Newport Bridge and Harbor —

849-2862.
91 Washington St., Newport 02840.
Open: Year-round.
Price: Moderate to Expensive.
Credit Cards: None.
Smoking: No.
Handicap Access: Yes.
Note: No pets.

was built as a convent in 1861. Of the eight rooms (there's also a cottage) five overlook the Harbor and four have grand old fireplaces. All have private baths and soaring ceilings, impressively done up in floral prints, Victorian antiques, and bright colors. Everything is spacious here, from the hallways, majestic parlors, and dining room, to the grounds and front veranda, where guests relax and watch the boats while consuming goodies from the homemade breakfast buffet.

VICTORIAN LADIES
Owners: Donald & Hélène O'Neill.
849-9960.
63 Memorial Blvd., Newport 02840.
Closed: Jan.
Price: Expensive.
Credit Cards: MC, V.
Smoking: One non-smoking building, plus non-smoking rooms.
Handicap Access: No.
Note: No pets, or children under 10.

H ave you seen the Victorian Ladies?" is a frequent refrain around Newport. On busy Memorial Boulevard between the Cliff Walk and Bellevue Avenue, it's easy to spot — just look for all the flowers, frequent winners of the Newport in Bloom competition. The front parlor looks exactly as if it had been decorated by a discriminating Victorian lady; the guest rooms are elegant, quiet, and comfortable, individually decorated with antiques and fine reproductions. Three buildings house 11 rooms, all with private bath, A/C, and television. A full breakfast buffet may be enjoyed on the flower-laden back patio.

VILLA LIBERTE
Innkeeper: Leigh Anne Mosco.
846-7444; 800-392-3717.
22 Liberty St., Newport 02840.
Closed: Jan.–Feb.
Price: Moderate to Very Expensive.
Credit Cards: MC, V.
Smoking: Yes.
Handicap Access: No.
Note: No pets.

A flat roof, an unusual second-floor porch perched over the arched entry way, and a Mediterranean color scheme give the Villa Liberte a distinctive look. Built in 1910 as a "House of the Evening," this is more a small hotel than an inn. The 15 guest rooms (including three housekeeping suites in the annex next door), share the same contemporary pastel decor and feature dramatic black-and-white tiled baths tucked under arched alcoves. All include A/C, telephone, and color TV. Continental breakfast is set up buffet style; guests may take a tray to the airy sun deck out back, to one of the sitting areas throughout the villa, or to their rooms.

WAYSIDE B&B
Dorothy & Al Post.
847-0302.
406 Bellevue Ave., Newport 02840.

T he Wayside is a stately mansion, enlarged to its present size in 1896. Despite the austere, yellow-brick grandeur of the façade, the interior is relaxed and comfortable. There are 10 guest rooms

Open: Year-round.
Price: Expensive (rates
 include tax).
Credit Cards: None.
Smoking: Yes.
Handicap Access: Possible.
Note: No pets.
Special Features: Heated in-
 ground pool.

in this 22-room house, all with ceiling fans and private bath, plus a six-person apartment in the carriage house. Everything here is on a grand scale: the Library Room has a 14-foot ceiling and a huge fireplace. Continental breakfast is served in a lovely dining room.

**THE WILLOWS OF NEW-
 PORT**
Owner: Pattie Murphy.
846-5486.
8 Willow St., Newport
 02840.
Open: Apr.–Nov.
Price: Expensive.
Smoking: In garden only.
Credit Cards: None.
Handicap Access: No.
Note: No pets, children
 inappropriate.

The Willows is known as the "Romantic Inn" — it's even recommended by the "Best Places to Kiss" guide. Five guest rooms, all with private bath and A/C, nestle in two historic townhouses built 100 years apart (1740 and 1840) and joined together. The Willows offers luxury taken seriously; the gracious pink parlor, the silver-service breakfast in bed (delivered by owner Pattie in black tie and top hat), champagne buckets, fresh flowers, frills and lace, and little stuffed animals holding romantic messages. Morning wake-up through a central intercom features bells and music and a short Newport history lesson. There's a bar upstairs and a wonderful garden out back, with a heart-shaped fish pond and nooks for private conversations. A real plus is concierge service that can reserve a table at Newport's many first-come, first-served restaurants.

Portsmouth

**BROWN'S BED &
 BREAKFAST**
Owners: Roger & Dot
 Brown.
683-0155.
502 Bristol Ferry Rd.,
 Portsmouth 02871.
Open: Year-round.
Price: Moderate.
Credit Cards: None.
Smoking: On deck only.
Handicap Access: No.
Note: No pets.

Owner Dot Brown says she "puts her heart and soul" into her guest house, and it's obvious. This weathered-shingle "cottage" was built at the turn of the century on three acres with a spectacular view of Narragansett Bay. The five guest rooms, two with private bath, all with cable TV, are spotlessly clean and decorated in gracious, grandmotherly style — stately but comfortable. Guests are welcome to use a lovely old-fashioned parlor but most prefer the back porch, flanked by open decks overlooking the Bay. This is where continental-style breakfast is served, and may include Dot's homemade muffins and local Portuguese specialties (try the wickedly delicious malassadas, a fried sweetbread dough). Guests return here year after year.

FOUNDER'S BROOK MOTEL AND SUITES
Owners: Lynne & Gerry
  Gaboriau.
683-1244; 800-334-8765.
314 Boyd Lane, Portsmouth
  02871.
Open: Year-round.
Price: Moderate.
Credit Cards: AE, CB, D,
  DC, MC, V.
Smoking: Four non-smok-
  ing rooms.
Handicap Access: Two
  rooms.
Note: Pets discouraged.

For a clean, quiet place to stay close to Newport (15 minutes by car), but beyond the bustling crowd, try these 24 efficiency suites and eight motel units. Not fancy but simply and attractively furnished, each has cable TV, telephone, and queen-size bed (the suites also have a full pull-out sofa). A continental breakfast is complimentary on weekends. The Founder's Brook was named for Anne Hutchinson, who in 1683 was the first woman to found a town in America.

PORTSMOUTH RAMADA INN AND CONFERENCE CENTER
Manager: Mark Jeffrey.
683-3600; 800-289-0404.
144 Anthony Rd.,
  Portsmouth 02871.
Open: Year-round.
Price: Moderate.
Credit Cards: AE, CB, D,
  DC, MC, V.
Smoking: Non-smoking
  rooms available.
Handicap Access: Yes.
Note: No pets.

In addition to the 85 guest rooms are an indoor pool, sauna and exercise room, free movie-channel TV, and two adjacent golf courses. Cranberry's Restaurant serves breakfast, lunch, and dinner, and offers live entertainment and dancing Friday and Saturday nights.

WHITE CAP CABINS
Owner: Joan DeMello.
683-0476.
Vanderbilt La. (very end),
  Portsmouth 02871.
Open: May–Oct.
Price: Inexpensive to Mod-
  erate.
Credit Cards: None.
Smoking: Yes.
Handicap Access: No.

Never was there a better place to get away from it all: a dirt and gravel lane leads through arching farmland to a copse of woods, then continues to the Sakonnet River. Three tiny cabins cluster in utter privacy at the shoreline. One has just two twin beds; another is the bathroom; the third has a kitchenette, wood-burning stove, and double bed. There's no phone and no electricity; the cabins are lit with kerosene and gaslight (with rechargeable lamps for children if they're occupying one of the sleeping cabins — there are rechargeable TVs, too). This is the place to bring kids and pets — or go by yourself and write the great American novel. There's also a pebble beach, swing, and stone grill.

SAKONNET

Little Compton

BALLYVOREEN
Owners: Eileen & Jim
  McDermott.
635-4396.
75 Stone Church Rd., Little
  Compton/Adamsville
  02837 (no sign).
Open: "Can be open year-
  round."
Price: Inexpensive.
Credit Cards: None.
Smoking: No.
Handicap Access: Yes.
Note: No pets.

Ballyvoreen is the name of a village in Ireland where the owners' grandparents were born — in Gaelic it means "the dear little place which overlooks the sea." You can't see the water from the McDermott's 1893 Victorian home (complete with cross-gabled roof and patterned shingles), but it's not far away and there's a canoe for paddling around nearby coves and ponds. Ballyvoreen is a true B&B; guests share bath, TV (with VCR), phone, and full, hearty breakfasts with the family. The one guest room has twin beds. It's not fancy, but the McDermotts make you feel at home. Other pluses include a library of books on Little Compton and Ireland, a shady screened porch, and a parakeet.

THE ROOST
Innkeeper: Terry Hall.
635-8486, reservations; 635-
  8407, innkeeper.
170 West Main Rd., Little
  Compton 02837 (no sign).
Open: Year-round.
Price: Moderate.
Credit Cards: MC, V.
Smoking: Downstairs only,
  not in rooms.
Handicap Access: No.
Note: No pets, or children
  over 12.

Satisfying is the word to describe this 1920s cottage on the edge of Sakonnet Vineyards (bookings are made through the winery), simple and casual, full of sunlight and strong colors, just as a beach cottage should be. A fairly steep staircase leads to the three second-floor bedrooms, each with private bath and either a queen, full, or set of twin beds. Continental breakfast is at a communal table in the sunny kitchen or on the deck out back. It's an idyllic walk to the winery or a short drive to the beach.

**THE STONE HOUSE
  CLUB**
Owners: Virginia & Tod
  Moore.
635-2222.
120 Sakonnet Point Rd.,
  Little Compton 02837.
Open: Year-round.
Price: Moderate to Expen-
  sive.
Credit Cards: MC, V.
Smoking: Discouraged.

Built in 1836 out near Sakonnet Point, this imposing granite mansion has high ceilings and walls two feet thick. There are 11 guest rooms in the main house (nine with private bath) and two more in the renovated barn, which also accommodates conferences and group events. The furnishings look seasoned rather than antique, and complement the secluded, slightly brooding, they-can't-find-me-here feel of the place. Note that this is a club: non-members are welcome but must add $20 to lodging and $5 to meal costs, bringing the

Handicap Access: One room.
Note: No pets.

prices up no higher than average. Continental breakfast is included with lodging. There's also a dining room and tap room in the main house (see *Restaurants*), and a great pond, ocean views, and a beach within walking distance.

Tiverton

**BONNIEFIELD COT-
TAGE**
Owners: Nancy & Ray-
mond Lundgren.
624-6364.
Neck Rd., Tiverton 02878
(no sign).
Open: Year-round.
Price: Moderate.
Credit Cards: None.
Smoking: Outside only.
Handicap Access: No.
Note: No pets or children.
Special Features: Clay ten-
nis court.

This cottage behind the Lundgrens' home is surrounded by flowers and shade trees, a lawn with a fieldstone grill and picnic table, a coop with five pure-bred Rhode Island Red chickens, and a clay tennis court (bring flat tennis shoes if you want to play). The cottage is modest but pleasant and very clean, and offers a small living room with kitchenette, dining area, full bath, and a second-floor room, bright with white wainscoting, with twin beds (for a little bit extra there's a cot for a third person). Nancy doesn't serve breakfast but often leaves fresh eggs and vegetables from the garden so guests can make their own. A short walk leads to a private beach on the Sakonnet River.

BLOCK ISLAND

The Neck

WILLOW GROVE
Owners: Dan & Debbie
Hart.
466-2896.
Corn Neck Rd., Block
Island 02807.
Open: Memorial Day–mid-
Sept.
Price: Expensive.
Credit Cards: None.
Smoking: No.
Handicap Access: No.
Note: No mopeds.

Dan and Debbie Hart are 11th-generation owners of this fully restored, stately Victorian out almost to the end of Corn Neck Road near Sachem Pond. The antique-appointed guest room has a private bath and its own parlor, fridge, and separate entrance. (The Harts discovered that their home was a 19th-century boarding house called Willow Grove — hence the name.) Considering the beautiful, utterly peaceful setting, the lovely antiques, and Debbie's home-baked breakfast (her cooking has been written up in *Yankee Magazine*), it's not surprising that guests return year after year. Dan has a taxi service and will run you to and from the ferry.

New Harbor Area

THE BARRINGTON INN
Innkeepers: Joan & Howard
 Ballard.
466-5510.
PO Box 397, Block Island
 02807.
Open: Apr.–mid-Nov.
Price: Moderate to Expen-
 sive.
Credit Cards: MC, V.
Smoking: On decks and
 grounds only.
Handicap Access: No.
Note: No pets, or children
 under 12.

Set on a knoll at the cross of Beach and Ocean Avenues, the Barrington commands a view of the sweeping marshes and ponds that lead down to New Harbor and the sea. The six private-bath rooms in this 1886 farmhouse fill up quickly with repeat guests and are exceptionally light and airy. The three second-floor rooms open onto individual decks; another deck is off the dining room, and guests may have their continental breakfast there. Like many other island innkeepers, Joan provides a communal fridge, wine glasses, and hot and cold beverages for guests to enjoy throughout the day. There are two parlors, one with TV and VCR; a nearby barn has been converted into two housekeeping apartments.

**CHAMPLIN'S MARINA,
 MOTEL & RESORT**
Owner: Joe Grillo.
466-2641; 800-762-4521.
PO Box J, Block Island
 02807.
Open: May–Sept.
Price: Expensive to Very
 Expensive.
Credit Cards: MC, V.
Smoking: Yes.
Handicap Access: No.
Note: No pets.
Special Features: Pool, ten-
 nis courts, playground.

There is nothing else like Champlin's on the island. It's a self-contained resort, with its own pool, tennis courts, private beach, bike, car, and moped rentals, cinema, restaurant and dinner the-atre — Aldo's even has a bakery annex out here. Guests come by car or boat; the marina has 225 slips. Rooms are motel-style, with cable TV and deck (you can specify countryside or Harbor view); efficiency suites are also available.

**THE NARRAGANSETT
 INN**
Owner: Eleanor Mott.
466-2626.
Block Island 02807.
Open: Mid-June–mid-Sept.
Price: Expensive to Very
 Expensive.
Credit Cards: AE, D, MC,
 V.
Smoking: Yes.
Handicap Access: Yes.
Note: No pets.
Special Features: Children
 under 8 stay free.

The Narragansett boasts a dignified location on a rise above Payne's Dock at New Harbor. The 51 rooms, with both private and shared bath, are basic and somewhat threadbare, as is the sitting room (with TV). A grand dining room, doing its part to keep up the elegance of this 1905 landmark, serves full breakfast. From the outside the place is still magnificent, and the views it offers of the Har-bor can't be beat.

Old Harbor Area

THE ATLANTIC
Innkeepers: George & Jane
  Cronk.
466-5883.
High St./PO Box 188, Block
  Island 02807.
Open: Apr.–Oct.
Price: Expensive to Very
  Expensive.
Credit Cards: AE, MC, V.
Smoking: Discouraged.
Handicap Access: No.
Note: No pets.
Special Features: Tennis
  courts and croquet field;
  children under 12 stay
  free.

One of the best places on the island for a fabulous view of stone-walled fields, Old Harbor, and the beaches beyond, is the porch of the Atlantic Inn. Perched high on a hill above the village, the 1879 hotel is one of the island's specialties: a big white clapboard building with a mansard roof and a veranda. The 21 rooms all have private baths, telephones but no TVs, and many have sea views. The dining room is open to the public for lunch and dinner (see *Restaurants*), as well as the veranda, where you can recline on wicker love seats and sip cocktails after 4pm (there's also a raw bar). You may spot llamas, emus, and other beasts in the field below; they belong to the Manisses Hotel petting zoo.

THE BELLEVUE HOUSE
Owners: Neva Flaherty &
  Read Kingsbury.
466-2912.
High St./PO Box 1198,
  Block Island 02807.
Open: Mid-May–Columbus
  Day.
Price: Moderate.
Credit Cards: MC, V.
Smoking: Not in rooms.
Handicap Access: No.
Note: No pets.

It looks like a farmhouse, set behind stone walls in a grassy meadow, but the Bellevue was actually built as an inn in 1882. Recently purchased, the inn is being renovated; the clapboards may be peeling a bit, but all the things that really count have been well attended to. The five guest rooms are of modest size but attractively furnished in cozy, easy-to-live-with antiques. An abundant continental breakfast is served in the kitchen, though guests may take a tray to the front porch and gaze at the ocean. Two quaint cottages on the property rent weekly, as do two housekeeping apartments and three two-bedroom apartments — a good choice for couples traveling together.

THE BLUE DORY INN
Owners: Ann & Lisa Loedy.
466-5891; 800-992-7290.
Dodge St./PO Box 488,
  Block Island 02807.
Open: Year-round.
Price: Expensive.
Credit Cards: AE, MC, V.
Smoking: Discouraged.
Handicap Access: Minimal.
Note: Children welcome,
  no pets.

There's something inherently nice about the Blue Dory. Perhaps because it backs up to the beach, or maybe it's so cozy and compact. Certainly it's the friendly atmosphere. Guests are welcome to use the kitchen (where continental breakfast is served), TV parlor, and outside shower; beach towels and chairs are available on loan. Complimentary wine and cheese is served at 6pm, and a plate of cookies is offered for dessert. Most of the 11 guest rooms — all with private bath — are smallish, but comfortably decorated with antiques and floral prints. In

Craig Hammell

A carousel horse welcomes visitors to the Blue Dory Inn on Block Island.

addition to the main building are four cottages, one of which only rents weekly (another, the "Tea House," served as a speakeasy during Prohibition).

GABLES INN & GABLES II
Owners: Barbara & Stanley Nyzio.
466-2213.
Dodge St./PO Box 516, Block Island 02807.
Open: May–Nov.
Price: Moderate.
Credit Cards: MC, V.
Smoking: Discouraged.
Handicap Access: No.
Note: No pets.

There are 19 guest rooms between the main Gables Inn and the Gables II up the street, both built in the mid-19th century. The charming, cozy rooms are decorated with antiques and Victorian-print wallpaper, as are two lounges, one with TV. Some have private bath, though most share. A pleasant porch features rockers and hanging baskets. Barbara and Stanley also offer five efficiency apartments at the Gables II plus a private cottage. Stanley makes pastries for the continental breakfast himself, and Barbara is very knowledgeable about the island.

THE GOTHIC INN
Owners: Toube, Bennett, & Kenny Wohl.
466-2918.
537 Dodge St./PO Box 537, Block Island 02807.
Open: Mid-May–mid-Oct.
Price: Moderate to Expensive.
Credit Cards: MC, V.
Smoking: Discouraged.
Handicap Access: No.
Note: No pets.

The Gothic has an eye-catching, almost campy Victorian look. It was built by Captain Dodge in 1865, and is now being renovated by the Wohls, who also own the Block Island Pharmacy (where guests can rent TVs, VCRs, and tapes). The parlor is pleasantly furnished and the welcome enthusiastic and friendly; the nine shared-bath rooms are fairly basic but clean, and plans are in store to spruce them up. A "California-style" continental breakfast includes bagels, muffins, granola, yogurt, and fresh fruit. There are also two efficiency apartments for rent in a nearby annex.

THE HARBORSIDE

Manager: Chris Sereno.
466-5504.
Water St./PO Box F, Block
   Island 02807.
Open: May–mid-Oct.
Price: Moderate to Expen-
   sive.
Credit Cards: AE, MC, V.
Smoking: Permitted.
Handicap Access: No.
Note: No pets.

The Harborside's 37 rooms aren't fancy. There's no air-conditioning, no TV, and no buffer from the noisy chatter outside. But there's real atmosphere here. The third-floor bathrooms are tucked under eaves and the floorboards of the pleasant lobby list northward — the building dates from 1887 and is on the National Register. Most rooms have a private bath. (See Chapter Five for the Harborside Restaurant.)

Mountain bikes meet high Victorian architecture at the Hotel Manisses on Block Island.

Craig Hammell

HOTEL MANISSES

Owners: Joan Abrams &
   Rita Draper.
466-2063.
Spring St., Block Island
   02807.
Open: Year-round.
Price: Expensive to Very
   Expensive.
Credit Cards: AE, MC, V.
Smoking: Yes.
Handicap Access: No.
Note: No pets, or children
   under 12.
Special Features: Animal
   farm.

The Manisses is one of the best-known and most luxurious hotels on Block Island. Built in 1872, it's intensely Victorian, with its pagoda-like central tower, front veranda hung with flowers, mansard roof, and sunny wicker-filled parlor. The 17 guest rooms have private baths (some with Jacuzzis) and — a nice touch — are named after shipwrecks. All are decorated with period antiques and include a complimentary decanter of brandy. A full breakfast is served across the street at the 1661 Inn, as are lunch and complimentary afternoon "wine and nibbles." The Manisses dining room, probably the fanciest on the island, is open to the public for dinner (see *Restaurants*). Organized walking and van tours of the island — some with picnic lunches or sangria at sunset — are offered to Manisses guests.

ROSE FARM INN

Owners: Robert & Judith
 Rose.
466-2021.
High Street/Box E, Block
 Island.
Open: May–Oct.
Price: Moderate to Expen-
 sive.
Credit Cards: AE, MC, V.
Smoking: Not permitted in
 rooms.
Handicap Access: One
 room in modern exten-
 sion.
Note: No pets, or children
 under 12.

This turn-of-the-century farmhouse burrows into the rolling countryside, and offers sea views. There are 10 rooms in the main house and nine more in the new not-quite-motel-style extension. Guests may choose between private or shared bath (deluxe rooms offer whirlpool and private deck). The guest rooms are furnished with antiques and period replicas as is the parlor, which offers both TV and wet bar. A continental buffet breakfast is served on the enclosed front porch.

SEA BREEZE INN

Owners: Bob & Mary New-
 house.
466-2275; 800-786-2276.
Spring St./PO Box 141,
 Block Island 02807.
Open: Year-round.
Price: Moderate to Expen-
 sive.
Credit Cards: MC, V.
Smoking: Not encouraged.
Handicap Access: Limited.
Note: No pets, or children
 under 5.

Hidden from Spring Street by tall pine trees, the Sea Breeze is actually three smallish cottages with a garden in between and nothing but the ocean behind. The rooms are simple and summery, decorated in fresh, clean-lined combinations of the old and new. A brass bed against a painted hardwood floor can be a welcome relief after all that Victoriana elsewhere on the island. There are 10 rooms plus one efficiency apartment that rents weekly. Breakfast is delivered in a picnic basket to the five rooms with private bath; guests in the other five receive their morning victuals at a communal table. Don't look for TVs or telephone, just a relaxed atmosphere, friendly hosts, and the sea.

SHEFFIELD HOUSE

Innkeepers: Steve & Claire
 McQueeny.
466-2494.
High St./PO Box C-2, Block
 Island 02807.
Open: Year-round.
Price: Moderate to Expen-
 sive.
Credit Cards: AE, MC, V.
Smoking: No.
Handicap Access: No.
Note: No children or pets.

A short trek uphill from Old Harbor, this Queen Anne was built in 1888 as a summer cottage, with a wraparound veranda (complete with rocking chairs), patterned shingles, and a wonderful turret, all very well kept today. In summer a lush, colorful flower garden dominates the front yard. The inn's seven rooms are comfortably decorated with antiques, wicker, and family pieces — most have private baths. A generous continental breakfast is served in the kitchen. There's an outside shower out back.

THE 1661 INN

Owners: Joan Abrams &
    Rita Draper.
466-2421.
Spring St., Block Island
    02807.
Open: Year-round.
Price: Expensive to Very
    Expensive.
Credit Cards: AE, MC, V.
Smoking: Yes.
Handicap Access: Yes.
Note: No pets.

On the seaward side of Spring Street is the 1661 Inn, named for the year that Block Island was purchased and settled by 16 English families. The unpretentious exterior belies the lavishness on the inside: the nine sumptuous rooms in this mid-19th-century white clapboard home all have private bath and are decorated with a mix of antiques and colonial replicas. There are more rooms in a separate guest house and cottage. The most expensive suite has a private deck, endless ocean views, and loft given over entirely to an enormous Jacuzzi. A full breakfast is served overlooking the ocean. The Settler's Pub (a sea-view dining room and deck) is also open to the public for lunch and cocktails, till 6pm.

The restrained charm of a guest room at the Spring House on Block reflects the island's easygoing style.

Craig Hammell

THE SPRING HOUSE

Manager: Vincent
    McAloon.
466-5844.
Spring St./PO Box 902,
    Block Island 02807.
Open: May–mid-Nov.
Price: Expensive to Very
    Expensive.
Credit Cards: AE, MC, V.
Smoking: Yes.
Handicap Access: No.
Note: No pets.

Set on a 15-acre promontory above the sea, the Spring House is the oldest of the island's grand Victorian hotels. The original house, built in 1852, was revamped in 1870 to its present appearance: a white clapboard building with a wraparound porch, and a red-shingled mansard roof with a distinctive cupola. The porch, where an all-you-can-eat lunch barbecue is served to the public, is one of the best places on Block for an ocean view with your drink. The dining room serves continental breakfast on pink-clothed tables; dinner and Sunday brunch are open to the public, offering a gourmet menu in the expensive range. All 49 rooms

— 32 in the main building, 17 in a similar structure nearby — have private bath and telephone. On one side of the front entrance is a cavernous bar with clusters of upholstered love seats and chairs; to the other is the lobby, a magnificent place with a fieldstone fireplace, open archways, and an air of just slightly faded elegance. Despite ownership problems in recent years, the Spring House is still going strong.

THE SURF
Owners: Ulric & Beatrice Cyr.
466-2241.
Dodge St./Box C, Block Island 02807.
Open: Memorial–Columbus Day.
Price: Moderate.
Credit Cards: MC, V.
Smoking: Everywhere but breakfast room.
Handicap Access: No.
Note: No pets.
Special Features: Great porch with sea views; bike rentals.

The porch of the Surf is supposedly the most-photographed spot in Rhode Island. Guests are tempted to spend the day on it in a wooden rocker, gazing out over Old Harbor and Crescent Beach. The hotel itself, mostly built in 1876, is a local landmark and a gabled, shingled tribute to New England Victoriana. The lobby continues the theme with Tiffany lamps and comfortable antiques. The 35 rooms in the main building are smallish but charming with simple, old-fashioned decor; two other buildings house another 12 rooms. All have sinks and shared baths. A full breakfast is served in the tin-ceilinged dining room. A six-day minimum is recommended in season. TV and telephone in lobby only.

West, Center, and South Sides

McCOMBE'S B&B
Owners: Teri & Bill McCombe.
466-2684.
Old Town Rd./PO Box 261, Block Island.
Open: Memorial Day–mid-Sept.
Price: Moderate to Expensive.
Credit Cards: None.
Smoking: Porch only.
Handicap Access: No.
Note: No pets, or children under 12.

He's the chief of police, she's the school art teacher: together they run a terrific B&B. There's only one guest room in this lovely, secluded spot, but it's a good one, with its own entrance and deck overlooking the back meadow, private bath, and queen-size bed. The room is sizable, and has a dining area (complete with old ice cream parlor furniture), white-washed wood, lace curtains, and Teri's own artwork. Every morning she'll deliver a gourmet continental breakfast to your door in an old picnic hamper. It's perfect for a small family, two couples (the sofa pulls out), or as a great romantic get-away. In case it rains there's color/cable TV. A nice touch is Teri's photo album of island attractions.

OLD TOWN INN
Owners: Monica, Ralph, & David Gunter.
466-5958.

Built c. 1870, the Old Town Inn is the only building remaining from the island's former town center. It's now on a quiet road overgrown with bayberry and blackberry bushes, far from the din of

Old Town Rd./PO Box 351, Block Island 02807.
Open: Memorial–Columbus Day.
Price: Moderate to Expensive.
Credit Cards: MC, V.
Smoking: Everywhere but dining room.
Handicap Access: No.
Note: No pets, or children under 5.

Old Harbor. The Gunters have been cheerfully running the inn for 25 years. Eight of the 10 rooms have private bath, the other two share. They're more utilitarian than charming, but are clean and bright, and include small refrigerators. A full breakfast is served in the dining room, and the lounge has a TV and pay telephone. This is the only real inn beyond the Old and New Harbor areas.

A former Primitive Methodist Church, the Sasafrash Inn on Block Island boasts a beautiful — and unusual — interior.

Craig Hammell

THE SASAFRASH
Owners: Shirley & Sanford Kessler.
466-5486.
Center Rd./PO Box 1073, Block Island 02807.
Open: Year-round.
Price: Moderate to Expensive.
Credit Cards: None.
Smoking: Not in bedrooms.
Handicap Access: No.
Note: No children or pets.
Special Features: Restored church.

It's impossible to express enough delight about the Sasafrash. It was built in 1907 as a Primitive Methodist Church, smack in the heart of Block Island (where the old town center used to be, about a 10-minute walk to New Harbor). The Kesslers have restored the church and made it their home. Gothic arched stained-glass windows complement their wonderful, eclectic collection of art and antiques — the view from the front door through to the rounded-arch area that was once an altar is breathtaking. Four guest rooms are on the second floor, which extends like a choir loft over half the living area below. Two have private bath, the others share. All the furniture is from the island (Shirley is also an antiques dealer), and the rooms are comfortable and bright, with unusual windows and angled walls. Shirley serves a full breakfast, and wine and cheese in the afternoon. There's also a back deck and outside shower.

CHAPTER FOUR

The Gilded Age and All That Jazz
CULTURE

Culture may be pronounced "Kelcha" here in Rhode Island, but that doesn't mean we don't have it. From colonial times through the Gilded Age, Newport, especially, has been one of the leading cities in America in the realm of architecture, the decorative and fine arts, and more recently, music.

Gilbert Stuart, the American portraitist who captured George Washington's likeness for posterity (more than once) was born in North Kingstown. Stuart was the first American artist to achieve a significant reputation abroad. By the mid-19th century, several painters of note were working in Newport: John La Farge, the preeminent decorative artist of his day, did the stained glass sequences

Craig Hammell

The Jamestown windmill was built in 1787. The stone walls in the foreground may be just as ancient, as are many of the dry-wall mazes throughout Narragansett Bay towns and Block Island.

in the **Channing Memorial Chapel** and **Newport Congregational Church,** as well as the wall murals in the latter. William Morris Hunt, credited for introducing romanticism to American art, took up residence in Newport in 1855.

Noted master craftsmen of colonial Newport include the Townsend and Goddard furniture-making families, and clockmaker William Claggett. (See the Antiques section of Chapter Seven, *Shopping*, for information about their work.)

Despite a brief reign by summer visitors like Henry James and Edith Wharton in the 1870s, Culture with a capital C became the sole province of the New York society crowd, who came, saw, and built mansions. Some bad-tempered people say that this is actually when Culture on Narragansett Bay came to an end, and Recreation — in the form of tennis, polo, and above all else, yachting — took over. But the construction of the mansions brought the finest architects and artisans in the world to Newport, and their legacy of stone, gilt, and marble has become a tool for understanding a vanished world. It should also be noted that some of the mansions are outstanding museums in their own right: Belcourt Castle, for instance, has the finest collection of 13th-century stained glass in the country.

Today music reigns supreme on the shores of Narragansett Bay. Three festivals bring the best classical, folk, and jazz musicians in the world to Newport each summer. The city gets crowded, but the sounds of Sonny Rollins's sax are worth some minor traffic jams.

If Newport's crowds do get on your nerves, however, don your cushion-soled museum shoes and take a trip to Providence. **The Rhode Island School of Design Museum** (454-6100; Benefit St.) is easily one of the best small art museums in the country. And don't overlook the **John Brown House** (331-8575; 52 Power St.), which John Quincy Adams called "the most magnificent private mansion" he'd seen in America. Or, if you're staying on the West Bay, call the **University of Rhode Island** (792-2200) in nearby Kingston for a schedule of events.

ARCHITECTURE

When it comes to architecture, Rhode Island's size is ideal. You can travel centuries within miles here; individual towns — and even streets — were seemingly built for no other purpose than to serve as pattern books of American architecture. The built landscape of Newport, especially, is as fine as it gets in this country. (For specifics about Newport's architecture, see the Historic Buildings & Sites section below.)

One type of colonial building was actually named for the state: the 17th-century Rhode Island stone-ender. These farmhouses were still built on medieval lines, and featured a massive fieldstone hearth along one wall. While there are none in the Narragansett Bay area (the nearest is the **Clemence-Irons House** in the village of Manton, in Johnston), the largest 17th-century home in New England can be found in Bristol: the three-story Joseph Reynolds House (1694), which is also a B&B (see the *Lodging* chapter). Bristol is well known for its Federal and especially its Greek Revival homes. The former represents a restrained, slightly more severe version of the Georgian style practiced during the colonial period (see the **William's Grant Inn**, *Lodging*, for a typical five-bay Federal clapboard structure); the little village of Wickford, on the western side of the Bay in North Kingstown, also boasts a fine collection of colonial and Federal homes, particularly on Main Street.

The Greek Revival came into vogue in the early to mid-19th century as an architectural corollary to the principles of the new American government. Its temple-like roofs, gable end to the street, and massive Doric, Ionic, and Corinthian columns were meant to summon associations with the Athenian democracy of ancient Greece. Bristol's Hope Street — the main thoroughfare — has some wonderfully massive examples of this style; peek down side streets for smaller, cottage-size versions.

Not surprisingly for "America's First Resort," Rhode Island is rich with Victorian resort architecture. The Newport mansions represent the most lavish flowering of this phase, but don't miss their less ostentatious — and in many ways more picturesque — Queen Anne and Shingle style neighbors (for example, the magnificent **Watts Sherman House,** a classic Queen Anne manor built in 1884 to a design by H.H. Richardson, and the **Isaac Bell House** of 1882—83, a superb Shingle style home by McKim, Mead, and White. More fine Shingle style homes are in Narragansett Pier's Historic District, but for Victorian hotels — great, white clapboard affairs with wraparound porches and mansard roofs — look to Block Island.

In fact, those buildings on Block Island are still being used; therefore, there are no listings for Block in the Historic Buildings section. It's a fine tribute to wooden structures that over the past century have withstood everything from winter storms to the 1938 hurricane. There's a wonderful continuity to Block Island building: while the Surf Hotel may have gingerbread porch brackets and a multi-gabled roof, its gray shingles hark back to the island's earliest farmsteads and outbuildings. And when Robert Venturi started playing around with Post Modernism in the early 1980s, one of his first homes was a little shingled beach cottage off Corn Neck Road. (A 1952 Harvard study proposed rebuilding Block Island as an exclusively International Style resort — a world of elongated steel I-beams and glass walls — good thing the shingles held out.)

CINEMA

Because there are so few cinemas in this part of the world, theaters that are just beyond the region's borders are also included.

West Bay

Pier Cinema 1 & 2 (789-3649; 3 Beach St., Narragansett)

Campus Twin (783-5972; Columbia St., Wakefield)

Showcase Cinemas 1–12 (885-1621; 1200 Quaker La./Rte. 2, Warwick; Exit 8A southbound, 9A northbound off Rte. I-95)

East Bay

Bristol Cinema (253-4312; 91 Bradford St., Bristol)

Showcase Cinemas: 1–8 (508-336-6020; 800 Fall River Ave./Rte. 114, Seekonk MA); 9 & 10 (508-336-3420; 775 Fall River Ave./Rte. 114, Seekonk MA)

Aquidneck

Holiday 7 (847-3001, W. Main Rd./Rte. 114, Middletown)

Starcase Cinemas (849-7777; 1346 W. Main Rd./Rte. 114, Middletown)

Jane Pickens Theatre (846-5252; 49 Touro St., Newport)

Opera House (847-3456; 19 Touro St., Newport)

Block Island

Empire Theatre (466-2555; Water St., Old Harbor) Seasonal.

Oceanwest Theatre (466-2971; Champlain's Marina, New Harbor) Seasonal.

DANCE

East Bay

Roger Williams University Dance Theatre (254-3624; Old Ferry Rd., Bristol) Call for a schedule of dance concerts performed by faculty, students, and guest artists.

Aquidneck

Island Moving Company (847-4470) Newport's resident dance company, IMC puts on a short series of outdoor summer dance concerts plus a holiday show in Newport in December. All performances feature new works accompanied by live music. The summer series is on the campus of St. George's School in Middletown; bring a picnic dinner (or buy one there), and take in not only great dancing but a panoramic view of Second Beach. Cutting-edge performing artists in an idyllic setting.

FINE ART GALLERIES

The Bay area is well served by both contemporary artists and a fine legacy of Gilded Age art collecting (look for "de-accessioned" private collections now hanging in local galleries). It's no surprise that **Christie's Fine Art Auctioneers** maintains an office in Newport. Following is a selection of both commercial and not-for-profit art galleries, featuring fine and folk arts — paintings, works on paper, sculpture, and the like. Remember, most galleries are closed on Monday.

West Bay

The Artist's Gallery of Wickford (294-6280; 5 Main St., Wickford) A co-op of fine artwork by Rhode Island artists; currently a selection of Frederick Remington bronzes.

Wickford Art Association Gallery (294-6840; 36 Beach St., N. Kingstown/Wickford) An active local arts organization that sponsors shows year-round; tends to focus on juried competitions and work by local artists. All media.

East Bay

Roger Williams University School of Architecture Gallery (254-3605; 1 Old Ferry Rd., Bristol) Works by faculty, students, and guest artists.

Aquidneck

Arnold Art Gallery (847-2273; 210 Thames St., Newport) Third-floor space for exhibits by contemporary artists.

DeBlois Gallery (847-9977; 138 Bellevue Ave., Newport) The spot to get a preview of local talent. Two artists show for two weeks, then another group takes over. All local, mostly contemporary work.

Fisher Gallery (849-7446; 481 Thames St., Newport) Look for small works in neon, plus framing done on the premises.

Hydrangea House Gallery (846-4435; 16 Bellevue Ave., Newport) Guests of the Hydrangea House B&B (see *Lodging*) get to eat breakfast in the gallery, but anyone can stop in. Small but select monthly shows focus on contemporary works, especially still lifes and seascapes.

Liberty Tree (847-5925; 104 Spring St., Newport) A fabulously full contemporary folk art gallery of great variety and richness. Mind the sheep dog.

Long Wharf Fine Arts Ltd. (847-6661; 10 America's Cup Ave., Newport) In the Brick Market Place shopping area: look for a selection of contemporary, international work from pop art to neo-surrealism.

McKillop Gallery (847-3160; Salve Regina University, Ochre Point Ave., Newport) Works by faculty, students, and contemporary artists.

The Newport Gallery (849-8218; 4 Perry Mill Market Place, off Thames St., Newport) A small, eclectic gallery featuring seascapes and marine art.

Norton's Oriental Gallery (849-4468; 415 Thames St., Newport) 18th- and 19th-century Chinese silk embroideries are the highlight of this two-story gallery in a c. 1835 home.

Roger King Fine Arts (847-4359; 21 Bowen's Wharf, off America's Cup Ave., Newport) A fine collection of 19th-century realist and Impressionist landscapes (primarily) hang in this three-story wharf space.

Spring Bull Studio (849-9166; Spring St., Newport) "Art in Architecture" — multi-media works by southern New England artists and architects — is a recent show representative of the gallery.

William Vareika Fine Arts (849-6149; 212 Bellevue Ave., Newport) Established in 1985, the William Vareika gallery offers two floors of beautifully mounted 18th-, 19th-, and 20th-century American art of the highest quality. Look for works by American romantic and realist artist John La Farge.

Sakonnet

Sakonnet Painters Cooperative Gallery (624-6545; 18 Commons, Little Compton) Weekly exhibits of members' works plus those of invited guests.

Virginia Lynch Gallery (624-3392 Main Rd./Rte. 77, Tiverton) One of the best galleries in the state: look for work by internationally known artists in everything from glass to photography. It could be in Soho, but it's in Tiverton.

Block Island

Art Constructions (466-2924; High St., Old Harbor) A recent show featured sculptures, reliefs, and drawings by a well-known Peruvian artist.

Malcolm Greenaway Galleries (466-2122; PO Box 506/Water St., Old Harbor) Greenaway is Block Island's premiere photographer; this is where to purchase one of his cibachrome prints.

Portfolio Gallery & Coffeehouse (466-5455; Block Island Marketplace, Ocean Ave., bet. Old & New Harbor) A recent show featured English wood, steel, and copper engravings from the 19th century.

Ragged Sailor Gallery (466-7704; Chapel St., Old Harbor) No formal openings, but continuing displays of contemporary, realist work including photographs, watercolors, oils, and pastels.

Spring Street Gallery (466-5374; Spring St., Old Harbor area) Changing exhibitions by contemporary local and nationally-known artists; media range from stained glass to paper quilts.

Square One Gallery (466-2112; Beacon Hill & West Side Rd.) It's a hike and you have to make an appointment, but try to reach this wonderful, secluded spot on Beacon Hill. The space is capped by a 20-foot vaulted ceiling, over works by contemporary area artists.

Terra Gallery (466-5699; 239 Ocean Ave., bet. Old & New Harbor) A very eclectic collection ranging from drawings and paintings to jewelry and artist's books.

GARDENS & GARDEN TOURS

West Bay

Wild Plant Walk (South County Museum, 783-7121; Canonchet Farm, off Beach St./Rte. 1A, Narragansett) See Museums & Historic Houses for more on Canonchet Farm and the South County Museum. Annual (mid-July) guided walk along nature trails on this 174-acre park.

East Bay

Blithewold Manor in Bristol is the centerpiece of one of the largest and most exotic arboretums in New England.

Craig Hammell

Blithewold Gardens & Arboretum (253-2707; 101 Ferry Rd./Rte. 114, Bristol) These grounds — 33 acres overlooking Narragansett Bay — harbor one of the first and most innovative arboretums in America, with exotic trees, shrubs, and flowers not grown anywhere else in New England, including the largest giant redwood east of the Rockies. In April Blithewold hosts Daffodil Week — one of the largest daffodil displays in the country, featuring over 30,000 blooming bulbs. Open year-round for self-guided tours ($3 adults, 50¢ children). See Historic Buildings for information on Blithewold Mansion.

Bristol Historical House & Garden Annual Tour (253-7223; 48 Court St., Bristol) Sponsored by the Bristol Historical & Preservation Society, this annual tour offers an unparalleled chance to see Bristol's exceptional homes and well-tended gardens. Usually scheduled toward the end of September.

A leafy bear at Green Animals topiary garden in Portsmouth.

Craig Hammell

Aquidneck

Green Animals Topiary Gardens (847-1000; Cory's Lane off Rte. 114, Portsmouth) Down a long lane near the Bay is a modest 19th-century estate. Behind the house are 80 sculpted trees and shrubs — considered to be the best topiary garden in the country. Bring the kids to marvel over 21 animals and birds, including the bear, the unicorn, the giraffe, the dinosaur, even a peacock, all growing (some to 26 feet) from the green leaves of privet hedges and yews. Open daily June–Sept.; $6 adults, $3 children.

Secret Gardens Tour (846-0514; Newport) An opportunity to tour the private courtyard gardens of colonial and Victorian homes in Newport's Point Section — which is something of a secret itself (a residential treasure-trove of old homes and narrow streets abutting Newport Harbor). Mid-June.

Block Island

Block Island House & Garden Tour (466-2982) Held every August, the tour offers a window on the island under cultivation — in contrast to the tangle of wild bayberry that has its way elsewhere. Superb vernacular architecture to boot.

HISTORIC BUILDINGS & SITES

The Narragansett Bay region is as rich in historic places as it is in quahogs, maybe more so.

In 1933 a survey of historic properties concluded that there were nine truly exceptional public buildings from the colonial period still standing in the United States. Boston and Philadelphia tied for second place with two each — Newport was the winning city with three (the **Redwood Library**, the **Brick Market**, and the **Old Colony House**) These are magnificent buildings, but the significance of Newport's historic architecture and of many of the smaller towns around Narragansett Bay rests upon the preservation of whole neighborhoods rather than one or two individual structures. Newport has over 300 pre-Revolutionary buildings alone, most of which remain private residences. Stroll through the **Historic Hill** district between Thames Street and Bellevue Avenue, roughly bordered by Touro Street on the north and Memorial Boulevard on the south. Here in the thick of things are calm side streets like Clarke and Division, where a sprinkling of 17th-, but mostly 18th- and early 19th-century homes nuzzle up against the sidewalks. (One of Newport's resident slave traders lived on Division, directly opposite the first free black church in Newport which was also a stop on the underground railroad.) For an uninterrupted taste of the past, cross Broadway and head to Newport's northwestern tip (right in the shadow of the Newport Bridge), the **Point Section** of town.

The Point is a marvel: T-shirt shops and bars don't exist here; it's an exclusively residential area of quiet streets lined with well-kept homes one, two, and three centuries old. (For B&Bs in this area see *Lodging*.) Guidebooks are notorious for throwing around the term "best-kept secret," but this fine place is Newport's unknown treasure. Walk here, don't drive — a bench in the tiny John J. Martins Memorial Park on Washington St., which incidentally offers a great view of the Newport Bridge, makes an ideal place to rest. Both Terence Gavan's *Exploring Newport* and *Best Read Guide: Newport* — the latter is free — contain walking tour descriptions of historic homes throughout the city, both open and closed to the public.

The waterfront is the busiest part of town — and in some ways, with four-lane America's Cup Avenue streaming through it, the most obviously adapted to the 20th century — yet this is also the heart of colonial Newport. **Long Wharf** was already decades old when **Brick Market** (now home to the new **Museum of Newport History**; see below) was built in 1722 in a neoclassical design by famous local architect Peter Harrison. The graceful Palladian arches on the ground floor (now closed) were built wide enough to accommodate wagons laden with farm produce. (Don't confuse Brick Market with **Brick Market Place**, an outdoor mall adjacent to the building — see *Shopping*.) Heading south down the Harborfront you'll come to **Bowen's Wharf** and **Bannister's Wharf**. The cobblestones belong to a recent restoration, but most of the buildings here, though they teem with chic shops, gourmet restaurants, and bars, date to the 18th and early 19th centuries. **Perry Mill**, at the convergence of America's Cup Ave., Thames St., and Memorial Blvd., is a handsome granite structure built as a textile mill in 1835 by Alexander MacGregor, the stonemason who was also responsible for **Fort Adams**.

Bay towns like Wickford, Bristol, and Warren have equally superb, if smaller, nests of historic homes. And then there is Block Island, Rhode Island's ode to architectural Victoriana. (These areas have few — or no — historic structures open to the public; see the Architecture section above for a general description.) The "cottages" — mansions to those who don't live in them — are listed in their own section below.

Local historical societies are a terrific source of information and often may be able to arrange private tours to homes not usually open to visitors. The following list will get you started:

Block Island Historical Society (466-2481; Old Town Rd.)

Bristol Historical & Preservation Society (253-7223; 48 Court St.)

East Greenwich Preservation Society (884-4988; 110 King St.)

Little Compton Historical Society (635-4559; 635 W. Main Rd./Rte. 77)

Portsmouth Historical Society (683-9178; 870 E. Main Rd. Rte. 138)

Preservation Society of Newport County (847-1000; PO Box 510, Newport)
PSNC maintains many of the mansions.

Narragansett Historical Society (783-4695; The Towers)

Newport Historical Society (846-0813; 82 Touro St.)

Rhode Island Historical Society (331-8575; Providence)

Tiverton Historical Society (624-8881)

West Bay

CANONCHET FARM
783-5400.
Strathmore St. off Beach
  St./Rte. 1A, Narragansett
  Pier.
Season: Daylight hours
  daily.
Free.

A cloudy day treat: a small 19th-century working farm set within a 174-acre park. Poke around the cemetery (graves date back to 1700), hike the fitness and nature trails, picnic, or visit South County Museum which is also here.

CASEY FARM
617-227-3956.
Boston Neck Rd./Rte. 1A,
  N. Kingstown/Saunders-
  town.

This large, white clapboard home looks almost too elegant to be an 18th-century farmstead. Built c. 1750, it overlooks Narragansett Bay and is encompassed by fields, woodlands, outbuildings,

The Silas Casey Farm in North Kingstown is an elegant reminder of plantation-style estates that once swept across western Rhode Island.

Craig Hammell

Season: June–Sept., Sun. 1–5.

Admission: $3 adults, $1.50 children.

tight-knit stone walls, and a family cemetery. This is a rare example of a Yankee plantation, inherited by a succession of gentlemen farmers. The property is maintained by the Society for the Preservation of New England Antiquities, which conducted archaeological fieldwork there during the 1992–93 season. Take a tour to see what they've found. (Don't miss the bullet hole in the parlor door — a memento from the Revolutionary War.)

GEN. JAMES MITCHELL VARNUM HOUSE
884-1776.
57 Pierce St., E. Greenwich.
Season: Memorial–Labor Day, Tues.–Sat. 1–4.
Nominal admission.

Built c. 1773, this is a mansion-sized house filled with excellent examples of colonial furniture and fabrics. Note especially the magnificent paneling, and don't forget to see the 18th-century garden.

Gilbert Stuart, George Washington's biographer-on-canvas, was born in this c. 1751 homestead in North Kingstown.

Craig Hammell

GILBERT STUART BIRTHPLACE
294-3001.
815 Gilbert Stuart Rd., N. Kingstown.
Season: Apr.–mid-Nov. Closed Fri.
Admission: $2 adults, $1 children.

Not just anybody's c. 1751 home, but that of Gilbert Stuart, the man responsible for all those portraits of George Washington. This deep colonial red homestead is tucked in the woods between Rtes. 1 and 1A. A real treat is the operating 18th-century snuff mill (the first in America), complete with water wheel. Stuart was born here but lived much of his adult life in Europe.

JAMESTOWN WIND-MILL
423-1798.
North Rd., Jamestown.

Erected in 1787 on a high, windy hill above the Bay, this weathered-shingle monument to colonial know-how was recently restored by the Jamestown Historical Society. It was a tradition

Season: Mid-June–mid-
   Sept., Sat. & Sun.
Free.

**OLD NARRAGANSETT
   CHURCH**
294-4357.
Church La., off Main St., N.
   Kingstown/Wickford.
Season: Mid-June–mid-
   Sept., Fri.–Sun.
Free.

SMITH'S CASTLE
294-3521.
55 Richard Smith Dr., off
   Post Rd./Rte. 1, N.
   Kingstown.
Season: May & Sept., open
   Fri.–Sun.; June–Aug.,
   Thurs.–Mon.
Admission: $3 adults, $1
   children under 12.

THE TOWERS
783-7121.
Ocean Rd., Narragansett
   Pier.
Season: July 4th–Labor
   Day, Sat.–Sun. 12–4.
Free.

WATSON FARM
423-0005.
North Rd., Jamestown.
Season: June–Oct. 15, Tues.,
   Thurs., Sun.
Admission: $4 adults, $2
   children.

here that whenever the mill stones were re-grooved — an event that caused some grit to get mixed in with the grain — the miller, were he a Democrat, would select a Republican's grist to grind — and vice versa.

Take the "old" in the name seriously. Built in 1707, this is one of the oldest Episcopal churches in the country; it possesses the oldest church organ (1680) in North America. Of note are the Queen Anne communion silver, the old-fashioned box pews, elegant wine-glass pulpit, and slave gallery. Gilbert Stuart (see above) was baptized here.

In 1678, Roger Smith rebuilt the blockhouse, or fortified trading post, that had been destroyed in King Philip's War. (Roger Williams had originally established it 42 years earlier). Smith called the place "Cocumscussoc" for the Native American name for the area. Visitors simply called it Smith's Castle. It's considered one of the oldest plantation houses in America, set on 27 square miles of coastal lands and gardens — have fun imagining it full of English-style squires and their families. There's an archaeological dig on the premises.

You can't miss these massive stone landmarks on Ocean Road, right next to the Coast Guard House restaurant. The 1885 towers and the arch they bear are all that's left of Stanford White's magnificent Narragansett Pier Casino, built in 1883 and burned to the ground in 1900. Today the Towers still summon up a powerful, romantic image of seaside days past.

A mid-19th-century farmhouse (moved to this spot), and 280 acres open for self-guided touring (enjoy the great Bay vistas) are the attractions. Still a working farm, it was being renovated in the 1993 season, an undertaking sponsored by the Society for the Preservation of New England Antiquities.

East Bay

BLITHEWOLD MAN-SION
253-2707.
101 Ferry Rd./Rte. 114, Bristol.
Season: Apr.–Oct., closed Mon.
Admission: $6 adults, $2 children (for mansion & gardens).

If any 45-room, turn-of-the-century mansion can be called charming and unpretentious, it's Blithewold. While a bit overshadowed by the spectacular gardens and arboretum (see the Garden section above), the mansion has its attractions too. It was built by coal magnate Augustus Van Wickle in 1908 to resemble a 17th-century stone-and-stucco English manor house, and indeed it does. A great place to watch the Bay and daydream about being rich.

Courtesy Coggeshall Farm

Hands-on activities at Coggeshall Farm in Bristol's Colt State Park.

COGGESHALL FARM MUSEUM
253-9062.
Colt State Park, off Hope St./Rte. 114, Bristol.
Season; Year-round exc. Jan., closed Mon.
Nominal admission.

The fields, woods, and rocky shores of Colt State Park (see *Recreation*) settle comfortably into Poppasquash peninsula. Nestled within the park is Coggeshall Farm, an 18th-century working farmstead featuring a team of oxen, colonial crafts and games, and historical herb and vegetable gardens. Write for a calendar of events, which includes the blessing of the animals (August), sheep-shearing

(May), maple sugaring (March), and other traditional events. Look for now-rare breeds of animals once common to 18th-century farms.

LINDEN PLACE
253-0390.
500 Hope St./Rte. 114, Bristol.
Season: Memorial–Labor Day., Weds., Sat., Sun.
Admission: $2.

An architectural confection more than a Federal mansion, this 1810 home designed by Russell Warren is the wedding cake of Bristol's "fair houses." It's every inch the impressive showplace owner George De Wolf intended (although he decamped in 1825 after he overspeculated and brought the town to financial ruin). The staircase is magnificent. The outbuildings include a 1906 ballroom and a carriage barn.

MASONIC TEMPLE
245-7652.
Baker St., Warren.
Admission: By appointment only.

This 19th-century temple is the oldest in New England. Make an appointment, if only to see twin Federal style doorways — masterpieces of elaborate carpentry — built from timbers of British frigates sunk in Newport Harbor during the Revolution.

MAXWELL HOUSE
245-7652.
59 Church St., Warren.
Season: June–Aug., first Fri. of the month.
No admission fee.

Prepare to be awed by the massive central chimney — complete with two beehive baking ovens — which dominates this gambrel-roofed colonial home built c. 1750. Fireplace cooking, candle-dipping, and other 18th-century skills are frequently demonstrated — call to ask what's up.

Aquidneck

CHANNING MEMORIAL CHURCH
846-0643.
135 Pelham St., Newport.
Services: Sun., 11am.

This rough-cut granite church, built in 1880, was named for William Ellery Channing, founder of American Unitarianism. Take special note of the stained glass windows by artist and sometime Newporter John La Farge (for more La Farge glass see Newport Congregational Church). Julia Ward Howe was a member of the congregation.

COMMON BURIAL GROUND
Farewell St., Newport.

Where else would pragmatic colonists put the graveyard but on Farewell Street? It's a pity that this wonderful historic cemetery isn't in better repair, but beneath the overgrowth are more than 3000 headstones and tombs, hundreds from the

18th century and many from the 17th. The eerie winged skull motif, a staple of colonial folk art, is here in force. (Many of the early carvings are by local masters William Mumford and John Stevens and son). The southern part of the yard was reserved for citizens, the northern for slaves.

EDWARD KING HOUSE
846-7426.
Aquidneck Park, 35 King
   St., Newport.
Season: Year-round,
   Mon.–Fri.
Free.

Envy the senior citizens of Newport: their community center is in the Edward King House, designed by Richard Upjohn c. 1846 and considered one of the premier Italianate villas in the nation. The central hall is a majestic, riveting space. (Another Upjohn villa is Finnegan's Inn at Shadow Lawn in Middletown; see *Lodging*.)

**FRIENDS MEETING
   HOUSE**
846-0813.
21 Farewell St.,
   Newport/Point Section.
Open by appointment only;
   call one week in advance.
No admission fee.

Constructed in 1699 and expanded in 1729, this is the oldest religious structure in New England. In 1730 over half the townspeople of Newport were Quakers and met here to worship. (During the Revolution, the Quakers' pacifism led many Newporters to consider them traitors to the cause — homes were burned and leading Quakers were jailed.)

Craig Hammell

The façade of Hunter House tells the story of Newport's 18th-century sophistication and wealth.

HUNTER HOUSE
847-1000.
54 Washington St., New-
   port/Point Section.
Season: Apr. & Oct.,
   Sat.–Sun.; May–Sept.,
   daily.

Considered one of the 10 best examples of colonial architecture in the country, this 1748 home is furnished with Newport's famous Townsend-Goddard furniture (see the Antiques section in the *Shopping* chapter for more information). The elaborate front door treatment (originally on the water

Admission: $6 adults, $3 children.

side of the house) is complete with a carved pineapple on top. Take a look at the colonial garden, too.

JEWISH CEMETERY
Corner of Bellevue Ave. & Kay St., Newport.

If you feel as though you might overdose on Americana, take a stroll among these plots: the inscriptions, dating as far back as 1761, are in Hebrew, Latin, Portuguese, and Spanish as well as English. Newport Jews purchased this land in 1677.

NEWPORT CONGREGA-TIONAL CHURCH
849-2238.
Spring & Pelham Sts., Newport.
Season: Memorial–Labor Day, Tues. & Thurs. 10–12.

The congregation was founded in 1695, but the current structure dates to 1857. It's noteworthy for its massive Romanesque-revival design, but even more so as one of only two churches in the country with an interior decorative scheme by John La Farge still intact. La Farge (1835–1910) was an American romantic and realist who did his first notable painting in Newport in 1859. His trademark opalescent stained glass windows and Byzantine-inspired wall murals are astounding.

OLD COLONY HOUSE
846-2980; 277-6790.
Washington Square, Newport.
Season: Mid-June–Labor Day, daily.
Free.

This is another of Newport's early historical and architectural treasures — and incidentally, where you can find Gilbert Stuart's most famous portrait of George Washington. Built in 1739, the Colony House is the second-oldest capitol building in the country (until the State House was built in Providence in 1900, RI's assembly used to meet here for half the year, and in Providence the other half). Announcements made from the central balcony include King George III's coronation in 1760, and the Declaration of Independence in 1776.

OLD SCHOOL HOUSE
683-9178.
Corner E. Main Rd./Rte. 138 & Union St., Portsmouth.
Season: Memorial–Labor Day, Sat.–Sun. 1–4.
Free.

Built in 1716, this is the oldest schoolhouse in America. It features a collection of antique desks, school bells, and textbooks.

OLD STONE MILL/VIKING TOWER
Touro Park (bordered by Bellevue Ave. bet. Mill & Pelham Sts.), Newport.

While Newport had taken to heart the notion that the stone tower was built by Vikings in the 11th century (hence the city's original "847" telephone exchange, which spells out V-I-S), the theory was recently disproved by a team of scientists from Scandinavia. The latest word is that it was built by English colonists as recently as 1600. Oh well.

PRESCOTT FARM
847-6230; 849-7300/7301.
2009 W. Main Rd./Rte. 114,
   Middletown.
Season: Apr.–Nov. daily.
Admission: $2 adults; $1
   children (for tour of
   guardhouse & windmill;
   grounds are free).

A 47-acre reconstructed colonial farm, Prescott is named not for its Yankee owner but for the British commander who was captured here in 1777. The main house is closed to the public, but you can visit the little 1730 gambrel-roofed guardhouse where Prescott was captured. Wander around with goats, lambs, and geese, and watch cornmeal ground in a c. 1812 English windmill (and buy the meal at a country store on the property, built in 1715 as the Portsmouth ferry master's home and moved to this site).

Redwood Library in Newport, considered one of the most important colonial buildings in America, looks like stone but is actually built of wood.

Craig Hammell

**REDWOOD LIBRARY &
   ATHENAEUM**
847-0292.
50 Bellevue Ave., Newport.
Season: Year-round,
   Mon.–Sat.
Free.

This architectural masterpiece is the oldest continuously-used library in the country, with a collection of paintings nearly as fine as that of the Newport Art Museum next door. It was built in 1749–50 in a neoclassical design by Peter Harrison, the same architect responsible for Brick Market and Touro Synagogue (of the three only the latter isn't included among the top 10 public colonial structures in the country). Take a close look at the exterior — it's actually wood painted to look like stone. Henry James worked here.

**SAMUEL WHITEHORNE
   HOUSE**
847-2448; 849-7300; 849-
   7301.

Captain Whitehorne, one of Newport's infamous triangle-traders, built this austere Federal style home in 1811. Today it's filled with price-

416 Thames St., Newport.
Season: May–Oct., Fri. 1–4,
　Sat.–Mon. 10–4.
Admission: $5 adults, $1
　students.

less Townsend-Goddard furniture and work by Newport silversmiths and pewterers, plus Far Eastern antiques and rugs. Don't miss the back garden. There's a great little cupola on the roof, caged in by matching chimneys.

**SEVENTH DAY BAPTIST
　MEETING HOUSE**
846-0813.
82 Touro St., Newport.
Season: Year-round; closed
　Mon.

This meeting house is the oldest of its faith (also called Sabbatarian) in the country, built c. 1729. Note the lovely pulpit and don't overlook the clock by famed Newport clockmaker William Claggett — it's two centuries old and still ticking.

ST. MARY'S CHURCH
847-0475.
Spring St., Newport.
Season: Year-round,
　Mon.–Fri. 7–11:30.
Free.

On September 12, 1953, Jacqueline Bouvier married John Kennedy in this lovely church, built in the English Gothic style in 1848–52. Established in 1828, this is the oldest Catholic parish in RI.

Touro Synagogue in Newport — the oldest in North America — reputedly inspired Thomas Jefferson to design Monticello.

Craig Hammell

TOURO SYNAGOGUE
847-4794.
85 Touro St., Newport.
Season: May–Labor Day,
  Mon.–Fri.; Sept.–Oct.,
  Mon.–Thurs.; otherwise
  Sun. 1–3.
Services: Summer, Fri. 7pm,
  Sat. 9am; otherwise Fri.
  6pm.

Continuing Newport's litany of "oldests," this elegant Peter Harrison structure is the oldest synagogue in North America (the same may be said of its torah). It was constructed in 1763 to serve Newport's Jewish community, established by 15 families from Holland in 1658 who were later joined by Sephardic Jews from Spain and Portugal. Despite the fact that Jews weren't allowed to vote until the Revolution, the synagogue preserves a letter from President Washington which states that the new country would give "bigotry no sanction and persecution no assistance." Harrison's design is said to have inspired Jefferson's plan for Monticello.

The Christopher Wren-inspired steeple of Trinity Church, 150 feet high, has been a landmark to mariners in Newport Harbor since 1726.

Craig Hammell

TRINITY CHURCH
846-0660.
Queen Anne Sq., Spring &
  Church Sts., Newport.
Season: Year-round.
Services (Episcopalian):
  Sun. 8, 11am (summer
  10am).

A great landmark (look for the 150-foot clock tower) and rendezvous spot when touring Newport. Trinity was built in 1725–26 from a design by Richard Munday, based on work by Christopher Wren. Inside is the only three-tiered wine-glass pulpit in the country, plus Tiffany stained-glass windows, and a pipe organ donated by George Berkeley (see Whitehall Museum House), tested by Handel himself before it was shipped from England. A $3 million restoration, funded by the congregation, was completed in 1987. (Stand in the center aisle and let your eye run down the row of chandeliers — they don't line up because the main beam has gone askew with age.)

UNION CONGREGA-
TIONAL CHURCH
Division St., Newport.

This fine Cottage Gothic structure, built in 1871, houses the first free black church in the United States. Twelve of Newport's leading African-Amer-

Season: Year-round.
Free.

icans met in 1824 to form the Colored Union Church and Society; their first meeting house was built on the present site that same year.

WANTON-LYMAN-HAZ-ARD HOUSE
846-0813.
17 Broadway near Washington Sq., Newport.
Season: June–Aug., Tues.–Sat.
Admission: $4.

Built c. 1675, this is the oldest house in Newport. In 1765 it was the home of Newport's stamp master, whose enforcement of the Stamp Act sparked a riot by Newporters during which the house was sacked. You'll see a wonderful winding staircase, medieval-looking beams and corner posts, and chimney details. The house is owned by the Newport Historical Society. It also features a colonial herb garden.

WHITEHALL MUSEUM HOUSE
846-3790; 847-7951; 846-3116 (July–Aug.)
311 Berkeley Ave., Middletown.
Season: July–Aug.; daily.
Admission: $3 adults, $1 children.

Whitehall came into this world in the 17th century as a farmhouse, but upon the arrival of Irish clergyman and philosopher George Berkeley in Newport in 1729, it was enlarged to become an elegant manor home. Berkeley introduced elements unusual in New England at the time: a formal façade, hipped roof, and false double-front doors. He lived here just three years before returning to England, whereupon he deeded the house to Yale University, which lent it out as a tavern. Today the stately red home is in good repair but its former view of open fields has been replaced by rows of condos.

WHITE HORSE TAVERN
849-3600.
Corner of Marlborough & Farewell Sts., Newport.
Season: Year-round.

This is the oldest operating tavern in the country, built in the mid-1600s. In 1687 William Mayes, a local pirate, got a license to sell spirits. Today the White Horse is a superb restaurant (see *Restaurants*). Call ahead to arrange a private tour with the curator, or just stick your head inside for a quick visit to the 17th century (note the curved-wall fireplace, massive beams, and medieval stairway wrapped around the chimney). On Fridays at 10:30 (through Oct.) you can have a tour, refreshments, and hearth-side lecture, all for $5.

Sakonnet

ALPACAS OF HENSE-FORTH FARM
624-4184.
460 East Rd., Tiverton.
Season: Year-round.
Free.

This farmstead, built in 1740, was moved to the site all the way from Woonsocket in northern RI. Visitors are welcome to tour the house, though it's a family home. The main attractions here, however, are the 12 alpacas, plus guinea hens, ducks, chickens, and fish. In season visitors can purchase eggs, flowers, and yarn (call before visiting to find out when they're carding the wool). Mind the "Alpaca Crossing" sign at the head of the driveway.

CHASE-COREY HOUSE
624-4013; 624-8881.
3908 Main Rd./Rte. 77,
Tiverton Four Corners.
Season: May–Sept., Sun.
2–4:30.

Built in 1730, this gambrel-roofed colonial home is now maintained by the Tiverton Historical Society, which mounts special exhibitions through-out the season.

Here in the Commons Burial Grounds at Little Compton lies Betty Pabodie, daughter of Pilgrims John Alden and Priscilla Mullens.

Craig Hammell

**COMMONS BURIAL
GROUND**
The Commons, Little
Compton.

The triangular Burial Ground is at the heart of Little Compton's Commons, the most pic-turesque village center in Rhode Island. You can get shivers in this graveyard just from reading the dates. Betty Pabodie lies here, the first white woman born in New England, daughter of Priscilla and John Alden. Also look for Elizabeth Mortimer (1712–76), whose inscription reads "In memory of Elizabeth, who should have been the wife of Mr. Simeon Palmer" (they were married but lived apart at her request — Simeon didn't consider her conduct becoming of a real wife).

GRAY'S STORE
635-4566.
4 Main St., Little Comp-
ton/Adamsville.
Season: Year-round; closed
Sun. Oct.–Apr.

If this isn't *the* oldest operating general store in the country, it's right up there. Built in 1788, it contains Little Compton's first post office plus the original soda fountain, candy and tobacco cases, and ice chest. You can buy Gray's jonnycake meal and even vintage clothing here.

WILBOR HOUSE, BARN, & QUAKER MEETING HOUSE
635-4559.
W. Main Rd./Rte. 77, Little Compton.
Season: Mid-June–mid-Sept., Tues.–Sat. 2–5.
Admission: $4 adults, 75¢ children.

This is one of those New England jigsaw puzzle houses: bits were fitted together in each ensuing century, from the 17th through the 19th. It was restored and filled with colonial appointments by the Little Compton Historical Society. The barn has a display of old farm tools, utensils, and vehicles.

HISTORICAL TOURS

For annual house and garden tours, see Gardens & Garden Tours above.

Newport on Foot Guided Walking Tours (846-5391; PO Box 1042, Newport) You might not get very far in an hour and a half — actually just over a mile on a ten-block loop — but you'll take in 150 years of history. Tour guide Anita Rafael leads you through graveyards and past colonial homes and landmarks (no mansions). By the end you'll know a hipped roof from a gambrel at 20 paces. Groups are small and leave from the Gateway Visitors' Bureau. Morning strolls include a stop for coffee or tea at the **White Horse Tavern**. Tours cost $7 per person and are offered year-round. Bus escort guides are also available.

Newport Historical Society (846-0813; 82 Touro St., Newport) Walking tours through Newport's National Historic Landmark District begin every Friday and Saturday morning at 10am, from mid-June through the end of September. This is a great "plein air" crash course in American architecture. Tours leave from the Historical Society offices and cost $5 per person; children under 12 free.

"THE COTTAGES" — THE NEWPORT MANSIONS

Contemporary architects have long glorified in "mansion bashing," considering these monuments to nouveau riche vanity to be just what Henry James called them — white elephants. But the tide is turning, and academic opinion is beginning to agree with the 800,000 visitors who troop through the "summer cottages" of the Astors, the Vanderbilts, and their friends each year. Some are magnificent buildings in their own right, created by designers of genius like Richard Morris Hunt, Henry Hobson Richardson, and Stanford White, the latter of the famous firm McKim, Mead, and White. (A little gossip never hurt any discussion of architecture: Stanford White was shot dead in 1906 by millionaire Harry Thaw, the spurned husband of actress Evelyn Nesbitt who was having an affair with White. Thaw chose a dramatic setting: the old Madison Square Garden in New York City, which White had designed. For more on the Gilded Age crowd see the *History* chapter.)

Mansion-watchers stroll along Newport's famed Cliff Walk.

Craig Hammell

The best way to get a good look at some of the most famous — and decide which ones you want to see on the inside — is to stroll the Cliff Walk. The Cliff Walk occupies the eastern coast of Newport's peninsula: it runs roughly parallel to lower Bellevue Avenue. It starts at Memorial Boulevard and continues south for three miles to Bailey's Beach, the exclusive spot for Gilded Age bathers. To one side are crashing waves, to the other magnificent mansions. But be warned: it can be scary going in some spots (it's quite a drop to the rocks below).

The mansions tend to cluster along a number of famous thoroughfares: Bellevue Avenue, Ochre Point Avenue (thanks to an irregular coast both parallel the Cliff Walk), and Ocean Drive. The latter is also known as "10 Mile Drive." It follows the southernmost tip of the Newport peninsula and continues up the western side, past **Brenton Point State Park**, the **Inn at Castle Hill, Fort Adams State Park**, and **Hammersmith Farm**. The scenery out here is windswept and rocky, with the romantic roof-lines of great manor houses dominating the horizon.

Many of these are still privately owned. The following are several of Newport's better-known mansions that are open to the public. Many are now maintained by the Preservation Society of Newport County (those with the phone number 847-1000; see the beginning of this section for the address). If you plan to visit more than one, purchase a combination ticket, from any two properties to all eight, including the colonial Hunter House and Green Animals topiary gardens in Portsmouth.

ASTORS' BEECHWOOD MANSION
846-3772.
580 Bellevue Ave.
Season: Mid-May–Dec., daily; Feb.–mid-May, weekends.

This well-proportioned, stucco-over-brick mansion was built in 1852, well before size became the determining factor of success. Beechwood was home to "The Mrs. Astor," doyenne of Newport society throughout the Gilded Age, and who

Admission: $7.75 adults, $6 children.

reigned over the "List of 400" like an American queen. You can experience something of what it was like to be a guest in her home: unlike the other mansions, Beechwood employs costumed actors as guides, who pretend — with a great deal of good humor — that it's still the 1890s. See Seasonal Events below for special performances there.

BELCOURT CASTLE
846-0669.
Bellevue Ave.
Season: Apr.–Oct., daily;
    Nov., Dec., Feb., Mar.,
    weekends.
Admission: $6.50 adults, $2 children.

This is Newport's only mansion with owners still in residence. It was built by Richard Morris Hunt for Oliver Hazard Perry Belmont and the former Alva Vanderbilt (see Marble House below) in 1894 in the style of a Louis XIII hunting lodge at Versailles. This 60-room castle boasts the largest collection of 13th-century stained-glass in the country. The public rooms really constitute a museum of European treasures from armor to German throne chairs to a full-size, gilded coronation coach.

THE BREAKERS
847-1000.
Ochre Point Ave.

The mansion to end all mansions. Cornelius Vanderbilt — believe it or not, a man of simple tastes — had it built for his wife, Alice, in 1895

Courtesy Preservation Society of Newport County

The Breakers — Cornelius Vanderbilt's "summer cottage" — has been called the most opulent private residence in the world.

Season: Apr.–Oct., Dec., daily.
Admission: $7.50 adults, $3.50 children.

according to a design by Richard Morris Hunt. Hunt based the 70-room seaside villa (it fronts on the Cliff Walk) on 16th-century northern Italian palaces. Massive and imposing (the Great Hall rises 45 feet), its interior walls sheathed in marble and alabaster, The Breakers may possibly be the most opulent private residence in the world — and decidedly the top single tourist attraction in Rhode Island.

CHATEAU-SUR-MER
847-1000.
Bellevue Ave.
Season: May–Sept., daily; Oct.–Apr., weekends.
Admission: $6 adults, $3 children.

One of the earliest Newport mansions, the Chateau is an extravaganza of American Victoriana, built for China trader William Wetmore in 1852, with extensive renovation by Richard Morris Hunt in the 1870s. The exterior is formidable, with a steep mansard roof and rough granite walls. Inside the central hallway rises 45 feet to a glass ceiling; open balconies of rich paneled wood wrap around each floor.

Craig Hammell

A dramatic moment in stone in the garden of The Elms.

THE ELMS
847-1000.
Bellevue Ave.
Season: May–Oct., daily; Nov.–Apr., weekends.
Admission: $7 adults, $3 children.

Modeled by architect Horace Trumbauer on the 18th-century Chateau d'Asnieres near Paris, The Elms is an elegant, white marble summer residence, built in 1901 for Pennsylvania coal millionaire E.J. Berwind. The ball to celebrate the opening of The Elms was the event of the 1901 season: three orchestras and pet monkeys played as 125 couples danced under the stars. The formal sunken garden was designed by French landscape architect Jacques Greber.

HAMMERSMITH FARM
846-7346.
Harrison Ave./Ocean Dr.
Season: Apr.–mid-Nov.,
	daily; mid-Dec. for
	Christmas.
Admission: $6.50 adults, $3
	children.

This 28-room Shingle style cottage on the western bend of Ocean Drive, far from the one-upmanship games played on Bellevue, was built for John Auchincloss in 1888. When Jacqueline Bouvier married John Kennedy in nearby St. Mary's Church the reception was held here. The rooms are extraordinarily airy and bright, as befits a summer cottage overlooking Newport Harbor; note the majestic jade plants. The surrounding gardens are beautifully landscaped, and the farm, established in 1640, is still in operation — the last working farm in Newport.

KINGSCOTE
847-1000.
Bellevue Ave.
Season: May–Sept., daily;
	Oct. & April, weekends.
Admission: $6 adults, $3
	children.

Kingscote started the ball rolling: it's considered America's first "summer cottage," built in the Gothic Revival style in 1839 by Richard Upjohn for the Savannah millionaire George Noble Jones. The mahogany-paneled dining room with a cherry floor is Kingscote's tour de force, added by McKim, Mead, and White in 1881 — note the wall of Tiffany glass tiles and cork ceiling.

On the grounds of Marble House, Alma Vanderbilt's Chinese Tea House overlooks the Cliff Walk.

Craig Hammell

MARBLE HOUSE
847-1000.
Bellevue Ave.
Season: Apr.–Oct., daily;
	Nov.–Mar., weekends
	(Tea House open
	May–Oct.)
Admission: $6 adults, $3
	children.

Another of Richard Morris Hunt's sumptuous palaces, Marble House is based on elements of both the Grand and Petit Trianon at Versailles. It was completed in 1892 after four years of work at a cost of $11 million, ostensibly for William K. Vanderbilt though it was his wife Alva who truly reigned here. (Alva was one of Newport's "Great

Triumvirate" of society dames — see *History* for more gossip.) The immense entrance portico is supported by gigantic Corinthian columns. Wear your sunglasses in the Gold Room, and note the Chinese Tea House on the grounds. (Alva closed Marble House after divorcing Vanderbilt, and moved across the street to the less imposing Belcourt Castle.)

Courtesy Preservation Society of Newport County

The ballroom at Rosecliff, where The Great Gatsby *was filmed in 1973, is the largest in Newport.*

ROSECLIFF
847-1000.
Bellevue Ave.
Season: Apr.–Oct., daily.
Admission: $6 adults, $3 children.

Stanford White designed Rosecliff for Tessie Oelrichs in 1902, and based it on the Grand Trianon at Versailles. This exquisite, white terracotta mansion overlooking the Cliff Walk is one of the most elegant in town. It's built in the shape of an H, and features the largest private ballroom in Newport. The lovely marble staircase is curved in a heart-shaped design. The garden terrace was based on one designed for Marie Antoinette. It's no surprise that Rosecliff was chosen as the set for the film of *The Great Gatsby*.

SEASONAL EVENTS

The Dansantes (846-3772; The Astors' Beechwood, 580 Bellevue Ave.) Victorian tea dances in the ballroom featuring Mrs. Astor's famous chilled strawberry tea. The Dansantes are performed throughout the year; call for a schedule and ask about Murder Mystery evenings as well.

The Fair at the Elms (847-1000; The Elms, Bellevue Ave.) Note that this gala auction, arts and crafts show, flower market, and food fair is only held once every three years — the last one was in early August, 1993. It's kicked off by an elegant evening preview cocktail party.

Gatsby Ball (423-1378; Rosecliff, Bellevue Ave.) This annual event brings Twenties-worshipers out in droves. Arrive in your best flapper-era attire to dance the night away in Newport's biggest, most elegant ballroom. Early to mid-July.

Night in White (846-0669; Belcourt Castle, Bellevue Ave.) This annual gala harks back to a famous, all-white Gilded Age ball at Rosecliff; now it's an evening of cocktails, endless hors d'oeuvres, and entertainment to benefit the Royal Arts Foundation. Early August.

Symposium on Newport Architecture & Design (847-6543; Preservation Society of Newport) The Society hosted its first and highly successful symposium in April 1993, and plans to turn it into a yearly event (co-sponsored by Christie's auction house). Architects, designers, and historians lecture on Newport houses, public buildings, and decorative arts. Call for tickets early because it's a sell-out affair.

LIBRARIES

Whether you stop in to peruse a mystery, or plan to spend hours doing genealogical research, local libraries are a great, often overlooked, resource. Those listed below contain rich materials on local history including out-of-print books and collections donated by townspeople (everything from menus and scrapbooks to Peruvian artifacts). Note that all libraries are open year-round and closed on Sunday, except where noted.

West Bay

Davisville Free Library (884-5524; Davisville Rd., N. Kingstown/Davisville) Open Mon., Weds., Fri. in summer; Tues., Thurs., Sat. in winter.

East Greenwich Free Library (884-9511; 82 Pierce St.)

Jamestown Philomenian Library (423-7280; 26 North Rd.) Includes the Sydney L. Wright Museum of colonial and Native American artifacts from prehistoric through 18th-century settlements on the island.

Narragansett Public Library (789-9507; Kingstown Rd.) Closed Sat. & Sun. in summer.

North Kingstown Free Library (294-3306; 100 Boone St., N. Kingstown/ Wickford)

Willet Free Library (294-2081; Ferry Rd., N. Kingstown/Saunderstown)

East Bay

George Hail Free Library (245-7686; 530 Main St./Rte. 114, Warren) Closed Sat. & Sun. in July & Aug. Includes the Charles R. Carr Collection of Pre-Columbian, Peruvian, and Native North American artifacts.

Rogers Free Library (253-6948; 525 Hope St./Rte. 114, Bristol) Closed Sat. & Sun. in July & Aug.

Aquidneck

Middletown Public Library (846-1573; 700 W. Main Rd./Rte. 114)

Newport Public Library (847-8720; Aquidneck Park, 300 Spring St.) The Newport Room has a wealth of local materials that are no longer available in book shops.

Portsmouth Free Public Library (683-9457; 2658 E. Main Rd./Rte. 138)

Sakonnet

Brownell Library (635-8562; The Commons, Little Compton)

Essex Public Library (625-6799; 238 Highland Rd., Tiverton)

Block Island

Island Free Library (466-3233; Dodge St., Block Island) Closed Sun. in summer; Sun. & Mon. in winter.

LIGHTHOUSES

Of all Rhode Island's lighthouses, the Southeast Light, perched atop Block Island's towering Mohegan Bluffs, is decidedly the most glamorous. Until recently it was also the most precarious. On August 14, 1993, the *Block Island Times* ran the simple headline "It Moved!" — referring to the Southeast Light's well-engineered trip 245 feet backward from the face of the eroding bluffs. Over the past 10 years islanders have struggled to raise nearly two million dollars to save the Victorian landmark; one resident said that losing the beacon would be like losing the moon. The cliffs were crumbling so quickly that if it hadn't been moved in 1993, within several years the Southeast Light would have wound up a heap of red-brick rubble on the beach, 204 feet below.

Its beauty notwithstanding, the Southeast Light was saved in order to provide dramatic rescues of its own. The island's long-time nickname is "The Stumbling Block," in honor of the fact that of the 1000 or so nautical disasters that have taken place off the New England coast in the past two centuries, half have occurred within range of Block Island. (Legend has it that some of these were the work of "moon-cussers," wreckers who used lanterns to lure ships into reefs, so they could steal the cargo.)

While Narragansett Bay isn't as exposed as Block Island, it's studded with lighthouses of its own, one of which drew its fame from a keeper rather than its location. The Ida Lewis Rock Light in Newport Harbor (inactive as of 1928 and now the Ida Lewis Yacht Club), was named for the daughter of Captain Hosea Lewis, who had a stroke only six months after his appointment as the lighthouse keeper. Ida and her mother took over until Ida was named sole keeper in 1877. She went on to serve for 59 years and become the most famous female lighthouse keeper in the country, frequently risking her life to save drowning swimmers and boaters. Before her death in 1911, Ida Lewis had received the Congressional Medal of Honor for bravery.

There are currently 24 working lighthouses in Rhode Island. (One of these, the **Rose Island Light**, whose beacon was re-lit in August, 1993, accepts overnight guests — see *Lodging*.) Following is a selection of favorites:

West Bay

Imposing Beaver Tail Light guards the rocky southern tip of Conanicut Island (Jamestown).

Craig Hammell

Beaver Tail Lighthouse (423-9941; Beaver Tail Point, Beaver Tail State Park, Jamestown) Strategically located at the tip of Conanicut Island, Beaver Tail was Rhode Island's first lighthouse, originally built in 1749. The current granite tower was erected in 1856. Tours June–Aug. Weds.–Sun.

Point Judith Lighthouse (789-0444; 1460 Ocean Rd., Narragansett/Pt. Judith) This sturdy red-and-white tower was built in 1810. It has a white light which flashes three times every 15 seconds. Access to lighthouse and Coast Guard Station is restricted.

Block Island

North Light (466-2481; Sandy Point, end of Corn Neck Rd.) Built in 1867, the North Light is the fourth lighthouse to occupy this position since 1829. Its beacon was automated by the Coast Guard in 1989 after a 16-year period of darkness. The first floor of the lighthouse now serves as a natural and historical interpretive center. Summer only.

Craig Hammell

The queen of Rhode Island lighthouses, the Southeast Light is the highest above sea level and has the most powerful beacon of any light in New England.

Southeast Light (466-2462, 2481; Mohegan Bluffs, off Spring St.) The highest lighthouse in New England with the most powerful beacon on the East Coast, the Southeast Light was built in the Gothic Revival style in 1873 at a cost of $70,000. Its hand-ground French lens is so powerful that if it stops rotating, refracting sunlight can ignite fires 35 miles away on the mainland. A permanent exhibition on island architecture, "Rugged and Refined," is mounted by the Block Island Historical Society. Open June–Sept., daily.

Palatine Light Yes, this isn't exactly a lighthouse, but according to some the

Palatine Light is what can happen when lighthouses don't exist but should. On December 27, 1738, the *Princess Augusta*, loaded with emigrants from the Palatine area of Germany, sank off the coast of Block Island with all lost (mooncussers were reportedly involved). Since then on the anniversary of the disaster there have been sightings of a ghostly ship ablaze on the horizon, which folklore has remembered as "The Palatine."

MILITARY SITES & MUSEUMS

West Bay

Quonset Aviation Museum (294-9540; 488 Eccleston Ave., N. Kingstown/ Quonset Point) This new museum is housed in the only brick hanger on the East Coast and is devoted to aircraft and New England aviation memorabilia. So far a Russian MIG-17 and an A-4 Skyhawk are some of the planes restored and on display. Open depending on weather conditions — call first. $2 adults, $1 children.

Varnum Military Museum (884-4110; 6 Main St., E. Greenwich) A collection of artifacts from U.S. wars through World War I. Open by appointment only.

Aquidneck

Artillery Company of Newport Military Museum (846-8488; 23 Clarke St., Newport) This is home to the oldest active military company in the U.S. — it received its charter in 1741 from King George III. The armory was built in 1836 and now houses perhaps the finest collection of foreign and domestic military memorabilia in the country, including four brass cannons — lent to the president for state occasions — cast by Paul Revere in 1797. Uniforms of Anwar Sadat, Prince Philip, and others. Open June–Sept.; closed Tues. Adults $2, children $1.

Butts Hill Fort (off Sprague St., Portsmouth) These ruined redoubts mark where the Battle of Rhode Island took place on August 29, 1778 (see *History*). Drive down to Middletown and look for Green End Fort off Vernon Ave. — the redoubts there mark British defense lines for Newport.

Fort Adams (847-2800; Fort Adams State Park, off Harrison Ave./Ocean Dr., Newport) With an unparalleled strategic and scenic location, Fort Adams is easily the most impressive military site in the state. It took 23 years to build the massive granite complex; but by the time it was finished in 1847 it was already obsolete (the huge walls, impenetrable to conventional muskets, would have been blown to bits by the powerful cannons invented during the Civil War). Fort Adams was closed in 1945, but it now serves as a perfect acoustic soundstage for the Newport Jazz and Folk festivals. The same Scottish stonemason who built the fort, Alexander MacGregor, also built Perry Mill, the Newport Artillery Company, and many stone houses around town.

Naval War College Museum (841-4052; Coasters Harbor Island, Newport; public access through Gate 1 of the Naval Education & Training Center) The museum is housed in Founders Hall, a magnificent structure which served as Newport's poorhouse from 1820–82, then as the first site of the Naval War College in 1884. The War College is the Navy's highest educational institution, considered one of top military schools in the world. Exhibits highlight the history of naval warfare and the naval heritage of Narragansett Bay. Look for exhibits dedicated to Oliver and Matthew Perry, local boys who made good (Matthew was responsible for the opening of Japan in 1854). Open year-round Mon.–Fri.; June–Sept., Sat.–Sun. too. Free.

Sakonnet

Fort Barton (Highland Rd., Tiverton) This Revolutionary War redoubt was originally named Tiverton Heights Fort for its strategic location: it was feared that the British in Newport would cross to the mainland at Tiverton and attack Boston. One night in 1777 a Col. Barton stealthily sailed from the fort to capture the British general Prescott in Middletown (see **Prescott Farm**) — hence the name change. A nature walk leads from the fort over the wonderfully named Sin and Flesh Brook. Open year-round, sunrise to sunset.

MONUMENTS & MEMORIALS

West Bay

Canonchet Memorial (On the Green at Exchange Place, Narragansett) This 6000-pound limestone memorial to Narragansett chief Canonchet was sculpted in 1977 by artist Robert Carsten.

Narragansett Indian Monument (Kingstown Rd. & Strathmore St., Narragansett Pier) A 23-foot sculpture carved from a single Douglas fir by artist Peter Toth, this is one of a series of 41 monuments throughout the country honoring Native Americans.

East Bay

Black Soldier's Memorial (W. Main Rd./Rte. 114, to left of junction with northbound Rte. 24, Portsmouth) At the spot marked by the flagpole, the first company of African-Americans to fight for the country encountered the British on August 29, 1778, at the Battle of Rhode Island.

Founder's Brook (signposted off Boyd's La., Portsmouth) A bronze marker shows the spot where Anne Hutchinson and her fellow settlers landed in 1638 and subsequently made history. (See the *History* chapter for more on Hutchinson and the Portsmouth Compact).

Sakonnet

Rhode Island Red Monument (Main St., Adamsville/Little Compton) One of only two monuments to chickens in the world (the other is in Georgia), this 1924 plaque honors the famed Rhode Island Red, first bred here in 1854.

Block Island

Settlers' Rock (Corn Neck Road) This sand-swept bronze plaque lists the names of 16 families (you'll find the same surnames in the current telephone directory) who arrived at this spot in April, 1661, to establish the first white settlement on the island.

MUSEUMS

The following represent most of the principal museums in the Narragansett Bay area. Also take a look at Military Sites & Museums, the Library listings, which contain information on library-owned collections, and Historic Buildings & Sites.

West Bay

JAMESTOWN MUSEUM
423-0784.
92 Narragansett Ave.,
  Jamestown.
Season: Mid-June–Aug.,
  closed Mon.
Free.

This 19th-century schoolhouse makes an ideal seaside museum — it's a little musty but the material is fascinating, featuring a permanent exhibit on the Jamestown ferries. The Jamestown-to-Newport route was established in 1675 and ran until 1969: the oldest transportation line in America served by the longest-operating ferry service. Special exhibits each season.

NEW ENGLAND WIRE-LESS & STEAM MUSEUM
884-1710.
Frenchtown & Tillinghast
  Rds., E. Greenwich.
Season: June–Sept., Sun
  1–5.
Nominal admission.

A small engineering museum with exhibits of early radio, telephone, and telegraph equipment plus engines of all description. There's also a reference library of early scientific texts for researchers and students.

SOUTH COUNTY MUSEUM
783-5400.

Exhibits on rural life in 18th- and 19th-century Rhode Island, including a country kitchen, general store, cobbler shop, antique carriage collection,

Craig Hammell

Rural life is on display at the South County Museum in Nar-ragansett.

Canonchet Farm off Boston Neck Rd./Rte. 1A, Nar-ragansett.
Season: May–Oct., Weds.–Sun.
Admission: $2.50 adults, $1.50 children.

and a featured show of early American crafts. There's an operating printing shop in a separate building. Annual quilt show in late August.

East Bay

BRISTOL HISTORICAL & PRESERVATION SOCIETY MUSEUM & LIBRARY
253-7223.
48 Court St.
Museum: Year-round, call for hours.
Library: Jan.–Nov., Weds. 1–5.
Admission: Free; $3.50 for use of library.

This county jail was constructed in 1828 from stone ballast used in Bristol sailing ships. Today it houses a library with very good genealogical materials, and a collection of 300 years of Bristolian artifacts.

FIREMAN'S MUSEUM
245-7600.
42 Barker St., Warren.
Admission: By appointment only.

A restored firebarn that once housed Narragansett Steam Fire Co. #3, this is a great place for kids to look at old fire-fighting equipment and climb aboard Little Hero, Warren's first fire engine purchased in 1802.

HAFFENREFFER MUSEUM OF ANTHROPOLOGY

It seems like you're penetrating primeval woodland to reach the place, but once here, a magnificent view of the Sakonnet River opens before you.

Craig Hammell

Exhibits of Inca artifacts are featured at the Haffenreffer Museum of Anthropology in Bristol.

253-8388.
Mt. Hope Grant, Tower St., off Metacom Ave./Rte. 114, Bristol.
Season: June–Aug., Tues.–Sun.; Sept.–May, Sat.–Sun.
Admission: $2 adults, $1 children.

Temporary shows and permanent exhibits trace various cultures of the Americas, including the Canadian and Alaskan North, the Southeast, the Great Plains, Mesoamerica, and more. A network of nature trails — be careful of the poison ivy — comb the 500-acre grant which was once the ancestral homeland of the Wampanoag tribe. The museum is administered by Brown University.

HERRESHOFF MARINE MUSEUM
253-5000.
7 Burnside St., Bristol.
Season: May–Oct., Tues.–Sun. 1–4.
Admission: $3 adults, $5 family.

The Herreshoff Shipyard built eight consecutive successful America's Cup Defenders between 1893 and 1954 (see *History*). This is their collection of 35 sailing and power yachts — sleek and graceful machines — plus photos and memorabilia from the Golden Age of Yachting. The Herreshoff Manufacturing Co. was founded in 1863 by John Brown Herreshoff and his brother Capt. Nat (Nathanael Green), who was known as the "Wizard of Bristol." The **America's Cup Hall of Fame** is currently under construction in a new wing of the museum.

Aquidneck

DOLL MUSEUM
849-0405.
520 Thames St., Newport.
Season: Year-round, Weds.–Mon.
Admission: $2 adults, $1 children, under 5 free.

An interesting little collection of dolls from the 18th century to the present, as well as dollhouses, miniatures, and antique toys.

INTERNATIONAL TENNIS HALL OF FAME (NEWPORT CASINO)
849-3990.
194 Bellevue Ave., Newport.
Season: Year-round.
Admission: $6 adults, $3 children, under 5 free.

This is a must-see for tennis, history, and architecture buffs alike. The Tennis Hall of Fame is housed in the old Newport Casino, a magnificent Shingle style complex designed by Stanford White in 1880. (The La Forge Restaurant is in the casino complex too; see *Restaurants*.) The casino was really a country club for Newport's Gilded Age vacationers, built by James Gordon Bennett, the New York publisher, after he was censured by the Newport Reading Room for challenging a friend to ride his horse across the front porch. Note the superb clock tower, Chinese detailing, horseshoe piazza, and latticed porches.

Above all, feast your eyes on 13 beautifully tended grass tennis courts. The first national tennis championship was held here in 1881 (it became the U.S. Open at Flushing Meadows). The Hall of Fame galleries include photo exhibits and a host of tennis memorabilia. Don't miss the court tennis court, where the older version of the game is still played as it was in the 13th century. See *Recreation* for information on renting the courts and USTA tournaments.

MUSEUM OF NEWPORT HISTORY
841-8770.
Brick Market, Long Wharf, & Thames St., Newport.
Season: Year-round.
Admission: $5 adults, $3 children.

This new museum curated by the Newport Historical Society just opened in December 1993. Don't miss it: interactive computers, photo installations, a children's discovery room, and exhibits ranging from local craftwork to Benjamin Franklin's brother's printing press will bring Newport's history to life. Look for interpretative exhibitions focusing on the working waterfront, Newport in the Revolution, the Gilded Age, the city's multicultural communities past and present, and more.

THE MUSEUM OF YACHTING
847-1018.
Fort Adams State Park, off Harrison Ave., Newport.
Season: Mid-May–Oct., daily.
Admission: $2.50, $5 family.

Did you know the word yacht derives from the Dutch for "chasing?" A "jaght schip" means a fast, agile craft. Visitors here will sample such lore as well as gain a new appreciation for the beauty and grace of sailing vessels. The museum is dedicated to recording the history and development of yachting around the world. Featured is *Shamrock V*, the English challenger for the America's Cup in 1930 — she's the only J class sloop in the world with a wooden hull that's still sailing, and her mast rises 155 feet; call ahead to arrange a tour. The museum is next to Fort Adams and overlooks Newport Harbor, and also offers the Phil Weld Library, a school of yacht restoration, and regattas.

**NEWPORT ART
  MUSEUM**
848-8200.
76 Bellevue Ave., Newport.
Season: July–Sept. daily;
  Sept.–June, Tues.–Sun.
Admission: $3 adults,
  under 18 free.

Here are works of art housed in a work of art — a rare Stick style mansion with medieval-style half-timbering, designed in 1864 by Richard Morris Hunt (his first Newport commission; Hunt later designed many of the "proper" mansions as well). The collection includes both contemporary and historical works from Newport and New England. Look for works by Winslow Homer, George Inness, and others. The museum also features summer outdoor classes in watercolors, pastels, and oils for all skill levels; one-week classes for kids in watercolor and sketching.

**NEWPORT HISTORICAL
  SOCIETY MUSEUM**
846-0813.
82 Touro St., Newport
  (next to Sabbatarian
  Meeting House).
Season: Year-round,
  Tues.–Sat.
Free.

In addition to rich research facilities including early town records, merchant account books, and collections in architectural history and photography, the NPHS exhibits its generous holdings of silver, china, and Townsend-Goddard furniture. For information on NPHS tours see Historical Tours above.

**PORTSMOUTH HISTOR-
  ICAL SOCIETY**
683-9178.
Corner of E. Main Rd./Rte.
  138 & Union St.
Season: Memorial–Labor
  Day, Sat.–Sun. after-
  noons.
Free.

The PHS has a small but fascinating collection , including early household conveniences and farm implements. This was the former Christian Sabbath Society Meeting House; Julia Ward Howe preached here.

**RHODE ISLAND FISH-
  ERMEN & WHALE
  CENTER**
849-1340.
Seamen's Church Institute,
  18 Market Sq., off Amer-
  ica's Cup Ave., Newport.
Season: Year-round,
  Thurs.–Tues.
Admission: $2 adults, $1
  children, under 5 free.

This marine discovery center is a great place for both kids and adults. You can learn how to go quahogging, "pilot" a ship, and visit a unique kind of petting zoo featuring sea urchins and horseshoe crabs. The museum is within the Seamen's Church Institute, a National Register building that's been "a haven for men and women of the sea" since 1919. Here you can find Newport's only public showers plus restrooms, washers, and dryers. The Green Galley coffee shop offers light fare at low prices.

Block Island

**BLOCK ISLAND HIS-
  TORICAL SOCIETY**

Let yourself be lured inside by the Block Island "double-ender" out front — because the island

466-2481.
Old Town Rd., Old Harbor
  area.
Season: June–Sept., daily.
Admission: $2.

had no natural harbor until breakwaters were built in the 1870s , fishermen used like-ended boats that could be easily hauled up onto the beach. Exhibits are a window on island life in the past. The BIHS also mounts exhibitions in the **Southeast Light** (see Lighthouses above).

**THE LOST MANIS-
  SEEAN INDIAN
  EXHIBIT**
466-5060.
West Side Rd.
Season: Memorial–Labor
  Day, daily.
Free.

The last Manisseean died in 1886 (his name was Isaac Church; Isaac's Corner at Cooneymus & Center Rds. & Lakeside Dr. is named for him), but you can honor the old tribe by visiting this collection of arrow and ax heads, knives, and other artifacts dating back to the 16th century. Painted hieroglyphics explore ancient ways of life.

MUSIC

Newport blows away the competition like a sou'east gale when it comes to music. This is the City by the Sea's specialty, and if classical, folk, or jazz are your thing, make every effort to attend one of the festivals highlighted below. Don't be put off by crowds: Folk and Jazz Festival weekends are two of Newport's busiest, to be sure, but traffic control (of both vehicles and humans) is utterly superb. Not even parking is a problem. A decade ago the original Kool Jazz Festival was suspended because the crowds got so rowdy. Now, security at the new JVC Jazz show (and the Folk Festival) is extraordinarily tight. No cans, glass, or alcohol are permitted — and don't bother trying to sneak anything in; guards at the door will open your thermos to check. The Newport Music Festival is held in the mansions, but here are some tips regarding the two open-air shows, both at Fort Adams: bring a blanket at least; better yet, lawn chairs so you can rest your back; bring an umbrella — if it rains, you're covered, if it's sunny, you have instant shade; bring sunscreen, a hat, a pack of cards, a backgammon set, the paperback you're reading. These are all-day events with long breaks between sets, and people really settle in. You can take your own picnic, though the food stalls are exceptional. Plan on eating lots of Ben & Jerry's ice cream. If you have a boat, join the ad hoc flotilla in the Harbor and listen for free.

Ben & Jerry's Newport Folk Festival (847-3700; PO Box 1221, Newport) This must be the most laid-back, politically correct, hip-and-cool, and all around good-time event in the world. People (around 7500 to 9000 each day) sit outside eating, talking, dancing, and listening to the country's best folk musicians. When it gets too hot, people just jump in the Bay. Every year new artists make their debuts, but the famous are on hand as well. The 1992 and '93

The massive walls of Fort Adams make a perfect sound stage for the annual JVC Jazz Festival in Newport.

Pamela Petro

Festivals concluded with an a cappella ensemble called Four Voices in Harmony; their sound is so pure it brings out the goose-bumps: the Indigo Girls, Mary Chapin-Carpenter, and Joan Baez were also featured. Wow. Held the first weekend in August.

JVC Newport Jazz Festival (847-3700; PO Box 1221, Newport) America's first jazz festival is now 40 years old. It's held the weekend after Ben & Jerry's Folk jubilee (the second weekend in August), in the same place (Fort Adams). The same food sellers are on hand too, and the harbor is filled with boats rocking to the beat. Only the audience and performers are different — the jazz crowd is older and more ethnically diverse, on hand to hear jazz giants such as Ray Charles, Grover Washington, Sonny Rollins, Tito Puente, even Spyro Gyra. Rosemary Clooney and the Count Basie Orchestra opened the 1993 event at a gala in the Newport Casino on Friday evening. This is as good as it gets.

The Newport Music Festival (846-1133, after June 1 call 849-0700; PO Box 3300, Newport) The 1993 Festival was the 25th anniversary of what has been called "the most prestigious musical event in America." The schedule is ambitious: three concerts daily over a two-week period, performed by over 200 artists in spaces constructed for this purpose — the music rooms of Newport's mansions. As the Festival's long-time director, Mark Malkovich III, has said, music warms up the museum-like atmosphere of these grand, cold palaces and brings them alive. The Festival is respected for its musical daring and the coterie of international talent it attracts, including past debuts by world-renowned pianists Jean-Phillipe Collard and Andrei Gavrilov. Held in mid-July.

OTHER SEASONAL EVENTS

Annual Barbershop Quartet Concert (466-2982; Block Island School Gymnasium, High St., Old Harbor, Block Island) They know how to sing barbershop on Block — they've been doing this event for 30 years.

Lafayette Band Summer Concerts (884-6843; N. Kingstown Town Beach, N. Kingstown) The Lafayette Band is one of the oldest community bands in the country (established 1882). Have a beach picnic and hear them play for free. Call for dates.

Summer Concerts By-the-Bay (253-2707; Blithewold, 101 Ferry Rd./Rte. 114, Bristol) Concerts on Blithewold's beautiful grounds are held all summer; call for a schedule.

Wickford Country Music Jamboree (295-2570, 800-854-8584; Wickford Festival Grounds, Tower Hill Rd./Rte. 1, N. Kingstown/Wickford) This is a new event, but it's been very successful. A day-long country music, dancing, cooking, even clothing fest, capped with a song contest — the winner receives a recording contract.

NIGHTLIFE

Newport has either a very good or very bad reputation as a party town, depending on who you ask. However, one thing is certain: walk down Thames on a summer night and you'll get vibrant earfuls of different beats through each open door. Like everything else in Newport, the atmosphere is casual and the partying potent: the area earns its reputation as the "Riviera of Rhode Island." The Newport scene makes a sharp contrast to most of the other Bay towns, especially Wickford (which is dry), and Little Compton and Tiverton, where it's quiet enough to hear nature go about its night business — and incidentally, great places to stargaze (a form of nightlife). Block Island in July, however, can give Newport a run for its money (the Old and New Harbor areas only — the rest is stargazing territory).

The following list is selective — the best thing to do is find a good little club for yourself. Many restaurants also have entertainment in season, particularly on weekends — some standouts are noted below, but see the *Restaurants* chapter as well (plus the Bar category of the Food & Beverage Purveyors section). Included at the end are several Providence-area clubs too good to miss.

West Bay

Alias Smith and Jones (884-0756; Main St., E. Greenwich) Live, local rock & roll and no cover before 9. **Blue Parrot** (884-2002; 28 Water St., E. Greenwich) Live waterside jazz. **Bon Vue Inn** (789-0696; 1238 Ocean Rd., Narragansett) Live rock & roll down by the sea.

East Bay

The Clubhouse (253-9844; 95 Tupelo St., Bristol) A popular spot to catch local rock bands.

Aquidneck

Bad Bob's (Waites's Wharf, off Thames St., Newport) Live rock plus "1 Boat,

2 Dance Floors, 3 Levels, 4 Bars" — how can you beat it? **Christie's** (847-5400; Christie's Landing, off Thames St., Newport) The food may be only so-so, but this is a great spot to sit outside and listen to live bands Fri.–Sun. In between sets you can hear the waves. **Club 3** (848-7851; 162 Broadway, Newport) Insiders call this the local musicians' favorite gig. It's small but packs a wallop; mostly local original rock bands plus the odd acoustic booking. **Coconuts Comedy Club** (849-2600; Doubletree Newport Islander Hotel, Goat Island, Newport) Attracts top comedians from around the country — chances are you've seen them on cable. **David's** (841-5431; Prospect Hill, Newport) A chic spot favored by the gay crowd of Newport. **One Pelham East** (847-9460; Thames St., Newport) Live rock in an Irish pub setting, believe it or not; in winter the locals hang out here, in summer it attracts a nicely diverse crowd. **Maximillian's** (849-4747; 108 Williams St., Newport) Perhaps you'll get lucky and arrive on pasta-and-oil night: "female wrestling with a culinary flair." **Smuggler's Landing** (847-7800; 142 Long Wharf, at Washington St., Newport) Piano bar plus contemporary and jazz. You can actually converse here above the music. **Thames Street Station** (840-9480; Perry Mill Market, off Thames St., Newport) A real dance club, with alternative and progressive rock. They play a lot of U2 and book live bands now and then. **Tickets** (849-1000; Newport Marriott, 25 America's Cup Ave., Newport) A self-described "high-energy" nightclub with DJ music and dancing.

Block Island

Captain Nick's (486-2000; Ocean Ave., Old Harbor) Live rock & roll (believe it — I once burned my foot through a hole in a sneaker, twisting the night away here). **McGovern's Yellow Kittens** (466-5855; Corn Neck Rd., Old Harbor) Live rock & roll plus occasional Motown, hip hop, and reggae.

Providence & Vicinity

CAV (751-9164; 14 Imperial Place, Providence) CAV stands for "Coffee Antiques Venture." It's a one-of-a-kind coffeehouse with interesting food (including brunch) and even more interesting antiques. Best of all is the amazingly diverse live music, ranging from African to contemporary folk. **Lupo's** (239 Westminster St., Providence) Lupo's Heartbreak Hotel is a legend in Providence. When it re-opened after a five-year hiatus even the mayor showed up for the festivities. The very best in live rock & roll. **The Comedy Connection** (438-8383; 39 Warren Ave., E. Providence.) *USA Today* called this one of the best comedy clubs in the country.

SEASONAL EVENTS & FESTIVALS

From the largest outdoor art show on the East Coast to the annual Blessing of the Fishing Fleet, Narragansett Bay has a festival for everyone. Note that the *Restaurants* and *Recreation* chapters also contain listings for seasonal events, as do headings for Music, Gardens, and the special section on Mansions.

Churches host a wealth of local happenings from fairs to the famous "May Breakfasts" featuring that special Rhode Island treat, jonnycakes.

Craig Hammell

West Bay

Blessing of the Fleet (783-7121; Great Island Rd., Narragansett/Galilee) A bishop blesses the fishing fleet, which is suitably decorated for the occasion, plus any pleasure craft on hand, then they all join in a floating parade.

Narragansett Art Festival (789-7713; Veteran's Memorial Park, off Ocean Rd., Narragansett Pier) Over 100 artists exhibit their wares by the seaside. Late June.

Narragansett Heritage Days (783-7121; Veteran's Memorial Park, off Ocean Rd., Narragansett Pier) Crafts, food, and nightly entertainment. Late July.

Quonset Air Show (886-1423; Quonset Airport, N. Kingstown/Quonset Point) An air-borne extravaganza, with the likes of the Red Devils (the British Army Parachute Team) and RI's own Air Force Thunderbirds. Around Memorial Day.

Summer Fest & Feast (885-0020; Main St., E. Greenwich) A good time: 125 arts and crafts exhibitors, a 5-K road race, live music, and best of all, food sampling at Norton's Marina. Old-fashioned trolley cars cruise along Main St. and the waterfront. Late August.

Wickford Art Festival (294-6840; sidewalks of Wickford, Brown, & Main Sts., N. Kingstown/Wickford) This is one of the oldest and largest annual art shows on the East Coast. With exhibits by over 250 artists, it literally takes over the whole town. Good quality work but on the safe side; go to the galleries for the avant garde. Early to mid-July.

East Bay

Bristol Fourth of July Parade (245-0750; Hope & High Sts., Bristol) First held in 1785, this is the oldest Fourth of July Parade in the country. You know when center lines along the parade route are painted red, white, and blue that this is no ordinary event. Crowds line up 12-deep (those in front have probably been there since 5am) to watch over 3000 marchers, floats, teams of Clydesdale horses, clowns, even a guy with a bass drum strapped to his lawnmower. The marching bands represent the pick of the national crop: don't miss yearly appearances by the famous Philadelphia Mummers, Tom McGrath's Marching Clambake Band from Newport, and especially the Centennial Legion Division — fife and drum corps in full 18th-century regalia. The parade is heralded by Bristol's town crier and lasts about three hours.

If you want to join the 200,000 other folks who attend this annual extravaganza, heed some warnings: the parade starts at 10:30 but roads are blocked off by 8:30, so arrive early — you can begin setting up blankets and chairs along the sidewalks any time after 5am. Plan to park at a distance; police recommend side streets, Colt State Park, and the Newport Creamery lot on Rte. 114 north of the town center, and either walk or bike in on the East Bay Bike Path, though it too gets crowded. Don't forget to bring cold drinks (no alcohol), sunscreen, and a hat. Or, if crowds give you the heebie-jeebies, watch full coverage on TV (it's carried by Channel 12, Providence's ABC affiliate).

Civil War Reenactment (277-2669; Colt State Park, off Hope St./Rte. 114, Bristol) The RI militia hosts those from several other states, and they stage a version of Appomattox revisited. Mid-June.

Aquidneck

Black Ships Festival (846-2720; citywide, Newport) Every year Newport celebrates the anniversary of hometown hero Commodore Matthew Perry's "opening of Japan" (the 1854 Treaty of Kanagawa), with Japanese art, origami,

Sumo wrestling is a highlight of the Black Ships Festival in Newport.

Courtesy of the Japan-America Society

and flower-arranging demonstrations, a kite festival, sumo wrestling, formal tea ceremonies, and more. Late July.

Christmas in Newport (849-6545; PO Box 716, Newport) Christmas in Newport, Inc., is a not-for-profit organization that for over 20 years has managed to orchestrate an event for nearly every day of December, and turn the City by the Sea into a glittering fairyland of white lights (a Moravian custom). Some stand-outs include the top-notch **Craft Show**, held the last weekend in November; **Historic House Tours**; a production of Handel's *Messiah* at **Trinity Church**; a **Kwanzaa**, which is an African-American celebration based on ancient African harvest rituals; the halls of **The Breakers, Chateau-sur-Mer,** and **The Elms** decked with boughs of holly, and marble, crystal, and gold; and above all, the **Turtle Frolic**. Every year since 1752, when the first "frolic" was held — it featured a giant vat of turtle soup — subsequent frolics have commemorated the event in the same spot on the same evening, December 23. It features 18th-century food, drink, and English country dancing. Come in your periwig and knee-breeches if you have them. For an advance peek at all the festivities, order the Christmas in Newport Video from Video Productions, PO Box 1024, Newport, 847-3229.

Country Folk Art Festival (846-1600; Newport Yachting Center, America's Cup Ave., Newport) This is rated as the best folk art show in the country: 150 artisans from across the nation. Every kind of craft-making material you can think of is for sale as well. Late August.

Fort Adams Festival (943-3308; Fort Adams State Park, off Ocean Dr., Newport) A low-key afternoon of arts and crafts, food, and a great view of Newport Harbor. Late July.

Harvest Fair (846-2577; Norman Bird Sanctuary, 583 Third Beach Rd., Middletown) Hay and pony rides, greased pole competitions, and even a Home & Garden Competition (enter your prize giant squash), plus scarecrow and apple pie contests. Tour the sanctuary, too.

Maritime Arts Festival (849-2243; Bowen & Bannister's Wharf, off America's Cup Ave., Newport) Where else can you listen to live music and watch the nation's finest scrimshaw artists demonstrate their craft, while your kids attend a ship-in-a-bottle-making workshop? Lots of local arts, crafts, and performers. Mid-May.

Newport Outdoor Art Festival (683-4009, 245-3793; Long Wharf Mall & Eisenhower Park, Washington Square area, Newport) This is a long-running, fine-arts-only show, with competitions and exhibits in oils, acrylics, pastels, watercolor, graphics, photography, and sculpture. Mid- to late June.

Newport Summer Fest (846-1600; Newport Yachting Center, America's Cup Ave., Newport) A great all-inclusive multi-cultural event. Food, crafts, music, dance, storytelling, from all over the world. Anything sponsored by the Yachting Center is a good bet. Late July.

Newport Winter Festival (847-7666; citywide) In case you thought Newport was dead in winter, show up the last weekend in Jan. through the first week in Feb. for this annual festival, which includes horse-drawn hay rides, ice carving and snow-and-sand sculpting contests, a progressive dinner party, and — get ready for it — the polar bear plunge.

Annual Lawn Party (846-9700; St. Mary's Episcopal Church, 324 E. Main St./Rte. 138, Portsmouth) They've been doing this in Portsmouth for over 120 years. Don't miss the baby parade, dunk tank, bakery and white elephant tables, local crafts, plus great food from clam cakes to chowder.

Sakonnet

Arts & Artisans Festival (800-677-7150; Tiverton Four Corners) A good, small outdoor arts festival. Mid-July.

THEATER

Rhode Island is home to one of the very best small repertory companies in the world: Trinity "Rep" in Providence (351-4242; 201 Washington St.) Call ahead for a list of the season's performances — a Trinity production is well worth a drive to Rhode Island's "Big City." In the Bay area, you'll also find the following excellent choices:

East Bay

Roger Williams University Performing Arts Center (254-3626; box office, 254-3666; Roger Williams University, 1 Old Ferry Rd., Bristol) This shared space is busy year-round. During the academic year, plays are performed by Roger Williams students and faculty; in July, the college community teams up with professionals to perform as the **Barn Summer Theatre**; and in August, the **Bristol Theatre Company** of community performers takes the stage, literally. Call the box office for a performance roster.

Aquidneck

Newport Playhouse & Cabaret Restaurant (848-PLAY; 102 Connell Hwy., Newport) A year-round dinner theater featuring local professionals. Call to find out what's on.

Rhode Island Shakespeare Theatre (849-7892; St. George School, Purgatory Rd., Middletown) A superb small theater company in summer residence on the beautiful campus of St. George's prep school (take a peek into nearby Purgatory Chasm before the show). It's a tiny space, so call for tickets ahead of time, but play selections are ambitious and the acting is consistently good. Their recent *Lion in Winter* was memorable.

Block Island

Ocean West Dinner Theatre (466-2971; PO Box 1052, Champlin's Marina, New Harbor) A seasonal dinner theatre and late-night cabaret at Champlin's Marina resort complex. It's a cheap taxi fare from anywhere on the island.

CHAPTER FIVE

Of Jonnycakes, Cabinets, and Quahogs

RESTAURANTS & FOOD PURVEYORS

Tomatoes were first eaten in Newport; until then they were thought to be poisonous. So you know this is a place with an adventurous palate. In fact, Rhode Islanders have created their own edible universe over the years. Some local terminology: "cabinets" are milkshakes (frappes to some). A grinder is a submarine sandwich. Jonnycakes — white cornmeal pancakes — are an old Yankee treat (see the sidebar).

Craig Hammell

George Crowther knows how to make East Bay jonnycakes at the Commons Lunch in Little Compton — his are the best.

And then there's the mighty quahog (pronounced "co-hog"). Quahogs are big, hard-shell clams, not to be confused with little necks (small hard-shell clams), or soft-shell clams. The quahog is frequently used to make "chowdah," of which several kinds abound. There's the classic white variety, known as New England style; the local favorite, Rhode Island Red (in a tomato-based broth); the so-called Block Island style, which comes as a clear broth; and finally seafood chowder, packed with all sorts of cooked crustaceans.

But that's not all. Get ready for fried clams (the whole plump creature), clam strips, clam cakes (these are actually fritters, about the size of a golf ball — nothing like crab cakes), and another local favorite, stuffed quahogs, universally known as stuffies (chopped clams in a bread-based stuffing, put back in the shell). The shores of Narragansett Bay are brimming over with purveyors of these delicacies, from elegant restaurants to seafood shacks.

It's no accident that ethnic cooking in the Bay area features native catches — indigenous to the Bay are swordfish, bluefish, lobsters, and mussels, in addition to those quahogs. Portuguese speakers came to work Rhode Island's maritime industries, and the culinary traditions they brought — from places like

The Quahog Stops Here

Cartoonist Don Bosquet is a native Rhode Islander and lives in Narragansett. He once held a regular job, but one day he snapped and decided to become a cartoonist. Bosquet has penned 8 books of cartoons lampooning life in the Ocean State, mostly starring that cute hard-shelled crustacean, the quahog. *The Quahog Stops Here* (Douglas Charles Press, paperback, $8.95) was Rhode Island's bestseller for 1993. *The Illustrated Rhode Island Dictionary*, a collaboration with Providence columnist Mark Patinkin, is his most recent publication (Covered Bridge Press, paperback, $8.95). Not surprisingly, Don Bosquet's favorite meal involves pasta and — you guessed it — seafood.

the Azores, Cape Verde, and Madeira, as well as Portugal — still flavor local menus. Look for linguiça and chouriço (spicy garlic sausages — chouriço is hotter), malassadas (fried sweetbread), kale soup, called caldo verde, and "blade meat," which translates to marinated pork.

All of the Bay traditions come together in Newport, which has one of the greatest concentrations of fine restaurants in New England. You can have an elegant meal in the nation's oldest continuously operating tavern (the White Horse), get seafood-in-the-rough on the wharf, or dine late in a hip bistro. In Newport, make reservations whenever possible: a genteel feeding frenzy takes hold of the town on summer weekends, and waits can be long. Also be advised that the BYOB designation you see in the listings below means Bring Your Own Booze.

The following restaurant listing is a generous cross-section of the area's many and varied eateries. The food and beverage purveyor section lists the best spots for provisions for everything from gourmet picnics to those essential ice-cream stops.

The price range reflects the cost of a single dinner meal, including appetizer, entrée, dessert, and coffee or tea. Wine or other beverages are not included in the price scale.

Dining Price Code

Inexpensive	Up to $15
Moderate	$15 to $25
Expensive	$25 to $35
Very Expensive	Over $35

Credit Cards

AE — American Express
CB — Carte Blanche
D — Discover
DC — Diner's Club
MC — MasterCard
V — Visa

For a long stay, consider the **Newport County Dinner Club** (847-3789; 28 Pelham St., Newport). It's a two-for-one coupon booklet that covers many towns in the Narragansett Bay area, and can add up to significant savings.

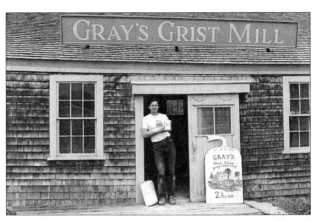

Tim McTague keeps local food traditions alive at Gray's Gristmill in Adamsville, built c. 1670.

Craig Hammell

Jonnycakes

It's no typo: real, honest-to-goodness Rhode Island jonnycakes have no H. If white cornmeal is made exclusively from White Cap Flint corn (an ancient, per-snickety strain native to this area), and stone-ground in Rhode Island, it may be called "jonnycake meal" — anything else is merely the stuff that makes johnny-cakes (the spelling is actually protected by Rhode Island state law).

The name probably derives from the colonial term "journey cakes," so named because the flat cornmeal pancakes were ideal for traveling. Typically, Rhode Islanders can't agree on how to cook their most famous home-grown product. There's the East Bay method, which produces large, thin, lacy jonnycakes that look like crêpes, and the West Bay style, which calls for smaller, thicker cakes the size of half-dollars. Every year jonnycakes are the staple of RI's traditional **May Breakfasts**. There are 35 or so held throughout the state on or near the first weekend of the month (held in everything from churches to yacht clubs). Call the RI Dept. of Economic Development (277-2601 or 800-556-2484) for a list.

Believe it or not, there is a Society for the Propagation of the Jonnycake Tradition in Rhode Island (PO Box 4733, Rumford 02916). You can watch jonnycake meal being ground at the following gristmills, and they offer mail order service:

Carpenter's Gristmill (783-5483; Moonstone Beach Rd., Perryville 02879) Carpenter's, c. 1703, is the only mill that still runs on water power. The meal is available at Wickford Gourmet.

Gray's Gristmill (508-636-6075; PO Box 422, Adamsville/Little Compton 02801) Operating continuously since 1670; buy the product (as well as other flours and meals) in Gray's own shop.

Kenyon's Gristmill (783-4054; Usquepaugh 02892) The mill was built c. 1711, but they use alien white corn, and must call their product johnnycake meal.

WEST BAY

East Greenwich

CATHAY GARDEN
884-7776.
363 Main St., E. Greenwich.
Closed: Mon.
Price: Inexpensive.
Cuisine: Chinese.
Serving: L, D.
Credit Cards: AE, D, MC, V.
Reservations: Not necessary.
Smoking: Section.
Handicap Access: Possible.

The dinner buffet here is popular with locals, who arrive in surprising numbers to eat in rather than take away (the decor is smart and there's a full bar). A Mandarin special, Moo Shi Pork — shredded meat with dried lily flowers, mushrooms, cabbage, and bamboo shoots with tortilla-like pancakes — is hot, spicy, and delicious.

**FRANK & JOHNNY'S
RESTAURANT &
PIZZERIA**
884-9751; 884-1221.
186 Main St., E. Greenwich.
Open: Daily.
Price: Inexpensive to Moderate.
Cuisine: Italian.
Serving: D.
Credit Cards: None.
Reservations: No.
Smoking: Yes.
Handicap Access: One step.

The pizza pie was voted one of the 10 best in the state, and is classic thin-crust, with a legion of toppings. Get it to go or have dinner there. The white tablecloths and plastic flowers are a sure sign of good unpretentious Italian food. The menu includes fried shrimp, veal stuffed with eggplant, imported ham, steaks, sandwiches, and pasta. Where else could you get macaroni with butter, or spaghetti with garlic, oil, and mushrooms? Good, simple food at great prices. They don't deliver.

JIGGER'S DINER
884-5388.
145 Main St.
Open: Daily.
Price: Inexpensive.
Cuisine: American.
Serving: B, L.
Credit Cards: None.
Reservations: No.
Smoking: Yes.
Handicap Access: No.

This 1917 diner car, perpendicular to Main Street, is reminiscent of an old ship's cabin inside, full of warm, mellowed wood. Not a tourist hangout but a local favorite, it claims the "best West Bay jonnycakes," and the "best diner breakfast." The sandwiches and Blue Plate Specials are also first-rate. Pies, cakes, and ice cream are all homemade. It's open from 6am–1pm — some regulars squeeze two meals into that little window of opportunity.

WALTER'S
885-2010.
5600 Post Rd., E. Greenwich.
Open: Year-round.
Price: Moderate to Expensive.
Cuisine: Italian/Jewish.
Serving: D.
Credit Cards: AE, MC, V.
Reservations: Recommended.
Smoking: Section.
Handicap Access: Yes.

Friends who usually refuse to eat Italian food out (they cook it so well themselves) were wowed here. With its unusual Jewish-Italian culinary heritage, Walter's puts a unique spin on everything, from the grilled mushroom appetizer stuffed with spinach, onion, and parmigiano to entrées featuring veal, chicken, a variety of pasta, and daily seafood specials. Expect a leisurely meal with attentive (but not aggressive) service — food this good requires a time commitment. Desserts are rich and varied, but it's the mushroom dishes that carry the day. Excellent gourmet and take-out shop (closed Mon.).

WAREHOUSE TAVERN
885-3700.
20 Water St., E. Greenwich.
Open: Daily.
Price: Moderate to Expensive.
Cuisine: Seafood/American.

Historic Water Street in East Greenwich fronts on a small harbor of pleasure yachts. Three waterside eateries jockey for position here all in a row: **Harborside Lobstermania**, the old standby, which offers dinner dining with lighter fare upstairs and fried seafood downstairs; the **Blue**

Serving: L, D.
Credit Cards: AE, D, DC, MC, V.
Reservations: No (recommended for 20 Water St.).
Smoking: Section.
Handicap Access: Yes.

Parrot, the newcomer of the group, with a more contemporary, pasta-based menu and live music on Sunday afternoons; and the **Warehouse Tavern**, which has its own elegant restaurant on the second floor, **20 Water Street**. The Warehouse Tavern itself has an enormous deck where yachts pull up as you eat. The menu is short but satisfying. The lobster roll was better than the shrimp pizza, but both were tasty; cherrystones, quahogs, and fish and chips are recommended. Inside, where the offerings are more extensive, the Tavern does a good job with both the grilled tuna steak and the Black Angus top sirloin. This really was a 19th-century warehouse — note the two enormous screw holes in the old beams by the bar.

Jamestown

BAY VOYAGE INN
423-2100.
150 Conanicus Ave., Jamestown.
Closed: Mon.
Price: Expensive.
Cuisine: Classic Continental.
Serving: D, SB.
Credit Cards: AE, DC, MC, V.
Reservations: Recommended.
Smoking: Yes.
Handicap Access: Yes.

Known for its magnificent brunch, the Bay Voyage is a treat any time. This Shingle style "cottage" was barged across the Bay from Middletown in 1889 (see Chapter Three, _Lodging_). The dining room offers compelling Bay views from all angles. The brunch is all-buffet, with a prix fixe of $15.95, and there are both breakfast and lunch offerings, plus made-to-order omelettes and waffles, and dessert (trifle and cakes). Otherwise reasonable people go crazy here, and pile their plates sinfully high. The dinner menu offers classics such as caesar salad for two (tossed table-side), lobster Thermidor, rack of lamb provençal, filet mignon, and sea scallops meunière, all delicious. The oysters on the half shell appetizer is a stand-out.

JAMESTOWN OYSTER BAR
423-3380.
22 Narragansett Ave., Jamestown.
Open: Daily.
Price: Moderate.
Cuisine: Seafood.
Serving: L, D, SB.
Credit Cards: AE, MC, V.
Reservations: No.
Smoking: Section.
Handicap Access: Two steps.

Some friends won't go anywhere else to celebrate an occasion. This, they say, is an unsung wonder, far from the crowds, formality, and high prices of Newport. Appetizers include Rhode Island "stuffies" (stuffed quahogs), lobster ravioli, fried calamari, and, of course, oysters. Best of all is the grilled, broiled, and blackened seafood, and you can get inexpensive items like fish and chips, burgers, and sandwiches. The "raspberry bash" — a concoction of chocolate cake, white chocolate, and raspberries — is out of this world. Both the staff and clien-

---

Meals on Wheels, Water, and in the Sand

Bay Queen Dinner Cruises (245-1350, 800-439-1350 in RI; 461 Water St., Warren) Have lunch, brunch, or dinner buffet aboard the sleek dining ship *Vista Jubilee*. The brunch cruise puts you ashore for two hours in Newport; the lunch trip offers a narrated tour of Newport Harbor; and the dinner cruise has dancing. May–Dec.

Block Island Dinner Cruise (466-2474; Champlin's Marina, New Harbor) Watch the sun set from the *Debonair* and enjoy a complete dinner plus champagne toast. $48 per person.

Kempenaar's Clambake Club (847-1441; 37 Malbone Rd., Newport) Arrange a private clambake for two or for a crowd up to 125, Apr.–Oct. The secluded clambake grounds are on Valley Rd. in Middletown — there's even a pool. Kempenaar's holds a Public Clambake every 4th of July (choose between steak and lobster plus all the fixings).

Morning Star **Charters** (295-5918; Wickford, N. Kingstown). Sail away on a 46-ft. cutter for breakfast, lunch, dinner, or even overnight cruises. They serve everything from hors d'oeuvres to lobster and native corn. BYOB.

Star Clipper Dinner Train (849-7550, 800-462-7452 outside RI; 102 Connell Hwy., Newport; leaves from 19 America's Cup Ave.). Pretend you're on the Orient Express: have a four-course meal on a three-hour train ride along Narragansett Bay. Note that most tables are for four. Murder Mystery and jazz evenings. Jackets required.

---

tele are friendly and informal; the latter tends to be a happy mix of islanders and local celebrities.

**JUNCTION 40 RESTAU-
RANT & PUB**
423-1020.
40 Narragansett Ave.,
   Jamestown.
Open: Daily.
Price: Inexpensive.
Cuisine: American.
Serving: B (weekends), L,
   D.
Credit Cards: MC, V.
Reservations: No.
Smoking: Section.
Handicap Access: Yes.

A good family spot to relax and get a decent meal after a day in Newport or poking around Beaver Tail. Breakfast is served on weekends, and seafood, deli sandwiches, pasta, burgers, and soups any time. Three clam cakes and a bowl of chowder is the house specialty and a deal at $2.95. There's also a children's menu, a full bar, and a large-screen TV.

SCHOOLHOUSE CAFÉ
423-1490.
14 Narragansett Ave.,
   Jamestown.
Closed: Mon.
Price: Moderate to Expen-
   sive.

Even though it's one of the few "upscale" places in town, the Schoolhouse Café is right at home on Jamestown, which is decidedly laid-back. This means that while the menu offers ports and cognacs, the dining room is airy and casual (it really was a one-room schoolhouse and general

Cuisine: American.
Serving: B, D, L (Sat.), SB.
Credit Cards: AE, MC, V.
Reservations: Suggested.
Smoking: Non-smoking
library/lounge upstairs.
Handicap Access: No.

store, built in 1829) and the waitstaff friendly and witty. The evening menu rounds up the usual suspects from sirloin and chicken to seafood and pasta. At brunch, the apple-cinnamon pancakes were tasty, though the French toast, made from Portuguese sweet bread, was undercooked. Both prices and food are middle-of-the-road, but the atmosphere is inviting. New owners recently took over.

**TRATTORIA SIM-
PATICO**
423-3731.
13 Narragansett Ave.,
Jamestown.
Open: Daily.
Price: Expensive.
Cuisine: Regional Italian.
Serving: D.
Credit Cards: MC, V.
Reservations: Recom-
mended.
Smoking: Section.
Handicap Access: Yes.

Other than the pizza places, Simpatico is the only "ethnic" restaurant on Conanicut Island. The white tablecloths and fresh flowers will lure you inside; the grilled portobello mushroom on spinach with balsamic sauce will whet your appetite (other appetizers include sautéed calamari and stuffed or steamed mussels). The "piatti principali" highlight the talents of the chef as well as the quality of local ingredients: the one-and-a-quarter-pound lobster comes in a spicy baste over squid-ink pasta; the mixed grill — lamb, pork, sausage, and chicken — is served with polenta and four different sauces.

Narragansett

ANGEL'S
782-2300.
140 Point Judith
Rd./Mariner's Square,
Narragansett.
Open: Daily.
Price: Moderate to Expen-
sive.
Cuisine: Italian.
Serving: D.
Credit Cards: AE, MC, V.
Reservations: For groups
over 4.
Smoking: Section.
Handicap Access: One step.

The cherubim and seraphim are here in force: on the wallpaper, hanging from the ceiling. Perhaps they're guardians of good pasta, which dominates the menu, from a lovely, light gnocchi to paella made with orzo instead of rice. Appetizers carry out the "cucina nuova" promise (as the cuisine is described on the menu), with selections like polenta e gorgonzola (with a creamy and pungent cheese sauce), cozze fritte (fried squid with hot pepper rings), and Roman egg-drop soup. Don't eat too much of the herbed bread, temptingly served with rosemary-infused olive oil: save room for homemade Italian desserts. A winner in a strip mall.

AUNT CARRIE'S
783-7930.
1240 Ocean Rd., Narra-
gansett/Point Judith.

A debate rages in Rhode Island as to who has the best clams — cakes, stuffies, fried, in chowder, you name it. Evelyn's and Flo's are the

Open: June–Labor Day;
  closed Tues.
Price: Inexpensive.
Cuisine: Seafood.
Serving: L, D.
Credit Cards: None.
Reservations: No.
Smoking: Yes.
Handicap Access: Yes.

BASIL'S
789-3743.
22 Kingstown Rd., Narra-
  gansett Pier.
Open: Weds.–Sun.
Price: Expensive to Very
  Expensive.
Cuisine: French/Continen-
  tal.
Serving: D.
Credit Cards: AE, MC, V.
Reservations: Recom-
  mended.
Smoking: Discouraged.
Handicap Access: No.

CASA ROSSI
789-6385.
90 Point Judith Rd., Narra-
  gansett.
Open: Daily.
Price: Moderate.
Cuisine: Italian.
Serving: D.
Credit Cards: AE, CB, D,
  DC, MC, V.
Reservations: Accepted for
  10 or more.
Handicap Access: Yes.
Smoking: Section.

CHAMPLIN'S SEAFOOD
783-3152.

other contenders; see below. Each lady has her own adherents, but they'll all treat you well. Aunt Carrie's is in a big old handsome beach house, open, airy, and casual, with a great view of the sea from the large dining room. A bluefish special was less than $5; a big bowl of chowder or an order of clam cakes is 75¢. All this, plus fried clams or fish and chips, will be devoured gleefully. Nice fresh fruit pies, too. Around for over 70 years; take-out and children's menu.

You can't miss Basil's: it's a townhouse in a small shopping plaza painted bright yellow, just across from Pier Marketplace. Inside, the elegant French provincial decor takes over, as does a team of very professional waiters who perform their tasks with alacrity and good cheer. The place is small (only 10 tables), and the menu ambitious, beginning with frogs legs, steamed mussels, and fettuccine Alfredo, and moving on to duck à l'orange, steak Diane, and the house specialty, Veal à la Basil's (medallions in a light cream and mushroom sauce). Béarnaise and cream sauces abound. Appropriately, the wine list features whites. Like the entrées, the desserts are wildly rich and flavorful. Word around Narragansett is that Basil's has great food, but is a little overpriced.

This is a find: a clapboard house marooned in a sea of miniature golf courses and fast-food joints, with authentic Italian cooking. All of the pastas are homemade, as is the excellent bread. Hard-to-find dishes turn up here: bracciola, for instance, which is rolled beef stuffed with eggs and spices. Appetizers begin with snails, squid, and antipasto; the huge menu is divided into beef, veal, chicken, and fish selections, plus lots of seafood combos over pasta. Portions are large, but leave room for the homemade cannoli, which is first-rate. Fresh gnocchi, pastas, and sauces to go, too.

Galilee is the home of Rhode Island's fishing fleet, so you know the seafood is fresh here. But

256 Great Island Rd./PO
   Box 426,
   Narragansett/Galilee.
Open: Daily.
Price: Inexpensive.
Cuisine: Seafood.
Serving: B, L, D.
Credit Cards: V, MC.
Reservations: No.
Smoking: Section.
Handicap Access: Limited.

where to get it can be confusing. Go with Champlin's — it's consistently good and has the optimum spot at the mouth of Point Judith Pond. Eat inside or out on the deck — or get some fried clams or a lobster roll to eat on the boat ride to Block. Order at the window and they'll call your number. Every permutation of Rhode Island seafood is here, including baked stuffed shrimp, fried squid, stuffies, fish and chips, and chowder. The prices are right, the fish is fresh, there's a full liquor license, and you can even get breakfast or ice cream downstairs. Highly recommended retail fish market, too.

CHEZ PASCAL
782-6020.
944 Boston Neck Rd./Rte.
   1A, Narragansett/Bonnett Shores.
Closed: Mon.
Price: Moderate.
Cuisine: French.
Serving: L (Sat.), D, SB.
Credit Cards: MC, V.
Reservations: Suggested.
Smoking: No.
Handicap Access: No.

If you went to sleep and dreamed of the perfect French restaurant, a little place that's unpretentious outside but charming within, where the food is exquisite but not too rich, and the prices low, you'd wake up at Chez Pascal. The relaxed atmosphere belies the professional wizardry of the kitchen. The fish potage, with tomatoes, lobster, clams, and mussels, and seasoned with garlic and saffron, is a masterpiece. So are the escargot, and the simple but exquisite pasta with vegetables and goat cheese (only $7.95). A steak-loving friend declared the rib-eye to be the only perfectly cooked cut of meat he's had in years. Other entrées include grilled lobster tail and the adventurous skate fish with horseradish sauce. Forget guilt and calories and have dessert, baked by Pascal himself. The crème brûlée and fruit tarts are as good as they look. At Sunday brunch, the brioche French toast with almond slices is fabulous. BYOB.

COAST GUARD HOUSE
789-0700.
40 Ocean Rd., Narragansett
   Pier.
Open: Year-round.
Price: Expensive.
Cuisine: Seafood/Continental.
Serving: L, D, SB.
Credit Cards: AE, CB, D,
   DC, MC, V.
Reservations: For parties of
   8 or more.

You can't get much closer to the water than this: the Coast Guard House was built in 1888 as a lifesaving station just feet away from Narragansett Bay. Fully recovered from recent hurricane damage, the main dining room offers one of the best water views in the state. With this location the food doesn't have to be good, but it is. The sole Véronique in a delicate white sauce with green grapes and the grilled swordfish with honey mustard glaze are both delicious. For non-fish-lovers there are plenty of other options. The decor is surprisingly elegant for a waterfront place, and the dining room takes on a lovely glow as the sun sets

Smoking: Non-smoking section with limited water view.
Handicap Access: Yes.

over the Bay. Beware: it can get noisy. The outdoor rooftop/deck bar has lighter fare, and was named by *Rhode Island Monthly* the best waterfront bar in Rhode Island.

OCEAN VIEW CHINESE
783-9070.
140 Point Judith Rd./#39 Mariner's Square, Narragansett.
Closed: Tues.
Price: Inexpensive.
Cuisine: Chinese.
Serving: L, D.
Credit Cards: None.
Reservations: No.
Smoking: Section.
Handicap Access: No.

This is *the* Chinese place in the West Bay — people even come from Newport for the authentic Mandarin and Szechuan specials. The menu is enormous and virtually every choice is a good one, with great service, good prices, and take-out. (Tip: pick up a couple of pint containers on the way to Block Island, where there is no Chinese food.)

PEPPERS
783-2550.
83 Narragansett Ave., Narragansett Pier.
Open: Daily to 2:30.
Price: Inexpensive.
Serving: B, L.
Credit Cards: None.
Reservations: No.
Smoking: No.
Handicap Access: No.

Locals may try to keep it a secret, but the word is out: Peppers is the hands-down choice for breakfast and lunch in Narragansett Pier. It's in the front room of the Grinnell Inn (a boarding house); dine on the porch as well. The setting is cozy and the food is great. The lunch menu has a Mexican flair, but includes burgers, quiche, tuna, and a great falafel pocket. Breakfast will please both traditional and new-fangled appetites. Take-out; BYOB.

SPAIN
783-9770.
1 Beach St., Narragansett Pier.
Open: Daily.
Price: Expensive.
Cuisine: Spanish.
Serving: L (except Sun.), D.
Credit Cards: AE, CB, DC, MC, V.
Reservations: For parties of 6 or more.
Smoking: Section.
Handicap Access: Yes.

It's a rare treat to find a shore restaurant that does more than fry or broil fish; to find one that serves authentic Spanish cuisine is truly special. The paella for two is available only on Friday and Saturday nights when the place is packed; be prepared to wait. The paella was brimming with blue mussels, shrimp, scallops, chicken, clams, and chouriço (spicy sausage), and a whole lobster — it made a second meal the next day. Also on hand are entrées such as chicken with saffron rice, olive oil, mushrooms, olives, and chouriço; and pork chops in lemon garlic sauce. End with a perfect cup of espresso and a slice of flan. The service is bustling and gracious, never fussy. Note: Spain is in a weathered-shingle, circular structure that's within the Pier Marketplace complex.

THE STEAK LODGE
789-1135.
945 Boston Neck Rd./Rte.
   1A, Narragansett/Bonnet
   Shores.
Open: Daily.
Price: Moderate to Expen-
   sive.
Cuisine: American.
Serving: D.
Credit Cards: MC, V.
Reservations: Accepted.
Smoking: Section.
Handicap Access: No.

This log cabin-like "lodge" has a wonderful ocean view and a very pretty, linen-tablecloth interior that belies the rustic look outside. The beef dishes are available with a variety of house sauces. The prices are low ($16.95 for filet mignon) and the quality is high — carnivores will have a field day here. Other red meats as well as chicken and seafood are also on the menu, as is a very reasonable children's selection. This is a family restaurant with sophistication and a view — a rare thing in a fast-food world.

TWIN WILLOWS
789-8153.
865 Boston Neck Rd./Rte.
   1A, Narragansett/Bon-
   nett Shores.
Open: Daily.
Price: Inexpensive.
Cuisine:
   American/Seafood.
Serving: L, D.
Credit Cards: V, MC.
Smoking: Yes.
Handicap Access: Do-able.

Twin Willows is really just a great big Irish bar with a nice view — but the food justifies its restaurant listing here. The homemade chowder is excellent, as are the fish and chips, stuffies, and the rest of the seafood offerings. Relaxed and informal, with ESPN on TV and the Bay outside, this is a favorite stop on the way home from the beach. Good selection of draught beers.

North Kingstown

GREGG'S
294-5700.
4120 Quaker La./Rte. 2, N.
   Kingstown.
Open: Daily.
Price: Inexpensive
Cuisine: American.
Serving: L, D.
Credit Cards: AE, D, MC,
   V.
Reservations: No.
Smoking: Section.
Handicap Access: Yes.

Yes, it's a little too resolutely cheerful, and the big, laminated menu can be overwhelming, with its vast selection of sandwiches (from clubs to grilled cheese to New York combos like corned beef and chopped liver), salads, burgers, daily specials, pastas, and even dinners, all but one (sirloin steak sandwich) under $10. But the real reason to go to Gregg's is the desserts, for the most gloriously, wantonly luscious cakes and pies you've ever seen. Get a slice or buy a whole one to go (see the display case). There are three other Gregg's locations in RI.

MANDARIN
294-6776.
7769 Post Rd./Rte. 1, N.
   Kingstown.
Open: Daily.

There are several Chinese restaurants on the East Greenwich/North Kingstown stretch of Rte. 1; skip the others and make a beeline to Mandarin. It's a little pricey for Chinese fare, but the

Price: Inexpensive to Moderate.
Cuisine: Chinese.
Serving: L, D.
Credit Cards: AE, MC, V.
Reservations: Not necessary.
Handicap Access: Yes.

RED ROOSTER TAVERN
884-1987; 295-8804.
7385 Post Rd./Rte. 1, N. Kingstown.
Closed: Mon.
Price: Moderate to Expensive.
Cuisine: Continental/American.
Serving: D.
Credit Cards: AE, D, DC, MC, V.
Reservations: Recommended.
Smoking: Yes.
Handicap Access: Yes.

dining room has character and the food is unusually good. Specials include orange flavored beef and seafood treasure (with shrimp, lobster, scallops, and fish fillet sautéed with straw mushrooms, snow pea pods, and vegetables). The menu is extensive.

A Rhode Island tradition, the Red Rooster Tavern is a throw-back in both menu and decor to a time before the 1980s, when words like "trendy" and "nouvelle" didn't refer to restaurants. With some exceptions, like sole baked with bananas, grapefruit juice, and curry, the menu is traditional: the baked seafood platter still comes with a buttery Ritz cracker topping. The prices are far lower than those at fashionable Newport eateries. A meal of grilled chicken with roasted red peppers and sausage was very good — not great, but good enough to make the Red Rooster a terrific deal. The award-winning wine list was named one of the best in the country by *Wine Spectator*. Don't miss the wonderful grapenut pudding, chosen "best traditional dessert" in the state. "Early Bird" specials, too.

Craig Hammell

Not the cartoon character but Pauline Bacon, pictured here with her husband Raymond, is in charge of Snoopy's Diner in North Kingstown.

SNOOPY'S DINER
295-1533.
4015 Quaker La./Rte. 2, N. Kingstown.
Open: Daily.
Price: Inexpensive.

This classic deco diner is done up inside and out in gleaming stainless steel and lustrous mint-green tiles. Owner Snoopy serves up wonderful diner fare in the form of meatloaf sandwiches and "broasted" chicken, plus a hearty plate of steak and

Serving: B, L.
Credit Cards: None.
Smoking: Yes.
Handicap Access: No.

eggs for breakfast (not to mention all kinds of pan-cakes and waffles), and more. Eat in a booth or on one of the spin-around counter stools.

The sensory delights of Wickford Gourmet in North Kingstown.

Craig Hammell

WICKFORD GOURMET
295-8190.
21 W. Main St., N.
  Kingstown/Wickford.
Open: Daily.
Price: Inexpensive.
Cuisine: Café.
Serving: B, L.
Credit Cards: A, MC, V.
Smoking: No.
Handicap Access: No.

The sights and aromas at this gourmet shop and café — chocolate truffles, more kinds of olives than you can pronounce, rich, dark bins of coffee beans, cheeses with rinds like topographical maps — create a sensory rush when you walk in the door. The tiny but tasty eat-in/take-out café is the only place in Wickford with upscale, imaginative fare. Don't overlook the catalogue of made-up baskets or the Wickford Gourmet Kitchen & Table shop next door.

EAST BAY

Bristol

AIDAN'S PUB
254-1940.
5 John St., Bristol.
Closed: Mon.
Price: Inexpensive.
Cuisine: Irish/American.
Serving: Late B, L, D.

On a side street a half-block from the harbor, this is a great hang-out bar, full of locals more than happy to tell you about the area. There are even lace half-curtains on the windows. They cook real Irish food here, including bangers & mash (Irish sausage with mashed potatoes and peas),

Credit Cards: MC, V.
Smoking: Yes.
Handicap Access: Yes.

shepherd's pie, fish and chips, and corned beef sandwiches — plus a well-recommended burger and local specials like chowder and clam cakes. Best of all are 12 beers on tap, including Guinness, Harp, Bass, Newcastle Brown, Double Diamond — all served in pint glasses.

BALZANO'S
253-9811.
180 Mount Hope Ave.,
    Bristol.
Open: Daily.
Price: Inexpensive.
Cuisine: Italian.
Serving: L, D.
Credit Cards: MC, V.
Reservations: For 6 or
    more.
Smoking: Section.
Handicap Access: Yes.

Also known as "Tweet's" (Tweety Bird is their logo), Balzano's is greatly beloved as *the* Rhode Island family restaurant. Everyone comes here — kids, moms, dads, grandparents, politicians — all downing heaping plates of spaghetti ordered by the pound. All the traditional dishes are on hand, from lasagna to manicotti, plus a host of seafood choices. It's noisy and absolutely packed with people, and there's not a porcini mushroom or sun-dried tomato in sight.

THE LOBSTER POT
253-9100.
121 Hope St., Bristol.
Closed: Mon.
Price: Expensive.
Cuisine: Seafood.
Serving: L, D.
Credit Cards: AE, CB, D,
    DC, MC, V.
Reservations: Suggested.
Smoking: Section.
Handicap Access: Yes.

Again and again The Lobster Pot is rated Rhode Island's best seafood restaurant. The terrific Bay views remind you why: everything from bouillabaisse (the house specialty — there's also a vegetarian variety) to scallops Nantucket (baked with cheddar cheese and sherry) is straight-off-the-boat fresh. You could make a meal of escargot, smoked salmon, crab cakes, or calamari — and these are only the appetizers. Other entrée options include baked stuffed lobster, surf-and-turf dishes, and a personal clambake ($25). Featured on the extensive wine list are half a dozen Rhode Island selections.

It's no criticism that this isn't a trendy place — the slightly old-fashioned atmosphere is just right.

REDLEFSEN'S ROTIS-
    SERIE AND GRILL
254-1188.
425 Hope St./Rte. 114,
    Bristol.
Closed: Mon.
Price: Moderate.
Cuisine: Grill/Continental.
Serving: D.
Credit Cards: AE, CB, D,
    MC, V.

Originally a German restaurant, Redlefsen's has branched out with pastas, Boboli pizzas, and grilled fare. A restaurant that can do a succulent German mixed grill (smoked pork chop, bratwurst, and chicken wings over tangy sauerkraut), rotisserie chicken, and a delicate pasta puttanesca (also served with chicken breast) — and do all well — is rare. The bread basket may include anything from sourdough to a French baguette to blueberry corn-

Reservations: For parties of six or more.
Smoking: Section.
Handicap Access: Yes.

THE SANDBAR
253-5485.
775 Hope St./Rte. 114, Bristol.
Open: Year-round.
Price: Inexpensive.
Cuisine: Seafood/Italian/Portuguese.
Serving: L, D.
Credit Cards: None.
Reservations: No.
Smoking: Yes.
Handicap Access: One step.

S.S. DION
253-2884.
520 Thames St., Bristol.
Closed: Sun.
Price: Moderate.
Cuisine: Seafood/American.
Serving: D.
Credit cards: AE, CB, DC, MC, V.
Reservations: Suggested.
Smoking: Section.
Handicap access: Yes.

Warren

BULLOCKS
245-6502.
50 Miller St. (corner of Water St.), Warren.
Open: Daily.
Price: Mostly Inexpensive.
Cuisine: American.
Serving: L Tues.–Sat. (in winter Sat. only), D Sat.–Tues.

bread. The bistro atmosphere is charming: strings of tiny white lights and a forest-green tin ceiling; white lace curtains hang in large, store-front windows. Save room for great desserts and coffee.

The Sandbar is the kind of place that makes life worth living. It's small and unpretentious — formica tables and vinyl chairs, and even though it's right on the Bay the windows face the road — and cheap. The food is outstanding. In addition to usual take-out fare such as fried seafood, two kinds of clam chowder, and sandwiches, the Sandbar offers entrées ranging from pastas and lasagna to baked fish Portuguese style. At $3.95 the seafood special with red sauce is magnificent, full of mushrooms, clams, shrimp, and scallops over spaghetti. Table wine, served in generous glasses, is better than most house wines that cost twice as much.

The S.S. Dion isn't a former steamship, though the Bay views from its front windows are almost as good as if you were standing on deck. "S.S." refers to owners Sue and Steve Dion, who keep their regulars happy with better-than-average seafood served in a casual dining room with nautical accents, including a tank of gargantuan carp. A selection of fresh grilled fish is the house specialty, which comes with a choice of homemade sauces. More elaborate concoctions include scrod stuffed with fresh crabmeat in a creamy Romano sauce; non-seafood dishes receive equal culinary attention. Lighter fare, too, along with rich desserts. Dinner-for-two bargains Weds., Thurs.

Bullocks is highly recommended as the best place in Warren to get a sandwich or light meal. Easy to miss, it *is* the charming, European-looking spot half-covered in ivy, with awning-shaded outdoor tables bordered by lovely flower boxes. There's a handsome bar and more tables inside. Soups, salads, and sandwiches are offered plus a short, simple dinner menu. The last call for

Credit Cards: MC, V.
Reservations: For six or
more only.
Smoking: Yes.
Handicap Access: Yes.

light fare comes at 10pm. Tip: spend the morning poking around the antique shops on Water Street then stop here for lunch.

**NATHANIEL PORTER
INN**
245-6622.
125 Water St., Warren.
Open: Year-round.
Price: Expensive.
Cuisine: Gourmet Ameri-
can.
Serving: D, SB.
Credit Cards: AE, CB, D,
DC, MC, V.
Reservations: Strongly rec-
ommended.
Smoking: Section.
Handicap Access: Two
steps.

With all the magnificent 18th-century homes here you'd think more would be occupied by restaurants, but the Nathaniel Porter Inn is one of only a few. The current owner, a descendant of the sea captain who built the house in 1795, has restored it to the highest standards. Several small dining rooms are decorated with antiques and glow with candlelight; in winter blazing fireplaces add to the atmosphere. A well-rounded menu offers starters including seafood chowder (a house specialty), smoked mussels, and grilled shrimp caesar salad; entrées range from smoked filet mignon with hazelnut sauce to Asian stuffed chicken and nut-crusted trout. For dessert try the Bartlett pear rolled in hazelnut paste and baked in puff pastry. The creativity and quality of the offerings equals that of far more expensive restaurants in Providence or Newport. Monthly international cuisine nights, too.

**OLD VENICE RESTAU-
RANT**
247-2060.
632 Metacom Ave./Rte.
136, Warren.
Open: Daily.
Price: Mostly Inexpensive.
Cuisine: Italian.
Serving: L, D.
Credit Cards: AE, MC, V.
Reservations: For groups of
8 or more.
Smoking: Section.
Handicap Access: Yes.

This comfortable, pine-paneled spot always turns up on best-for-less lists. The cars overflowing the crushed seashell parking lot — almost all with Rhode Island plates — attest to its popularity. Begin with the house specialty, fried squid in a delicious garlic butter and hot pepper sauce; continue with scrod oregano with chopped tomatoes, wine, balsamic vinegar, and a light crumb topping. Or try the plump, tender fried clams, or the steak served under a dollop of whipped garlic butter (a steal at $8). The setting is bright and upbeat.

**TAV-VINO/THE BLUE
COLLAR**
245-0231.
267 Water St., Warren.
Closed: Mon.
Price: Moderate.

Stroll past old houses and antique shops to a white, crushed-shell drive: Tav-Vino is at the end, right on the Bay. The dining room is attractive — lots of glass and wood — and there's deck dining in season. The emphasis is on fresh fish (as

Cuisine: Seafood.
Serving: D.
Credit Cards: AE, MC, V.
Reservations: Accepted.
Smoking: "Sometimes a
room is non-smoking."
Handicap Access: Yes.

WHARF TAVERN
245-5043.
215 Water St./PO Box 69,
Warren.
Open; Daily.
Price: Moderate.
Cuisine: Seafood.
Serving: L, D.
Credit Cards: AE, CB, D,
DC, MC, V.
Reservations: Recom-
mended.
Smoking: Section.
Handicap Access: Yes.

opposed to shellfish), from sole to tautog, salmon to trout. The mud pie has been ranked "best decadent dessert" in the state. The only hitch is the noise in this low-ceilinged spot; if you don't mind shouting, go for the fish.

Both the new enclosed deck and older, more rustic dining-room are right on the Warren River — the views are tremendous. And so is the food. The Wharf Tavern caters to seafood lovers, but the char-broiled menu gets equal time, making surf-and-turf options a good choice. Lobster is a specialty and is prepared in a variety of styles from Thermidor and Newburg to pot-boiled, all offered at reasonable prices. Poultry and pastas are on hand as well; the luncheon menu offers lo-cal plates and sandwiches in addition to entrées. Free bottle of Sabastiani if you dine 4:30–6pm! Take-out menu and docking available, too.

AQUIDNECK

Middletown

ANDREW'S
848-5153.
909 E. Main Rd./Rte. 138,
Middletown.
Open: Daily.
Price: Moderate.
Cuisine: American.
Serving: L, D, SB.
Credit Cards: AE, MC, V.
Reservations: Accepted.
Smoking: Section.
Handicap Access: Yes.

EASTSIDE MARIO'S
841-0700.
593 W. Main Rd./Rte. 114,
Middletown.

Out in Middletown's flat, green nursery land (note the fields of baby shrubs across the way), Andrew's is somewhat of an enigma. It used to be a car showroom, and some feel the atmosphere hasn't changed all that much. But everybody agrees that you get a very good meal here. An evolving menu offers mostly grilled fare and pasta, with a fair distribution across poultry, seafood, and meat bases. All desserts are made in-house; try the chocolate sour cream cake.

About as happening a spot as they come, Mario's tongue-in-cheek Little Italy atmosphere is fun and funky, complete with red-checked

Open: Daily.
Price: Inexpensive to Moderate.
Cuisine: Italian.
Serving: L, D.
Credit Cards: AE, MC, V.
Reservations: No; sometimes long waits.
Smoking: Section.
Handicap Access: Yes.

tablecloths. The noise level is high — the waitstaff is encouraged to shout — and the prices are low. And the food is excellent. From thin crust, wood-grilled pizza to pastas (both tossed and baked selections), specials like goomba chicken (grilled with peppercorn cream sauce), plus ribs and steak dishes, you can't go wrong. Fun touches include fresh baked bread served in a paper bag, and a dessert menu accompanied by a Viewmaster so you can see what you're getting. Good decaf espresso.

Mario's is a chain — six locations throughout the country — but it's a good one. Kids will love it here. Take-out.

Old-fashioned seafood with a smile at Johnny's House of Seafood in Middletown.

Craig Hammell

JOHNNY'S HOUSE OF SEAFOOD
847-3059.
53 Purgatory Rd., Middletown.
Price: Moderate.
Open: Daily.
Cuisine: Seafood.
Serving: L, D.
Credit Cards: AE, MC, V.
Reservations: Yes.
Smoking: Section.
Handicap Access: One step.

The high-tide hurricanes of 1938 and '54 swept Johnny's away. Today it's built on a sturdy concrete foundation, which is a good thing, since Johnny's deserves to be around a while. It's a seafood restaurant of the old school: red vinyl-covered captain's chairs, mounted game fish on the walls, a superb location right on the beach, and classic seafood dishes, from fried scallops to broiled lobster served with a big scoop of cole slaw. The seafood kabob (swordfish, shrimp, and scallops) is modest in size but tasty. Johnny's also operates the **Atlantic Beach Club** right behind it, even closer to the water, with live music and a lighter menu for a more rambunctious crowd.

SEA SHAI
849-5180.
747 Aquidneck
   Ave./Aquidneck Green,
   1B, Middletown.
Open: Daily.
Price: Moderate.
Cuisine: Japanese/Korean.
Serving: L, D.
Credit Cards: AE, D, MC,
   V.
Reservations: Accepted.
Handicap Access: Yes.

The write-ups always describe Sea Shai as serene — and it is, a world away from the Newport-bound traffic on busy Aquidneck Avenue. There's a sushi bar as well as Japanese dishes from tempura to teriyaki, plus a wide selection of Korean specialties, featuring mostly sautés and casseroles. The Korean side of the menu has a spicy kick to it, though you can have it toned down as much as you wish.

TITO'S CANTINA
849-4222.
651 W. Main Rd./Rte. 114,
   Middletown.
Open: Daily.
Price: Inexpensive.
Cuisine: Mexican.
Serving: L, D.
Credit Cards: None.
Reservations: No.
Smoking: Yes.
Handicap Access: Yes.

How can you beat good, cheap Mexican food in a setting that's a cross between burger-chain and Mexican kitsch? Tito's bills itself as a "Mexican Quick-Service Cantina" — a good description. The Bandito Burrito, a 16-oz. monster with the works, is a real crowd pleaser. Tito's quesadilla is also very tasty. In addition to a wide variety of tacos, fajitas, burritos, and the like, there's also a "Little Amigos" menu and a selection of desserts from flan to chimi-chiquita (deep fried banana in a flour tortilla with chocolate sauce). Wine and Mexican beer is available at the Middletown location (the Newport Tito's, at 7 Memorial Blvd., 849-1222, is BYOB). Take-out and Tito's own brand of tortilla chips and salsa.

Newport

ANNIE'S
849-6731.
176 Bellevue Ave., New-
   port.
Open: Daily.
Price: Inexpensive.
Cuisine: American.
Serving: B, L.
Credit Cards: None.
Smoking: Yes.
Handicap Access: Yes.

This is an exceptionally attractive coffee house right next to the Newport Casino on Bellevue Avenue. Breakfast features a slew of omelettes; lunch ventures into quiches, salads, sandwiches, and soups. All of the baked goods are from **Katrina's Bakery** right down the street at 1 Casino Terrace.

**ANTHONY'S SHORE
   DINNER HALL**
848-5058.

For seafood-in-the-rough, go to Anthony's. They have their own retail fish market, so the clams, lobster, and fish catches are fresh daily. Order your

Waites's Wharf, off lower
  Thames St., Newport.
Open: Daily May–Oct.
Price: Mostly Inexpensive.
Cuisine: Seafood.
Serving: L, D.
Credit Cards: AE, MC, V.
Reservations: No.
Smoking: Yes.
Handicap Access: Yes.

clam cakes and chowder combo, or the immense
Newport lobster boil, or even honey-dipped
chicken, then get a tray, queue up for drinks, go
find a spot at a free picnic table, watch boats come
and go on the Harbor for a little bit, then tuck in
when your number is called. The lobster roll has
been voted best in the state.

*First-rate fare is found at the Black Pearl on Bannister's Wharf
in Newport.*

Craig Hammell

THE BLACK PEARL
846-5264.
Bannister's Wharf, off
  America's Cup Ave.,
  Newport.
Open: Daily.
Price: Very Expensive.
Cuisine: Continental.
Serving: L, D.
Credit Cards: AE, MC, V.
Reservations: Necessary for
  Commodore Room.
Smoking: Yes.
Handicap Access: One step.

You can sit wharf-side at the café (there's a raw
bar), inside in the Tavern, which offers a
lighter fare menu, or even go to the Black Pearl hot-
dog annex. To splurge, go to the Commodore
Room. The low, long ceiling is spanned by one
glossy, black beam; walls are a deep green with
more black trim, tablecloths are white. The essen-
tials — menu and wine list — are first rate, as are
the small details: piping hot French rolls, fresh
flowers, elegant presentation. Roast duckling in a
black mushroom and truffle sauce was outstanding, as were scallops bathed in meunière. With all
these superlatives, it's a shame that smoking is permitted in such tight quarters.

THE BOATHOUSE
846-7700.
636 Thames St., Newport.
Open: Year-round.

The thoroughly nautical atmosphere includes
America's Cup memorabilia, yachting flags,
fishing nets, buoys, even a neon sailboat advertis-

Price: Moderate to Expensive.
Cuisine: Seafood.
Serving: L, D, Brunch daily.
Credit Cards: AE, D, MC, V.
Reservations: Accepted.
Smoking: Non-smoking section.
Handicap Access: Yes.

ing beer up at the bar. Besides specializing in large-scale lobster bakes, the Boathouse offers classic seafood dishes such as baked stuffed shrimp and bay scallops as well as BBQ and Cajun specials, plus a lighter fare and children's menu. The clam chowder isn't the best but there's Bass ale on tap. Reputed to be Ted Turner's favorite hangout in Newport.

BRICK ALLEY PUB & RESTAURANT
849-6334.
140 Thames St., Newport.
Open: Daily.
Price: Moderate.
Cuisine: American.
Serving: L, D.
Credit Cards: AE, CB, D, DC, MC, V.
Reservations: Accepted.
Smoking: Section.
Handicap Access: No.

Rumor has it that there are over 200 items on the menu at this hot spot on Thames. And the quality is very high. Stand-outs are fresh fish and deli sandwiches, nachos, fajitas, and a house specialty, Irish coffee. The decor — memorabilia from the owners' travels around the country and Mexico — is as fascinating as the menu. There's also an outdoor courtyard in the back.

BURKEY'S 5th WARD DINER
842-0140.
654 Thames St., Newport.
Closed: Mon.
Price: Inexpensive.
Cuisine: Diner.
Serving: B, L, D.
Credit Cards: None.
Reservations: No.
Smoking: Yes.
Handicap Access: One step,

A young, hip, very tanned crowd has found this place in a big way. The decor is cool: blue-painted tin ceiling, funky counter stools. It's noisy and smoky at times, and the waitstaff can be a bit air-headed. The breakfast and lunch menus feature classic diner fare, which ranges from good (the bagels) to greasy (the sausage and eggs). A small dinner menu offers light, nouvelle-inspired pasta and seafood dishes. When it's not in an uproar (i.e., Folk Festival weekend), the food is better and it offers shelter from the tourist throng. BYOB.

CAFÉ DEL MARE
849-7788.
75 Long Wharf Ave., Newport.
Closed: Mon.–Tues.
Price: Moderate.
Cuisine: Northern Italian/Seafood.
Serving: D.
Credit Cards: AE, CB, D, DC, MC, V.

A restaurant-within-a-restaurant. Café del Mare hides at the far end (where the harbor view is better) of JW's Sea Grill, in the Marriott Hotel. Dinner starts with a fine antipasto plate and piping hot rolls, served with both rosemary- and garlic-infused olive oils. The entrées are a deal: fresh pastas are around $10; the Escargot del Mare, for example, is a sheer delight (snails in garlic butter over pasta, splashed with Armagnac). Ravioli

Reservations: Yes.
Smoking: Section.
Handicap Access: Yes.

CAFÉ ZELDA
849-4002.
528 Thames St., Newport.
Open: Daily, year-round.
Price: Moderate.
Cuisine: Eclectic/Italian.
Serving: L, D, SB.
Credit Cards: AE, MC. V.
Reservations: Only on
   weekdays.
Smoking: Yes.
Handicap Access: One step.

CANFIELD HOUSE
847-0416.
5 Memorial Blvd., New-
   port.
Closed: Mon.
Price: Expensive.
Cuisine: Continental.
Serving: D, SB.
Credit Cards: AE, CB, D,
   DC, MC, V.
Reservations: Recom-
   mended.
Smoking: Section.
Handicap Access: No.

CHRISTIE'S
847-5400.
Christie's Landing, off
   Thames St., Newport.
Open: Daily.
Price: Moderate to Expen-
   sive.
Cuisine: Seafood.
Serving: L, D.
Credit Cards: AE, CB, D,
   DC, MC, V.
Reservations: Recom-
   mended on weekdays;
   not accepted weekends.
Handicap Access: Yes.

choices range from gorgonzola to artichoke — the latter baked with prosciutto and fontina. Desserts include hazelnut-cappuccino torte, and the like. The coffee is outstanding.

For bistro atmosphere à la Newport (continental/nautical), go to Zelda's. All the locals do, especially in winter, when it's the bar of choice. The food is excellent and supremely colorful (a meal of tri-colored ravioli with broccoli, onion, and sun-dried tomatoes looked like an artist's palette). Soups, salads, and sandwiches are on the menu, plus entrées from mussels marinara to fresh fettuccine with pesto. Bouillabaisse, portofino, and paella are the house specials — the chef prepares one each day. Sunday brunch is also a standout. The menu says, "Menu may vary due to hangovers and hurricanes."

The Canfield House, built as a casino in 1897 by the creator of Solitaire, has a reputation as a locals' paradise. The service is relaxed but wonderfully accommodating and the Gilded Age mood pleasantly and elegantly understated. For appetizers, choose between standards such as baked onion soup (a good, upstanding version) and exotic specials like shad roe (Cole Porter fans may be willing to spend $18 on this one). Entrée selections are many and diverse; let one — sole turbans stuffed with breaded lobster and whole cashews — speak for them all. Desserts are properly decadent.

Christie's is one of those big, noisy seafood places right on the water that has a terrific view, long-standing reputation, and merely average food. Many visitors wind up here because it's right off Thames. The casual atmosphere of the outdoor patio, where live entertainment is offered on summer weekends, carries through to the huge, rustic dining rooms inside — the view from either is superb. Seafood, meat, and poultry dishes are what you'd expect. Portions are generous and, for such a big place, the waitstaff is calm and cheerful. The oldest waterfront restaurant in Newport.

CLARKE COOKE HOUSE
849-2900.
Bannister's Wharf, off
America's Cup Ave.,
Newport.
Open: Year-round.
Price: Bistro: Moderate to
Expensive; dining room,
Very Expensive.
Cuisine: Bistro: Continen-
tal/Creative American;
dining room, French.
Serving: Bistro: L Mon.–Fri.
plus weekends in season,
D daily; dining room, D
Thurs.–Sat.
Credit Cards: AE, CB, D,
DC, MC, V.
Reservations: Accepted for
dining room only.
Smoking: Yes.
Handicap Access: No.

In the thick of the Harbor throng, the Clarke Cooke House is in an old clapboard house, and is a contender for best restaurant in town. The formal French dining room (jackets required) is upstairs, and features a smoked pheasant ravioli appetizer, and entrées such as a grilled swordfish steak over a crisp risotto cake with a delicate reduction of cream, green olives, and Dijon mustard; rack of New Zealand venison; and veal and sweetbreads, in a green peppercorn sauce with Swiss potatoes. The downstairs bistro has a porch area built out over the water, called the Candy Store — different name, same menu, same place. It's an extraordinarily attractive spot, with marble-top tables, green chairs, and a bar dominated by a huge old ship model. The food ranges from sandwiches and salads to entrées like cod in cornbread and pistachio crust on a light curry sauce. Even the burgers are delicious.

DRY DOCK SEAFOOD
847-3974.
448 Thames St., Newport.
Closed: Jan.
Price: Moderate.
Cuisine: Seafood.
Serving: L, D.
Credit Cards: None.
Reservations: No.
Smoking: Yes.
Handicap Access: One step.

Rhode Island Monthly always includes this place in its "Cheap Eats" round-up (a best-for-less guide). The atmosphere is relaxed and the straightforward seafood simply and perfectly cooked, with plenty of options that let you eat with your fingers: peel-and-eat shrimp, clam boils, and lobsters. The fried shrimp nears perfection. BYOB.

ELIZABETH'S
846-6862.
Brown & Howard Wharf,
off Thames St., Newport.
Closed: Mon.
Price: Expensive.
Cuisine:
Continental/Seafood.
Serving: D Tues.–Sat.,
Brunch Sat.–Sun.
Credit Cards: AE.
Reservations: Recom-
mended.
Smoking: Section.
Handicap Access: Yes.

The decor here is comfortable and eclectic, full of paisley and antiques — a look that the British owner calls "Welsh/English." Every night Elizabeth serves up a different selection of platters for two (this is a good spot to go tandem, but half-platters are available if your party adds up to an odd number). One example is the stuffed sourdough bouillabaisse, with a first course of salad and herb toast, and second course featuring the rich seafood stew served in a scooped-out sourdough loaf, with sausage and assorted grilled veggies on the side, plus pasta of the day. As if that weren't enough, all platters come with Elizabeth's stuffed vegetable-cheese-garlic bread. A delightful favorite. BYOB.

INN AT CASTLE HILL
849-3800.
Ocean Drive, Newport.
Open: Daily.
Price: Very Expensive.
Cuisine: Creative Continental.
Serving: L Tues.–Sat., D Mon.–Sat., SB.
Credit Cards: AE, MC, V.
Reservations: Recommended.
Smoking: Non-smoking room.
Handicap Access: No.

Marine biologist Alexander Agassiz built this Shingle style mansion in 1874 off the western stretch of Ocean Drive; it features wood paneling, Oriental antiques, and a magnificent view. In the four intimate dining rooms (jackets required), the menu combines exquisitely simple entrées like Dover sole or New York sirloin with creative concoctions such as shrimp in lime vodka with cilantro oil and wild rice. Appetizers include mascarpone with Granny Smith apple ravioli and chicken and leek sausage, the wine list offers Rhode Island selections, and the desserts are top-notch. On Sunday afternoons the informal bar-and-barbecue starts at 4:30. Come early, it's popular. The patio bar on weekdays is less crowded. (Inn reviewed in *Lodging*.)

INTERNATIONAL CAFÉ
847-1033.
677 Thames St., Newport.
Closed: Tues.
Price: Inexpensive to Moderate.
Cuisine: Seafood/Filipino.
Serving: D.
Credit Cards: MC, V.
Reservations: No.
Smoking: Yes.
Handicap Access: Feasible.

Down on lower Thames, the Almanzor family — she's the hostess, he's the cook — are from the Philippines, and their menu has an international theme. Look for Polynesian fried shrimp, "Szechuan Crustacean Deluxe," Thai appetizers, BBQ steak, Hungarian chicken strudel, and all-American desserts like Chocolate-Raspberry Bash. Some are better than others: one evening the sole special dazzled, the crustacean dish (with lobster and shrimp) didn't. Though there are ups and downs, the decor and unusual menu make it worth the hike. Take-out; BYOB.

LA FORGE CASINO RESTAURANT
847-0418.
186 Bellevue Ave., Newport.
Open: Daily.
Price: Moderate to Expensive.
Cuisine: American.
Serving: B, L, D, SB.
Credit Cards: AE, MC, V.
Reservations: Recommended.
Smoking: Section.
Handicap Access: No.

La Forge is all about atmosphere, and it is exceptional here even by Newport standards. The restaurant is part of the sprawling, Shingle style casino complex designed by McKim, Mead, and White in 1880 — it also houses the International Tennis Hall of Fame. La Forge's front rooms and porch offer a fairly standard light menu; inside is an authentic aristocratic experience. A graceful semicircular porch overlooks pristine grass tennis courts. The bar alone, a classic example of warm, gleaming wood and 1890s panache, will summon up the Gilded Age. The food is straightforward and dependable: seafood, steaks, veal, and chicken (the surf-and-turf, in a variety of combinations, is a good choice). Go simply to go back in time.

LA PETITE AUBERGE
849-6669.
19 Charles St., Newport.
Open: Daily.
Price: Very Expensive.
Cuisine: French.
Serving: D.
Credit Cards: AE, MC, V.
Reservations: Necessary.
Smoking: No (not strictly
    enforced if no one
    objects).

A visual and gastronomic delight, and one of Newport's best. Several small dining rooms with Provençal appointments (lace tablecloths and curtains) nestle in this 1714 colonial home; in winter fires roar and meats sizzle over open hearths. The menu is classic French with some local and other continental influences. Memorable appetizers include escargot, lobster bisque, and mousse de foie gras. As for entrées, the broiled lobster tails with truffles in a lobster bisque-like sauce were heavenly; other possibilities range from Beef Wellington to frogs legs to duckling in raspberry sauce. The desserts are equally tantalizing. An extensive wine list includes some interesting after-dinner sipping rums. On the night we went service was a little erratic, but dinner was worth the wait. Casual courtyard dining in season offers light grilled fare.

LE BISTRO
849-7778.
Bowen's Wharf, Newport.
Open: Daily.
Price: Very Expensive.
Cuisine: French.
Serving: L, D.
Credit Cards: AE, MC, V.
Reservations: Recom-
    mended.
Smoking: Section.
Handicap Access: No.

Le Bistro specializes in French "low cuisine" — good, hearty bistro fare, here with a few flights of fancy: bouillabaisse, steak au poivre with *real* "frites," sea scallops meunière, seven-hour lamb, and cassoulet. The salads are little masterpieces (try the warm spinach with breaded, deep-fried chevre and sharp vinaigrette). Desserts are created in-house. The place is lovely; the upstairs bar is a particularly nice spot.

**MAMMA LUISA ITAL-
    IAN RESTAURANT**
848-5257.
673 Thames St., Newport.
Closed: Mon.
Price: Mostly Moderate.
Cuisine: Italian.
Serving: D.
Credit Cards: None.
Reservations: Yes.
Smoking: Section.
Handicap Access: No.

Tip: walk to Mamma Luisa's. It's all the way down at the end of lower Thames, where old Newport lives on unhampered by T-shirt shops and traffic jams. The exercise will help later when you want to eat everything on the short, handwritten menu. Marco Trazzi, the host, has learned well from his mamma (a chef in Bologna), offering superior food in a delightful setting: two intimate dining rooms on either side of a center-hall colonial. The homemade spinach gnocchi, a family specialty, is superbly cooked and delicately flavored; also memorable is the pork tenderloin, smothered in fresh mushrooms with an intense green peppercorn sauce (worth the wait). The appetizer sampler plate for $8.95 is recommended, but leave room for the ricotta pie with raisins — dense, but authentic. BYOB.

MEXICAN CAFÉ
849-4203.
150 Broadway.
Open: Daily.
Price: Mostly Inexpensive.
Cuisine: Mexican/Cajun.
Serving: L, D.
Credit Cards:
Reservations: No.
Smoking: Section.
Handicap Access: No.

One of the best deals in town, this eatery is far from the thick of things over on Broadway, north of Washington Square. Plain on the outside, it's not a place to head for atmosphere. But the Mexican food, served with black beans and rice, is the best in town. They even make their own tortillas daily. It's hard enough to decide between quesadillas, enchiladas, burritos, tacos, and fajitas, without options like blackened catfish, swordfish with jambalaya, and chicken Creole. A salsa-loving gringo's dream. Take-out; BYOB.

THE MOORING
846-2260.
Sayer's Wharf, off America's Cup Ave, Newport.
Open: Year-round.
Price: Moderate to Expensive.
Cuisine: Seafood.
Serving: L, D.
Credit Cards: AE, MC, V.
Reservations: No.
Smoking: Section.
Handicap Access: No.

Dine right on the harbor here, where a sea of yachts supplies the dining room decor (in winter sit inside by an open hearth). Fresh local seafood dominates the menu, from lobsters to Atlantic salmon fillet and shellfish stew. Sandwiches, soup, salads, and quiche, plus meat and poultry dishes, are served at lunch and dinner. The appetizer menu is unusually extensive and interesting, including Portuguese-style mussels (served with chouriço) and smoked lemon pepper mackerel. The food is almost as good as the view.

Craig Hammell

Baseball fans flock to Mudville's for burgers, and to games at Cardines Field next door.

MUDVILLE PUB
849-1408.
8 W. Marlborough St., Newport.
Open: Daily.
Price: Moderate.

Owned by former Boston Celtic Kevin Stacom, Mudville is a sports pub extraordinaire. It's decorated in dark wood and sports memorabilia, and prides itself on having more TV sets per square foot than any other bar in Newport — 11 alto-

Cuisine: American.
Serving: L, D.
Credit Cards: AE, MC, V.
Reservations: No.
Smoking: Yes.
Handicap Access: Yes.

MURIEL'S
849-7780.
58 Spring St., Newport.
Open: Daily.
Price: Moderate.
Cuisine: Eclectic.
Serving: B, L, D, SB.
Credit Cards: D, MC, V.
Reservations: Accepted.
Smoking: Section.
Handicap Access: One step.

MUSIC HALL CAFÉ
848-2330.
250 Thames St., Newport.
Open: Daily.
Price: Moderate.
Cuisine: Southwestern.
Serving: L, D.
Credit Cards: AE, D, MC,
   V.
Reservations: Accepted.
Smoking: Section.
Handicap Access: No.

**NEWPORT BEACH CLUB
   RESTAURANT**
846-0911.
30 Wave Ave., Newport.
Open: Daily.
Price: Moderate to Expen-
   sive.
Cuisine: Contemporary
   American.
Serving: L, D, SB.

gether, with both satellite and cable hook-ups. Daily specials include pasta, chicken, and seafood, plus big, generous sandwiches, salads, soup, and appetizers. The general consensus is that "Babe's Burgers" are the way to go — there's even one stuffed with feta. Best of all, in season you can sit outside on the patio and watch live ballgames at Cardines Field next door.

Outside and inside, Muriel's looks like an attractive, hip French bistro. Tablecloths are overlaid with embroidery and glitter (all under glass). The menu ranges farther afield: entrées include pan-seared scallops in a curry glaze over rice, homemade pastas, steaks, and creative salads and sandwiches. The range is perhaps too great: some meals are hits, some only good — they should have been better in such delightful surroundings. Stick with the French offerings; for dessert, the crème brûlée is superb. The seafood chowder is an award-winner. BYOB.

There is only so much chowder a person can eat. So for a change, try the Music Hall Café and its somewhat eclectic but mostly Southwestern fare. The building really was a music hall once, but now it's nicely outfitted in pale desert shades and a trompe l'oeil painting of an adobe village. The menu offers hip dishes like marinated grilled pork chops with black beans, fried bananas, and polenta, and chicken breaded in blue corn flour. Everything is imaginatively concocted and nicely cooked, though there could be a bit more oomph in the seasoning. (They have chowder too.)

On the ground floor of the Inn at Newport Beach, the Beach Club Restaurant looks across Wave Avenue to Easton, or First Beach, though the view from the glassed-in porch actually highlights the road more than the sea. The food, like the decor, is contemporary, ranging from teriyaki-style dishes and quesadillas to stand-bys that include shrimp-stuffed scrod and broiled salmon. A meal of shrimp and scallops over chow mein noodles

Credit Cards: AE, CB, D, DC, MC, V.
Reservations: Accepted.
Smoking: Section.
Handicap Access: Yes.

was good but uninspired. Lunch and brunch fare are recommended.

PEABERRY'S BOMBAY CAFÉ
847-7880.
212 Thames St., Newport.
Open: Daily, year-round.
Price: Moderate.
Cuisine: Indian.
Serving: B, L, D.
Credit Cards: AE, D, MC, V.
Reservations: Accepted.
Smoking: Section upstairs.
Handicap Access: One step.

The only Indian restaurant on Aquidneck Island, this café is a joint venture between Peaberry's Gourmet Coffee Shops and Kebab-N-Kurry in Providence: an inspired marriage. From standards like chicken tandoori, to the chef's special, begum thaali (a "royal platter" of vegetarian treats), everything is perfectly cooked, flavorful, and aromatic. Even the plain white rice comes with plump sultanas, or try the lemon rice as a side dish. Order ahead for take-out or eat in the pale peach dining room. The (seasonal) buffet lunch is a deal. The wine list marked with selections recommended for hot or mild dishes is a great idea.

PEZZULLI'S
846-5830.
136 Thames St., Newport.
Closed: Mon.
Price: Expensive.
Cuisine: Italian.
Serving: D.
Credit Cards: AE.
Reservations: No.
Smoking: Yes.
Handicap Access: No.

In a choice, second-floor spot overlooking the old Brick Market Place, Pezzulli's specializes in pasta of all shapes and varieties, served under an array of inventive sauces. How about aragosta fra diavolo — sautéed lobster in a tangy marinara over squid-ink pasta, or rotelle with sausage in a creamy tomato sauce? The pasta is served al dente, and comes with a quiet garden salad and baguette of warm bread. End with espresso, or a scoop of gelato in a candied shell, laced with caramel and whipped cream. BYOB.

THE PLACE AT YESTER-DAY'S
847-0116.
28 Washington Square, Newport.
Closed: Mon.
Price: Expensive to Very Expensive.
Cuisine: Contemporary.
Serving: D.
Credit Cards: AE, MC, V.
Reservations: No.
Smoking: No.
Handicap Access: Yes.

Newporters rave about The Place, which puts a unique spin on everything, then cooks it perfectly, with an inspired use of seasonings. The Art Nouveau decor is enchanting, the service friendly and helpful, the dress casual, and the wine sampler (a tray of five small glasses) is an innovative introduction to the excellent wine list. The menu includes Moroccan steak salad and scallops with red cous cous (appetizers); salmon in an herbed crust with chard and tomato compote and pesto potatoes; and soft-shell crabs in an exquisite puddle of garlic mayonnaise — all superbly presented.

A typically luscious dessert choice is key lime soufflé with fresh fruit. (Yesterday's is the lighter fare eatery to the left of the front door, the wine bar is on the right.)

PRONTO
847-5251.
464 Thames St., Newport.
Open: Daily.
Price: Moderate to Expensive.
Cuisine: Italian.
Serving: B Sat., Sun.; L, D.
Credit Cards: AE, MC, V.
Reservations: Recommended.
Smoking: Yes.
Handicap Access: Yes.

In summer the door stays open and bustling Thames Street is right outside, but the interior — chic in a elegantly funky way — can transport you to the European location of your choice. There's only one room (the all-smoking policy is questionable), so reserve ahead. Creative pasta dishes, tossed with a cornucopia of nouvelle ingredients, dominate the regular menu, which is supplemented by a generous choice of specials. A recent appetizer special was a salad of grilled quail stuffed with lobster and scallop mousse.

PUERINI'S
847-5506.
24 Memorial Blvd. West, Newport.
Closed: Mon.
Price: Moderate.
Cuisine: Italian.
Serving: D.
Credit Cards: None.
Reservations; No.
Smoking: No.
Handicap Access: Yes.

Simplicity, charm, and reasonable prices add up to an unpretentious winner. Three small dining rooms are cozy and casual, with '50s-style vases on the tables and original photos on the walls. The menu is divided into chicken, beef, and vegetable selections, each offered in a variety of preparations over or stuffed into homemade pastas, with a choice of sauces. The special of scallops in garlic and olive oil over squid ink and lobster fettuccine — heralded by a delicious starter of garlic bread with roasted peppers and mozzarella — was cooked perfectly and packed with interesting flavors. Each dish is served on a different plate of old china — a nice touch. The wine list is small (chianti or chardonnay) but of good quality; the gelato selections temptingly exotic.

THE RHUMB LINE
849-6950.
62 Bridge St., Newport.
Open: Daily.
Price: Expensive.
Cuisine: Seafood/Creative American.
Serving: L, D, SB.
Credit Cards: MC, V.
Reservations: Recommended.
Smoking: Section.
Handicap Access: One step.

Tucked away in a colonial home in the Point Section of town, the Rhumb Line has a snug, romantic atmosphere, a creative menu, a first-rate wine list, and a special dessert — chocolate bread pudding with vanilla ice cream. Fish is a specialty here: the smoked bluefish pâté appetizer is always a standout; entrée specials like sole vert (with a rémoulade of spinach and peppers) kept up the excellent theme. The sirloin steak was a bit disappointing, but dessert made up for that. The wine list is extensive and fairly priced. A lighter fare menu is also available.

SALAS'
846-8772.
345 Thames St., Newport.
Open: Daily.
Price: Inexpensive to Moderate.
Cuisine: Seafood/Italian.
Serving: D.
Credit Cards: AE, D, DC, MC, V.
Reservations: No; sometimes a wait.
Smoking: Section.
Handicap Access: No.

Salas' is a Newport fixture. It may be crowded and noisy and right in the heart of Thames, yet everyone is happy and eating like crazy. Specialties include two market-priced versions of the individual clambake, and pasta or Oriental spaghetti by the pound (at $4.50, a quarter-pound with shrimp is too much for one person). And there are plenty of seafood and Italian dishes to choose from, and sandwiches. The wine list is pedestrian (chianti is the best bet), but good draft beer is a bargain. Salas' is popular with Newport regulars and the sailing crowd (chic because it's unchic), as well as visitors who recognize a great deal.

SARDELLA'S
849-6312.
30 Memorial Blvd. West, Newport.
Open: Daily.
Price: Moderate.
Cuisine: Italian.
Serving: D.
Credit Cards: AE, D, MC, V.
Reservations: Suggested.
Smoking: Section.
Handicap Access: Yes.

Sardella's dishes are inspired by both northern and southern Italian traditions, and seasoned with the freshest ingredients. The petti di pollo Romano (chicken stuffed with mozzarella, garlic, fresh parsley, and wine) was excellent; the ravioli alla Parma and prosciutto, flavored with basil in a cream sauce, superb. So was the vichyssoise starter. The wine list isn't extensive but it's good, with a fine Sardella's label chardonnay. The dark, warm tones of the dining room perfectly suit the heady Italian aromas and flavors. End with a great espresso and a truly mouth-watering napoleon. There's a wood-burning fireplace in winter and outdoor patio dining in summer. Piano music after 8pm.

SCALES AND SHELLS
846-3474.
527 Thames St., Newport.
Open: Daily.
Price: Expensive.
Cuisine: Seafood.
Serving: D.
Credit Cards: None.
Reservations: No.
Smoking: Section.
Handicap Access: Yes.

Billing itself as the only restaurant in Newport to serve seafood exclusively, the blackboard menu here notes what's fresh from the sea: tuna, bluefish, swordfish, scallops, red snapper — if it swims in local waters, it's been served here. House specialties include grilled clam pizza, calamari, and wood-grilled fish of all description. A southern Italian flavor is also detectable. The dining room is very informal and spills over into the open kitchen. Go early — it gets busy.

SWEETWATER GRILLE
846-1700.
14 Perry Mill Wharf, off Thames St., Newport.

A dual emphasis on both flavor and visual artistry results in a Caribbean sole both exotic and beautiful, a combination of the tropical tang of

Open: Daily.
Price: Mostly Moderate.
Cuisine: Seafood with Cajun/Jamaican influences.
Serving: L, D, SB.
Credit Cards: V, MC.
Reservations: Accepted.
Smoking: Section.
Handicap Access: Yes.

grilled banana and the earthy-tasting jerk spice (a Jamaican ingredient) — the strong flavors don't overwhelm, and are enhanced by almonds, green pepper, and onion. The blackened items are tender and explosively spicy. The grilled swordfish steak is served with a lovely ginger-mango sauce. Neither appetizers nor desserts matched the quality of the entrées — a minor glitch when the main courses are so good.

WHARF DELI & PUB
846-9233.
37 Bowen's Wharf, off America's Cup Ave., Newport.
Open: Daily.
Price: Inexpensive.
Cuisine: American.
Serving: L, D.
Credit Cards: AE, MC, V.
Smoking: Yes.
Handicap Access: No.

A very versatile spot: it's a bar where you can get a Black and Tan (Guinness and Bass combo) and listen to local artists entertain nightly (no cover); it's a restaurant with grilled fare, sandwiches, and salads (though the chowder is only so-so); it's a deli for cold-cuts, take-out, and platters or boxed lunches made up to go; it's a raw bar. The nachos are terrific.

Craig Hammell

Generation upon generation has carried on the tradition of fine food and drink at the White Horse Tavern in Newport.

WHITE HORSE TAVERN
849-3600.
Marlborough St., Newport.
Open: Year-round.
Price: Very Expensive.

The building that houses the White Horse Tavern was constructed in 1673; in 1730, tavern keeper Jonathan Nichols named it the White Horse. It's been serving food and drink ever since, but make no mistake: this is no tourist attraction get-

Cuisine: Continental/Cre-
  ative American.
Serving: L Mon., Wed., Sat.;
  D daily; SB.
Credit Cards: AE, CB, D,
  DC, MC, V.
Reservations: Recom-
  mended.
Smoking: Section.
Handicap Access: Yes.

WINDWARD GRILLE
849-2600.
Doubletree Newport
  Islander Hotel, Goat
  Island, Newport.
Open: Daily.
Price: Moderate to Expen-
  sive.
Cuisine: Seafood/Grill.
Serving: D, SB.
Credit Cards: AE, CB, D,
  DC, MC, V.
Reservations: Recom-
  mended.
Smoking: Section.
Handicap Access: Yes.

Portsmouth

15 POINT ROAD
683-3138.
15 Point Rd., Portsmouth.
Closed: Mon.
Price: Moderate.
Cuisine: American
  Bistro/Continental.
Serving: D.
Credit Cards: D, MC, V.
Reservations: No; some-
  times a wait.
Smoking: No (flexible).
Handicap Access: Yes.

ting by on its age and beamed ceilings. By all standards, the White Horse Tavern offers superb
gourmet food and gracious professional service. A
variety of seafood, meats, and poultry are on hand,
all expertly prepared and presented. For example,
the mingled flavors of the chicken stuffed with foie
gras over wild rice takes poultry dishes to a new
height; the wine and dessert selections are also
superb. The fine colonial atmosphere and exceptional food here offer a rare opportunity to hold the
ordinary at bay. Jackets required.

No nouvelle anything here; instead the menu
offers good grilled fare in very generous portions. The salmon has a reputation for freshness.
The Windward's specialty, however, is brunch,
voted best in the state by *Rhode Island Monthly*. The
buffet is more than plentiful; it's gargantuan. While
dinner seems to be frequented mainly by hotel
guests (mostly business travelers), Rhode Islanders
consistently make their way out to Goat Island for
the brunch.

The big picture windows command a fabulous
view of the Sakonnet River, with the little
Stonebridge Marina in the foreground. The restaurant is done in fresh, contemporary colors and light
woods. Seafood predominates among the signature
specials, which include cod Mediterranean,
sautéed with peppercorns, capers, black olives,
green onions, garlic, and white wine. A pasta and
chicken dish was good but not memorable. Char-
grilled specials and traditional New England
favorites are also on hand. If you have to wait for a
table at the bar, try the exquisite Deluxe Margarita.

**MELVILLE GRILLE &
LAGOON BAR**
683-2380.
East Passage Yachting Center, Portsmouth.
Closed: Jan.–Feb.
Price: Moderate.
Cuisine: American.
Serving: B Fri.–Sun., L, D, SB.
Credit Cards: D, MC, V.
Reservations: Accepted.
Smoking: Section.
Handicap Access: Yes, for patio.

Back in the '40s the Mosquito Fleet trained here — the Navy's elite team of World War II PT Boat crews. Before that the East Passage Yachting Center was a resort called Portsmouth Grove. Today only the naval heritage remains. It still looks like a base, except for the pleasure yachts. The Melville Grille is in a quonset hut and features WWII-era photos and '40s music. The eclectic menu offers burgers, seafood, sandwiches, grilled fare, and pastas, all a notch or two above average, as is their specialty, Bermuda fish chowder. Boxed lunches and party platters to go, too. Melville Grille is off Rte. 114 right on the Bay — watch for the Melville Boat Basin sign.

**REIDY'S FAMILY
RESTAURANT**
683-9807.
3351 E. Main Rd./Rte. 138, Portsmouth.
Open: Daily.
Price: Inexpensive.
Cuisine: American.
Serving: B, L, D.
Credit Cards: No.
Smoking: Yes.
Handicap Access: Yes.

This overgrown diner has old-fashioned counter stools and booths; the waitresses smoke. Reidy's claims to specialize in seafood, but everything here has a home-cooked, hearty flavor. They serve breakfast all day and offer a 21-shrimp basket (the critters are small, but tender and not greasy) for $5.95. The menu includes shepherd's pie and a chouriço grinder. Try the grapenut or Indian pudding — or both. Beer and wine, and take-out.

SEA FARE INN
683-0577.
3352 E. Main Rd./Rte. 138, Portsmouth.
Closed: Mon.
Price: Very Expensive.
Cuisine: Creative Continental/American/Greek.
Serving: D.
Credit Cards: AE, MC, V.
Reservations: Recommended.
Smoking: Section.
Handicap Access: Yes.

Master Chef George Karousos recently received the prestigious Ambassador Award from the International Institute for Dining Excellence. One visit and you'll want to give him a medal too. Karousos calls himself a "culinary archaeologist" and is fond of reinterpreting standard recipes, using only fresh seasonal ingredients and light sauces. A starter of baked mushrooms stuffed with lobster is heavenly; so is the entrée of poached salmon in lemon wine sauce with scallops and clams. Homemade Greek yogurt with raspberries is a perfect ending. Recommendations: the house dressing with feta for the salad, and the house potatoes, mashed with bacon, asparagus, and other wonderful tidbits. Choose between seven elegant, antique-filled dining rooms, all in a richly renovated Victorian mansion in a park-like setting. Despite the grandeur, the Karousos family is warm and friendly.

SAKONNET

Little Compton

**ABRAHAM MANCHES-
TER RESTAURANT &
TAVERN**
635-2700.
Adamsville Rd., Little
  Compton/Adamsville.
Open: Daily.
Price: Inexpensive to Mod-
  erate.
Cuisine: American/
  Seafood/Italian.
Serving: L, D.
Credit Cards: D, MC, V.
Reservations: Not neces-
  sary.
Smoking: Section.
Handicap Access: Yes.

This former 1820s general store is a gathering place for the community. Little League photos and work by local artists hang on the walls, wines from nearby Sakonnet Vineyards are on offer, and in addition to predictable American and Italian standards, specials like conch salad and fresh fish dishes reflect the Portuguese heritage of many locals. The combination of relatively sophisticated offerings and basic fare (in large or small portions), plus a relaxed atmosphere (kids are even given crayons) make this a great place for families. Mud pie is a house specialty.

THE BARN
635-2985.
Adamsville Rd., Little
  Compton/Adamsville.
Open: Daily to 11:30am.
Price: Inexpensive.
Cuisine: American.
Serving: B.
Credit Cards: None.
Smoking: Section.
Handicap Access: Yes.

Frequently voted "best breakfast in a country setting" in Rhode Island, this charming spot really was a barn, and has big old sliding doors to prove it. Have breakfast outside on a patio under a single, enormous umbrella, or inside — the converted loft is a wonderful space. Everything tastes good here, from the corned beef hash to omelettes and French toast.

COMMONS LUNCH
635-4388.
The Commons, Little
  Compton.
Open: Daily.
Price: Inexpensive.
Cuisine: New England.
Serving: B, L, D.
Credit Cards: None.
Reservations: No.
Handicap Access: Yes.

The Commons Lunch is possibly *the* quintessential Rhode Island restaurant — a little place with tables, booths, and counter service, just across from Little Compton's wonderful churchyard. The food is superb, the portions huge, and the cuisine is pure New England. Not only can you get East Bay jonnycakes made with cornmeal ground at Gray's Gristmill just down the road, but they also serve a tasty, generous helping of fish and chips, plus quahog chowder *and* quahog pie, a variety of grinders including chouriço, fried seafood, and kale soup (another Portuguese influence), as well as "American" meals such as liver and bacon and baked ham. Save room for Indian, grapenut, or bread puddings, or choose a slice of homemade pie for dessert. You know this is a great place when the waitress asks, "Do you need to see the menu?"

COUNTRY HARVEST
635-4579.
67 W. Main Rd./Rte. 77, Little Compton.
Closed: Tues.
Price: Expensive.
Cuisine: American.
Serving; D, SB.
Credit Cards: AE, CB, D, DC, MC, V.
Reservations: Suggested.
Smoking: Section.
Handicap Access: Yes.

The Country Harvest is a blessing in Little Compton, where eateries are few and far between. It occupies a choice spot looking west over a meadow and the Sakonnet River — sunsets can be breathtaking. The menu isn't adventurous, but every meal is cooked absolutely to order. The chef is wonderfully accommodating and will gracefully make substitutions upon request. Poultry, beef, veal, seafood, and pastas are all here, along with truly fresh vegetables; the fresh fruit sherbet is good, too. The dining room is rustic and attractive. A nice touch is the inclusion of many local selections on the wine list. Pub room and patio bar, too.

THE STONE HOUSE CLUB
635-2222
122 Sakonnet Point Rd., Little Compton.
Closed: Mon. in season; open Fri.–Sun. only, Sept.–mid-June.
Price: Moderate to Expensive; Tap Room, Inexpensive.
Cuisine: American/International.
Serving: D.
Credit Cards: MC, V.
Reservations: Yes.
Smoking: No.
Handicap Access: No.

The Stone House Club (see *Lodging*) is an atmospheric old place near the end of Sakonnet Point. The Tap Room is a British-style pub with low, beamed ceilings and a ponderous hearth (it would be a great spot to wait out a winter storm). Lighter fare is served here; the more formal restaurant is upstairs. Entrées range from chicken and duck to veal, fish, and beef, with seafood and vegetarian pastas on hand as well. Culinary influences are all over the map, self-described as "American, nouvelle, classic French, natural, and Oriental." Locals seem to regard this place as a mystery — sometimes good, sometimes fair. Add $5 to every meal consumed by a non-member.

Tiverton

BARCELLOS FAMILY RESTAURANT
624-6649.

Satisfy a whole range of tastes here, from the timid to the adventurous. Fresh, local seafood comes any way you want it, but check the menu's

1214 Stafford Rd./Rte. 81, Tiverton.
Open: Daily.
Price: Inexpensive to Moderate.
Cuisine: Portuguese/ American/Spanish.
Serving: L, D.
Credit Cards: D, DC, MC, V.
Reservations: Yes.
Smoking: Section.
Handicap Access: Yes.

back page — all the listings are in Portuguese. Authentic Portuguese cooking is at the heart of the Barcellos kitchen, and the shrimp Mozambique is a standout. The prices are right, and so are the desserts: Kentucky derby pie may be the most popular, but flan and grapenut custard are the chef's favorites.

EVELYN'S DRIVE-IN
624-3100.
2335 Main Rd./Rte. 77, Tiverton.
Closed: Tues.
Price: Inexpensive.
Cuisine: Seafood/American.
Serving: B, L, D (close by 8pm).
Credit Cards: None.
Reservations: No.
Smoking: Yes.
Handicap Access: Outdoor tables.

Evelyn's is a 1950s-style roadside dream. The outdoor picnic tables overlook lovely Nannaquaket Pond; the indoor "dining room" looks like it belongs in a seaside beach cottage. Order at the take-out window while crunching crushed white shells underfoot. In addition to the usual array of local fresh seafood, you can also get sandwiches and full dinners that range from chow mein to grilled lemon pepper chicken, meatloaf, ham, and a veal cutlet. The huge stuffie is great, seasoned with an Italian flair. Orders of clam cakes and fried shrimp are generous and tasty.

MOULIN ROUGE
624-4320.
1403 Main Rd./Rte. 138, Tiverton.
Closed: Tues.
Price: Moderate.
Cuisine: French.
Serving: D.
Credit Cards: AE, CB, DC, MC, V.
Reservations: Accepted.
Smoking: Section.
Handicap Access: Not bad.

There's a mini Eiffel Tower out front with Christmas lights (the moulin is around to the side), and a menu with listings like escargot, chicken cordon bleu, and crêpes suzettes — traditional French food à l'Amerique. This *isn't* an upscale French bistro, but the crab entrée was equal to the best, and the sole bonne femme was delicious in a white wine cream sauce with mushrooms and shrimp. The wine list includes a selection of cognacs and liqueur-laced coffees. Cozy dining room paneled in knotty pine.

BLOCK ISLAND

Those who have been around the Block a few times (island humor) offer the following recommendations: if at all possible, BYOB and any edibles you can carry (if your pack animal is a car, fill up the tank on the mainland — prices are half-again as high on the island). Groceries are high-priced and limited here, as is alcohol. Most inns have refrigerators at guests' disposal and some have kitchens — take advantage of them. If you plan to cook fish, buy in Galilee before you leave the mainland. It's very fresh there (home of the fishing fleet) and the prices are *far* lower than those on Block. If that's not practical, buy your lobsters at the crack of dawn on New Harbor docks from returning lobstermen.

Or, take some newspapers and matches out to the beach at sunset, dig a hole, line it with rocks, put in some driftwood, and have a cook-out — it's cheap, legal (though camping out is not), and fun. Load up a plastic bag with rocks for ballast and chill your wine or beer in the sea.

Otherwise, following are some eateries with good island dining and atmosphere.

The Neck

THE BEACHEAD
466-2249.
Corn Neck Rd., Block
   Island.
Open: Daily, year-round.
Price: Inexpensive.
Cuisine: Burgers.
Serving: L, D.
Credit Cards: None.
Smoking: Yes.
Handicap Access: Yes.

Block Islanders are in love with this place. The year-round lot gathers here to shoot pool, sit at the bar, and talk about the weather, and down possibly the best burgers on the island. Beachy, right across from the Atlantic Ocean, it offers very good fish and deli sandwiches, chili, and a big chef salad. Clam chowder is served "Block Island style" — a clear broth with onions, potatoes, and local clams. Only available in season — the mark of a wise cook.

CORNE NECK COUN-
   TRY KITCHEN
466-5059.
Corn Neck Rd., Block
   Island.
Open: Daily, year-round.
Price: Inexpensive.
Cuisine: American.
Serving: B to 2pm.
Credit Cards: None.
Smoking: Yes.
Handicap Access: Yes.

This is the island's upscale choice for breakfast. Fresh-ground coffees, homemade pastries (scones are a specialty), eggs Benedict, and made-to-order omelettes are featured. The latter include the Aztec (chili peppers, hot sausage, cheese), the Dublin (hash and cheese), and the Provence (black olives, mushrooms, red onions, cheese). Breakfast fare is served through lunch time.

WINFIELD'S
466-5856.
Corn Neck Rd., Block
   Island.

Low, beamed ceilings, white tablecloths, and candlelight create a refined setting here, but dress is casual. The menu is fairly creative with a

Closed: Tues.
Price: Expensive.
Cuisine: Creative American.
Serving: D.
Credit Cards: AE, MC, V.
Reservations: Accepted for 6 or more.
Smoking: No.
Handicap Access: One step.

good choice of pastas, including four-cheese penne (a favorite), pasta primavera, and fettuccine carbonara. A recent special was a pork and shrimp curry with banana, pineapple, and coconut. A chocolate cheesecake was a choice dessert. Though this is one of Block's few upscale eateries, it does have its bad nights.

Dead Eye Dick's at Payne's Dock in New Harbor — the food is as good as the sign.

Craig Hammell

New Harbor

DEAD EYE DICK'S
466-2654.
Payne's Dock, Block Island.
Open: Daily.
Price: Moderate to Expensive.
Cuisine: Seafood.
Serving: L, D.
Credit Cards: AE, MC. V.
Reservations: No.
Smoking: Section.
Handicap Access: One step.

Many islanders will tell you that Dead Eye Dick's is the best restaurant on Block. There's much to support this view: an outdoor deck overlooking Payne's Marina, polished wooden floors, bright scarves spread diagonally under glass-top tables — and grilled swordfish in sun-dried tomato vinaigrette. In addition to interesting seafood entrées, stand-outs include grilled chicken with black bean Creole sauce, New York sirloin with gorgonzola butter, and grilled pork chops in Vermont maple syrup and Dijon mustard sauce. The Maine raspberry cake alone is reason enough to go, as is the hot fresh bread served with garlic oil.

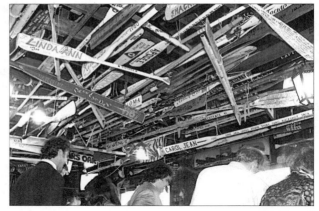

The Oar on Block Island lives up to its name.

Craig Hammell

THE OAR
466-7753.
Job's Hill, on West Side Rd.,
   Block Island.
Open: Daily.
Price: Inexpensive.
Cuisine: American.
Serving: B, L.
Credit Cards: None.
Smoking: Yes.
Handicap Access: No.

Though The Oar has a reputation for great breakfasts and sandwiches, the slogan here is "best stocked bar on the East Coast." Add "best view" as well. Behind the bar are picture windows overlooking New Harbor; combined with the varnished wooden bar top and glinting bottles of colored liqueurs, it's a lovely sight. Wash down the Key West conch fritters with some Murphy's Irish Stout on draft. Breakfast ends at 11:30 and lunch at 5pm — after that it's bar snacks only. Sit at picnic tables outside, or stay in and try to count the number of oars hanging from the ceiling.

Old Harbor Area

**ALDO'S RESTAURANT
   & PIZZERIA**
466-5871.
Weldon's Way, Block
   Island.
Open: Daily.
Price: Inexpensive to Moderate.
Cuisine: Italian.
Serving: L, D.
Credit Cards: MC, V.
Reservations: No.
Smoking: "Sometimes."
Handicap Access: Yes.

Aldo's is the granddaddy of island pizza joints. Eat inside or out on the patio. Try the chicken pasta andiamo (with broccoli and feta cheese) — it's plentiful and remarkably fresh and flavorful. The baked ziti also scores, and the spinach pie and pizza are always good. Don't overlook the homemade ice cream and baked goods at Aldo's Bakery next door.

ATLANTIC INN
466-5883.
High St., Block Island.
Open: Daily.
Price: Expensive.
Cuisine: Creative American.
Serving: D.
Credit Cards: AE, MC, V.
Reservations: Recommended.
Smoking: Section.
Handicap Access: No.

You'll be tempted to forgo dinner and just stay out on the wonderful porch, sipping pint sleeves of Bass Ale and sending cold, fresh oysters gliding down your throat as the lights come on in Old Harbor below. But don't, because the dining room inside features highly praised clam chowder, and crispy salmon served over spinach and topped with roasted yellow pepper sauce — the house special. The emphasis here is on local ingredients and native seafood. Word around the island is that the dining room can be erratic, but it's still regarded as one of the best. Entertainment on weekends.

ELI'S
466-5230.
Chapel St., Block Island.
Open: Daily.
Price: Moderate.
Cuisine: Pasta.
Serving: D.
Credit Cards: None.
Reservations: No.
Smoking: Yes.
Handicap Access: No.

Eli's has much to recommend it — and a few things to watch out for: it's tiny and popular, so the wait is long. Also, go with cash (a "local" check means Block Island only). As for the food: it's excellent, perhaps not what you'd expect from a tiny, storefront spot in the middle of the ocean. The pastas are creative, enormous, and wonderfully flavorful, such as the pasta puttanesca, which means "whore's pasta." It doesn't appear on many menus, and this version was a treat. The individual white pizza with clams (split as an appetizer) was also excellent. No desserts, but beer and wines by the glass. Take-out.

ERNIE'S OLD HARBOR RESTAURANT
466-2473.
Water Street, Block Island.
Open: Daily.
Price: Inexpensive.
Cuisine: American.
Serving: B.
Credit Cards: No.
Smoking: Yes.
Handicap Access: No.

Not too many tourists discover Ernie's, since most lodging includes breakfast these days. But the locals love this place, just a hop, skip, and jump from the Old Harbor ferry landing. A back deck overlooks the dock. The menu is extensive, from pancakes to eggs to oatmeal, and everything tastes good. Skip your B&B breakfast once to come here and meet the people who keep Block Island alive in winter — it's the place for island gossip.

FINN'S SEAFOOD RESTAURANT
466-2473.
Water St./PO Box 250, Block Island.
Open: Daily.

Finn's, a venerable seafood-in-the-rough spot, has outdoor café tables (though they overlook the parking lot). Most of the seafood comes from Finn's own fish market next door (see Food Purveyors). There's a raw bar, lobster baked or stuffed

Price: Moderate.
Cuisine: Seafood.
Serving: L, D.
Credit Cards: AE, MC, V.
Reservations: No.
Smoking: Section.
Handicap Access: Yes.

THE HARBORSIDE
466-5504.
Water St., Block Island.
Open: Daily, Memorial
Day–late Sept.
Price: Moderate to Expen-
sive.
Cuisine: American.
Serving: B, L, D.
Credit Cards: MC, V.
Reservations: Suggested.
Smoking: Section.
Handicap Access: No.

THE MANISSES
466-2421; 466-2063.
Spring St./PO Box 1, Block
Island.
Open: Daily; weekends
only in winter.
Price: Expensive to Very
Expensive.
Cuisine: Creative Ameri-
can.
Serving: D.
Credit Cards: AE, MC, V.
Reservations: Recom-
mended.
Smoking: Section.
Handicap Access: No.

MOHEGAN CAFÉ
466-2605; 800-825-6254.

in varying weights, fried everything, and seafood dinners including Alaskan king crab legs. Best bet: the fisherman's platter, either broiled or fried, which comes with slaw and fries. Tip: avoid the steaks; this *is* a seafood place. Burgers and sand-wiches are available too, plus good pies and aver-age wines.

This may be the first place you see coming off the ferry at Old Harbor — the red-and-white striped café table umbrellas will catch your eye. The breakfast and lunch menus offer standard fare; the dinner choices are more elaborate and, though not necessarily inventive, are consistently good. The interior dining rooms have attractive nautical antiques and uneven floorboards (the restaurant is within the 1887 hotel of the same name), but sit outside if you can — it's a great spot to watch the world go by. End with one of the most generous hot fudge sundaes around. Note: only salad bar on the island.

The dining room at the Hotel Manisses is proba-bly the most elegant on Block, but the unoffi-cial island-wide policy of casual attire holds here too. Some residents claim that the Manisses is "over-hyped" — that may be true, but the food is still very good, if pricey. Choose between eating inside in the high Victorian atmosphere, or outside on the back deck, where you can keep an eye on the llamas who roam around the hotel's animal farm. Order à la carte or prix fixe. The former includes a raw bar plus selections like baked herb polenta and smoked fish plate. Entrées feature the tried and true with a nouvelle flair: grilled tuna with red pepper coulis, filet mignon with shiitake mushroom glace, and lamb chops with prosciutto-wrapped stuffed shrimp. The Library Room and Top Shelf Bar offer a change of scene for desserts, liqueurs, flaming coffees, and more.

You can watch the ferries come and go from big picture windows and get a really top-notch

Water St., Block Island.
Open: Daily.
Price: Inexpensive to
 Expensive.
Cuisine: American.
Serving: L, D.
Credit Cards: AE, MC, V.
Reservations: No.
Smoking: Section.
Handicap Access: One step.

burrito here. But beware: locals warn that this spot has a reputation for "soaking the tourists on the fish," as one islander put it. And sure enough, the handful of dinner specials such as grilled swordfish, stuffed shrimp, surf and turf, and the like all hover near $20 (you can do better elsewhere). If you're interested in lighter fare, however, order from the regular menu. The excellent burgers, Mexican selections, and sandwiches satisfy without breaking the bank. Or just go for dessert, with choices like chocolate tortillas, Indian pudding, and Chaos Snickers Pie.

THE 1661 INN
466-2063; 466-2421.
Spring St., Block Island.
Open: Daily.
Price: Inexpensive to Moderate.
Cuisine: American/International.
Serving: B, L.
Credit Cards: AE, MC, V.
Reservations: No.
Smoking: Section.
Handicap Access: Yes.

The dining room and deck at the 1661 Inn overlook the Atlantic Ocean, a great view that nonguests are welcome to enjoy during breakfast, lunch, or for drinks in the afternoon (see *Lodging*). The breakfast buffet ranges from waffles and French toast to eggs, roasted potatoes, hash, and even fish dishes. At lunch time the lobster roll is a couple bucks more than at the take-outs in Old Harbor, but the relaxing atmosphere, the view, and the bar are worth it. Also on hand is an Oriental seafood salad, caesar salad (with anchovies), a burger, kosher dog, vegetarian pita pocket with hummus and veggies, Mediterranean-style pizza (with eggplant, roasted red peppers, feta and cheddar, black olives, and capers), and more. There is even bread pudding for dessert.

WATER STREET CAFÉ
466-5540.
Water St., Block Island.
Open: Late June–Labor
 Day.
Price: Inexpensive.
Cuisine: Seafood/American.
Serving: L daily; D Fri., Sat.
Credit Cards: None.
Smoking: Yes.
Handicap Access: One
 step.

Within and beside Block Island's original pharmacy, a much-photo'd and gingerbreaded building built in 1882, Water Street Café is "alfresco only." Pick up your meal from the takeout window and eat it under umbrellas at café tables in the adjoining yard, and enjoy an unhampered view of Old Harbor. The seafood salad roll — Block Island lobster and snow crab with fresh dill — is a very tasty bargain at $6.95. You can also get chili, hot dogs, and burgers, clubs, nachos, tuna melts, and the usual cornucopia of fried seafood. The chowder took first place in Block's 1991 Chowder Cook-Off.

Providence Restaurants

Only a 45-minute drive from Newport, Providence offers an abundance and variety of great eateries. Here's a selection of 10 *personal* favorites:

Al Forno (273-9760; 577 S. Main St.) One of the spots that put Providence on the culinary map — the owners recently received the prestigious James Beard Regional Chef Award for the Northeast. Wood-grilled pizzas, fabulous Italian fare.

Angels (273-0310; 125 N. Main St.) *Esquire* called it one of the country's 10 Hottest New Restaurants in 1989, and it hasn't cooled off since. A tiny storefront spot with fin-de-siècle atmosphere, the house specialty is a huge Delmonico steak, and every continental dish is inspired.

Big Alice's (273-5812; 100 Hope St.) This ice cream spot is very good and very popular, especially with the Brown University crowd. Flavors from the exotic (sesame) to the down-home (oreo cookie).

Blue Point Oyster Bar (272-6145; 99 N. Main St.) Hands down the best seafood in town, served in an elegant-but-funky setting near the Rhode Island School of Design. The stellar wine list has won all kinds of awards. Feels like a hip bistro in Paris.

Down City Diner (331-9217; Eddy & Weybosset Sts.) "Diner" comes from the great Deco surroundings, not the avant garde food. A prix fixe of only $12 gets you a meal of cold tomato and orange soup, salad, and squid in cilantro and tomato baste over polenta.

Estrella's (434-5130; 736 N. Broadway, E. Providence) A favorite of a host of Portuguese restaurants in East Providence, Estrella's does great bacalhau (codfish) dishes and more, for low prices.

Federal Hill is Providence's Little Italy. The center line of the main artery, Atwells Ave., is painted red, white, and green. Classic Italian cooking gets its due on every street corner: try **Camille's Roman Garden** for a special event or **Trattoria D'Antuono** for a homey meal.

New Rivers (751-0350; 7 Steeple St.) Great American bistro food in a warm, intimate setting, between RISD and the new Providence riverfront. Try the spring roll starter, and praline ice cream to finish.

Pot au Feu (273-8953; 44 Custom House St.) Classic French food upstairs, bistro food in the brick-walled basement. A rare five-star rating from *Rhode Island Monthly*.

Rue de l'Espoir (751-8890; 99 Hope St.) "The Rue" has a low-key, romantic atmosphere and consistently good food — more cosmopolitan than French. Great bread and wines by the glass.

FOOD & BEVERAGE PURVEYORS

The food and beverage purveyors listed here are, for the most part, one-of-a-kind establishments, and offer a variety of alternatives to restaurant dining. For picnic or party provisions, back-packable eats, or just a coffee or ice cream stop, see below.

Some local chains are also well worth a visit ("local" here means only or mostly in Rhode Island, and "chain" any place with over three locations). A sampling:

Newport Creamery: 23 locations in RI. A cross between Friendly's and an old-fashioned ice cream parlor (with old-fashioned prices), it offers great ice cream plus burgers and sandwiches. **Bess Eaton Donuts**: 28 locations in RI. Local doughnut chain with a great name. **Ocean Coffee Roasters**: 5 locations in RI. This new gourmet coffee/bakery chain is turning up everywhere. The

---

Del's Lemonade v. Coffee Milk

It comes as no surprise that a state with a jonnycake law would want to put something on the books about Rhode Island's favorite beverage. It sounds benign, but a small war broke out in 1992 between Del's Lemonade diehards and the Coffee Milk crowd when the RI Legislature tried to name the state's official beverage. When the smoke cleared, Coffee Milk had won the day, though this is still a touchy issue. Decide for yourself.

Del's Lemonade: Since 1948; there's at least one real lemon peel in each cup of this sweet, slurpy stuff, guaranteed by the owner. Del's has spread recently beyond RI. There's a story of a potential but hesitant franchiser in California who got a Providence phone book and called people out of the blue to see what they thought of Del's. He opened his franchise right away. There are Del's shops, trucks, and street-carts all over the state.

Coffee Milk: Invented by the Autocrat Co. in 1895 and again by Eclipse Foods in 1914, coffee syrup is like sweet liquid gold. Both brands are still available, but are now manufactured by the same people (Autocrat). Mix your own syrup into a glass of cold milk, or buy ready-mixed cartons (coffee milk outsells chocolate milk 4-to-1 in RI convenience stores). The good news is that 1 oz. of coffee syrup has less caffeine than 8 oz. of a cola drink.

Del's Frozen Lemonade is a Rhode Island tradition.

Craig Hammell

quality is right up there with your local coffee house. A good bet for breakfast.
Strudels 'N Cream: 4 locations in RI. A fine bakery that also serves gourmet
coffee and ice cream — look for one in Newport, Jamestown, Bonnet Shores (in
Narragansett), and on the URI campus.

BAKERIES

West Bay

Allie's Donuts (295-8036; 3361 Quaker La./Rte. 2, N. Kingstown) It's a
Rhode Island tradition to get Allie's doughnuts on the way to the beach. The
chocolate frosted are to die for; lots of other treats. Open daily.

Real Muffins (783-8380; 1014 Boston Neck Rd./Rte. 1A, Narragansett) The
apple muffins have been voted best in the state.

Robert's Bread Factory (885-3920; 11 Union St., E. Greenwich) The smell of
fresh-baked bread will lure you in; try an eggplant calzone or one of the deli
sandwiches.

East Bay

Oliver Street Bakery (253-1660; 60-$^1/_2$ Oliver St., Bristol) It's worth a turn off
the main drag to this side-street spot. The pizzas, breads, and spinach pies
taste truly homemade. Go Sunday mornings for fresh malassadas (fried sweetbread dough). Closed Mon.

Sip & Dip Donuts (247-1060; 487 Metacom Ave./Rte. 136, Warren) Get a
dozen homemade doughnuts, a breakfast sandwich, or an inexpensive grinder
for lunch. Malassadas on Sun. morning.

Sunset Bakery (253-6607; 499 Hope St./Rte. 114, Bristol) Since 1929, a
superb traditional bakery, with fresh French, Portuguese, and Italian breads,
plus a host of sweet treats. The birthday cakes are artwork.

Coffee shops open early on Thames Street in Newport.

Craig Hammell

Aquidneck

Bagel Bite (848-2245; 113 Memorial Blvd. West, Newport) A hip bagel bakery with a tiny patio. Great lizard-painted tables; the bagels are good too.

Corga's Bakery (849-0615; 687 W. Main Rd./Rte. 114, Middletown) 99¢ for a medium coffee and a doughnut or muffin. Also Portuguese sweetbread, plus malassadas on Fri., Sat.

The Wave (846-6060; 22 Washington Sq., Newport) Recently taken over by Ocean Coffee Roasters, Newporters still refer to it as The Wave — one of the most recommended places in town to get good biscotti and a cup of coffee. Sandwiches too.

Sakonnet

Olga's Cup and Saucer (635-8650; at Walker's Roadside Stand, 261 W. Main Rd./Rte. 77, Little Compton) Olga's is Little Compton in a nutshell: swanky stuff in a modest setting. Elegant offerings like iced cappuccino, fresh ginger lemonade, squash-and-onion pizza, and fabulous baked goods (including fresh-baked pies) explain why it's been featured in *Metropolitan Home.*

Block Island

Aldo's Bakery & Ice Cream (466-2198; Weldon's Way, Old Harbor) Next to the pizza place of the same name, the bakery offers fresh baked breads, pies, pastries, and homemade ice creams.

BARS

West Bay

The Irish Pub (294-9761; 8220 Post Rd./Rte. 1, N. Kingstown/Wickford) Looks like a dive, but *the* place to go for fish and chips (they use flounder, not white fish) and good beer. You'll appreciate this spot since Wickford village is dry.

Narragansett Café (423-2150; 25 Narragansett Ave., Jamestown) Voted "best dive bar in Rhode Island." Tavern fare available plus live entertainment on weekends.

Aquidneck

O'Brien's Pub (849-6623; 501 Thames St., Newport) A darn good Irish pub — from Memorial Day–Sept. drink alfresco out on the patio, return to pub atmosphere when it gets cold. Breakfast, sandwiches, full dinners.

Sakonnet

Li'l Bear Lounge & Restaurant (624-9164; 983 Main Rd./Rte. 138, Tiverton) Not quite a dive, not quite a family restaurant. Sit around the bar with the local fishermen (there's a great wagon-train lamp — the wagons move), or get tasty regional food like jonnycakes, chouriço, and the fried local catch at rock bottom prices.

Block Island

Mahogany Shoals (466-5572; Payne's Dock, New Harbor) This is such a wonderful — albeit tiny — spot that regulars wanted to keep it to themselves. No luck. It's in a tiny shack at the end of the pier: good drink, good music (a house favorite is a tune about Bertha's Mussels in Baltimore), great people. 11am–1am. You have to look to find it.

FARM STANDS & MARKETS

West Bay

Cranston Farm (295-1985; 7490 Post Rd./Rte. 1, N. Kingstown) Pick up fresh vegetables, condiments, and fruit pies.

East Bay

D. Alves Pure Honey (Long Rd., E. Warren) A tiny roadside stand selling fresh honey and homegrown vegetables. Drive down to Touisset Point for lots more fresh produce for sale, usually stacked on a cart at the end of someone's drive and sold on the honor system.

Aquidneck

Farmlands (847-1233; 474 Wapping Rd., Portsmouth) A beautiful, quiet spot to pick up peaches, and in the fall, apples and cider.

Sakonnet

Helger's Produce Market (625-5169; 2474 Main Rd./Rte. 77, Tiverton) Local produce and Portuguese baked goods, plus two take-out windows: one for ice cream, the other fried seafood and burgers. Helger's Turkey Farm is just down the road — order one fresh.

Walker's Roadside Stand (635-4719; 261 W. Main Rd./Rte. 77, Little Compton) Rhode Islanders call this the best in the state. Here you'll find the freshest of everything, including the sweetest corn and plums on earth.

Block Island

Block Island Farmer's Market (466-5364) Held Weds. morning in Negus Park, and Sat. out behind the Manisses, it's a cornucopia of island produce.

Littlefield Bee Farm (466-5364; PO Box 514, Corn Neck Rd.) Walk the Clayhead Trail, then on the way home pick up fresh Block Island honey, beeswax candles, and gift baskets.

FISH & MEAT MARKETS

Lobster boats haul in the catch at Sakonnet Harbor in Little Compton.

Craig Hammell

West Bay

Butcher Block Gourmet Deli (885-0530; 5647 Post Rd./Rte. 1, E. Greenwich) Self-described as "the only old-fashioned meat market" in town. It's really three shops in a row: gourmet & deli, butcher's, and pizza place. The pizza is great.

Handrigan Seafood (789-6201; Great Island Rd., Narragansett/Galilee) Near the Block Island ferry; sells everything you can name and some things you can't. Straight-off-the-(nearby)-dock fresh.

Main Street Fish Market (885-9295; 431 Main St., E. Greenwich) Features locally caught fresh seafood, plus prepared clam cakes, chowder, stuffies, snail and squid salad, and more. Steamed and live lobsters. Also does clambakes.

Seafood Marketplace (885-8100; 6995 Post Rd./Rte. 1, N. Kingstown) Have them ship your clambakes anywhere in the world, or just get fresh lobsters, clams, fish to go. There's also a take-out/eat-in menu with lots of fried seafood plus red, white, broth, or seafood chowder. Try the quahog chili.

Watson Farm (423-0005; 455 North Rd., Jamestown) A rare find: stop at this old island farm to select fresh cuts of lamb or Black Angus beef for your freezer. Also wool yarns for sale.

Zeek's Creek (423-1170; N. Main Rd., Jamestown.) A little shack in the marshes; get your bait and tackle here as well as fresh seafood.

East Bay

Andrade's Catch (253-4529; 186 Wood St., Bristol) Here the seafood comes both fresh and fried, straight from the owner's boat. They "dig and deliver" their own shellfish. Open Weds.–Sat.

Hall's Seafood (245-0225; 8 Turner St., Warren) When in Warren, this is where to pick up fish, lobster, scallops, crabs, etc. And try **Hall's Deli** (245-2066) right next door for salads, sandwiches, and picnics. Closed Mon.

Quito's Fish Market (253-9040; 411 Thames St., Bristol) The fish market is right on the Bay; there's also a wee restaurant built out over the water, with comfy booths and terrifically fresh fish. Red and white chowder, plus beer and wine. Daily till 6, Fri. till 8pm, May–Oct. On the East Bay bike path.

Aquidneck

Aquidneck Lobster Company (846-0106; Bowen's Wharf, off Thames St., Newport) You know it's fresh when they give it to you whole or fillet it in front of you.

Long Wharf Seafood (846-6320; 17 Connell Hwy., Newport) Recommended by some of Newport's best chefs for fresh fish and shellfish.

Portsmouth Meat Market (683-1484; 108 Chase Rd., corner of E. Main Rd./Rte. 138, Portsmouth) Choice cuts of meat plus fish and Portuguese sausage. Boxed specials to go.

Sakonnet

Manchester Seafoods (624-8000; 2139 Main Rd./Rte. 77, Tiverton) Look for the neon lobster: fresh and smoked fish plus live lobsters and shellfish, wholesale and retail. If they're out of something try **Bridgeport Sea Food Market** or **Lisbon Fish Market** next door.

Sakonnet Lobster Company (635-4371; Sakonnet Pt. Rd./Rte. 77, Little Compton) Pick up some dripping wet lobsters and seafood. (Locals' advice is to skip the markets and buy straight off returning boats early in the morning, down at Sakonnet Point.)

Block Island

Finn's Fish Market (466-2102; Water St., Old Harbor) Pricey by off-island standards, Finn's nonetheless has the freshest lobster, fish, and clams you'll find.

GOURMET, DELI, & GROCERY

West Bay

Chef-a-Roni Fancy Foods (884-8798; 2832 South County Trail/Rte. 2, E. Greenwich) This place is so great it has out-of-state regulars: a large gourmet market with deli counter, prepared foods, bakery, and its own brand of spices. Closed Tues.

The Coffee Bean and Deli (782-6226; 20 Woodruff Ave., Narragansett) The deli counter smells like the Lower East Side; fresh baked goods and over 30 kinds of coffee. Middle Eastern appetizers, too. Highly recommended.

Papa's Country Grocery (783-1230; 123A Boon St., Narragansett Pier) A fun country store with everything from Duke's Texas-size muffins to Mrs. Papa's coffee cake, penny candy, and hand-quilted pillows.

The Picnic Basket (782-2284; 20 Kingstown Rd., Narragansett Pier) A gourmet deli with sandwiches, soups, salads, plus fresh-baked breads and bagels. Also frozen yogurt, Ben & Jerry's ice cream. They do picnic baskets for the beach.

Ryan's Market (294-9571; 70 Brown St., N. Kingstown/Wickford) An old-fashioned market with groceries plus prepared foods to go — great macaroni and cheese at $1.99 per serving.

To Market! To Market! (885-4977; 96 Main St., E. Greenwich) A terrific deli/market/café (the tables have great inset tiles) with breakfast fare, salads, and sandwiches (try the Mexican turkey tortilla). Lots of gourmet prepared foods and desserts to go. Closed Sun.

East Bay

Aguiar's Market (253-1775; 585 Metacom Ave./Rte. 136, Bristol) This place is so authentic even the signs are in Portuguese. Come here for linguiça, chouriço, and other Portuguese specialties.

Golden Goose Deli (253-1414; 365 Hope St./Rte. 114, Bristol) An attractive café right on the main street; bring soups and salads home from the deli counter or have a sandwich made up on the spot. Great desserts, ice cream, and espresso.

Peaberry's (253-0360; 483 Hope St./Rte. 114, Bristol) Peaberry's originated in Providence as a bakery serving gourmet coffees; now you can get epicurean foodstuffs and sandwiches too.

Aquidneck

Cappuccino's (846-7145; 92 William St./opposite Almac's, Newport) Trendy sandwiches and salads to go (or eat in), plus fresh-baked goods.

Foodworks (683-4664; 3030 E. Main Rd./Rte. 138, Portsmouth) Smell the aroma of fresh-baked breads, pastries, and work-of-art gourmet pizzas. Also deli sandwiches and salads.

Kathleen's Fantastic Food (849-9043; 312 Broadway, Newport) This place is a smorgasbord of great smells and sights, including 8 potato and 12 chicken salads. The blueberry muffin here was voted best in the state. Also at 34 Narragansett Ave. in Jamestown (423-0414).

Marcie's General Store (683-9200; -9811; ferry landing, Homestead Village, Prudence Island) The only store on the island, with maps, gear, some groceries, and pops. Check in before you go wandering.

The Market on the Boulevard (848-2600; 43 Memorial Blvd., Newport) The most-recommended grocery, deli, gourmet shop in town — one of Newport's finest chefs was recently spotted coming out the door with a big bag, surely a good sign. They put apricots in the chicken salad.

Nature's Goodness (847-7480; 510 E. Main Rd./Rte. 138, Middletown) Natural foods grocery store, and it gets points for opening right next to a Tastee Freeze.

The gourmet pastas, sauces, and European breads at Pastabilities would have been a hit in ancient Rome.

Craig Hammell

Pastabilities (847-7894; 4 Spring Wharf, off Thames St., Newport) Pasta lovers: they make over 20 flavors of fresh pasta here, from sweet curry to saffron and even chocolate. A myriad of shapes are available, plus ravioli, tortellini, gnocchi, stuffed shells, and more. Sauces too, plus European breads. Call in your order or to find out what's being made fresh that day.

Sig's Market (847-9668; 7 Carroll Ave., Newport) Ask where to get a decent sandwich and this is where locals send you. It's really an overgrown grocery with a deli counter and soft ice cream. A selection of catered meals are also available (the whole caboodle, from hors d'oeuvres through entrée, salad, dessert, and even plastic cutlery). Great prices.

Sakonnet

Wilbur's Store (635-2356; 50 Commons) Get everything here from baked goods to a pound of hamburger to hardware. Where all of Little Compton comes to shop.

F.A. Simmons Groceries (635-2350; 37 Crandall Rd., Little Compton/ Adamsville) Ice cream, groceries, magazines, T-shirts: this is no tourist dive but an authentic wood-paneled general store.

The Provender (624-8084; 3883 Main Rd./Rte. 77, Tiverton Four Corners) This is the only upscale gourmet deli in the region, in a majestic Victorian house. Splurge and buy a whole Austrian plum torte, or pick up a deli sandwich or croissant. They do superb picnic lunches and take MC, V.

Block Island

Block Island Depot (466-2403; Ocean Ave., bet. Old & New Harbor) The natural and health foods shop on the island.

Block Island Grocery (466-2949; Ocean Ave. bet. Old & New Harbor) Of the two grocery stores on the island, this is the one without liquor, though the produce here seems better. Deli counter in the back.

Seaside Market (466-5876; Water St., New Harbor) This is the other grocery store on Block that does sell alcohol (the only other spot is the Red Bird Liquor store on Dodge St.). Deli counter.

ICE CREAM & SWEETS

West Bay

Scrumptious (884-0844; E. Greenwich Marketplace Plaza) The super-rich desserts here live up to their billing.

Wickford Sweet Shoppe (295-5427; 83-D Brown St., N. Kingstown/Wickford) Eat your ice cream, cookies, and candy right at the end of the pier overlooking the Wickford Harbor. They also sell Del's.

East Bay

Delekta Pharmacy (245-6767; 496 Main St./Rte. 114, Warren) Don't miss this

1858 apothecary with full, old-fashioned fountain service. The coffee cabinets are the best in the state. Lovely wood trim and tiled floor, and shelves full of soaps and bottles.

Aquidneck

College Variety Grocery (67 Memorial Dr., Newport) Possibly the greatest Italian ice in the world is sold here. The ebullient owner offers lots of flavors — the lemon is divine — but try the Texas Gunpowder, made from jalapeño peppers. They'll take your picture with a Polaroid as you take your first lick — that's what they did with me.

Treat's (847-8381; 458 Thames St., Newport) Some call it a bakery, some say it's a sandwich shop. Some like the ice cream, so here it is.

Sakonnet

Gray's Ice Cream (624-4500; 16 East Rd., corner of Main St./Rte. 77, Tiverton Four Corners) The quintessential Sunday-drive-in-the-country ice cream barn. The homemade product is as rich and creamy as it gets (try the grapenut). Also frozen yogurt and sherbet for the calorie-shy. A much-loved landmark.

Margaret's Corner Cones (Willow Ave.) Just down from the Commons, don't miss this small summer-only spot featuring local Bliss ice cream.

Block Island

The Ice Cream Place (466-2145; Weldon's Way, Old Harbor) Flavors and concoctions are listed on an enormous chalk board that takes forever to read. Great homemade peanut butter brownies and other goodies. Best ice cream and frozen yogurt on the Block.

TAKE-OUT & CHEAP EATS

West Bay

East Ferry Deli (423-1592; 47 Conanicus Ave., Jamestown) An indoor/outdoor café overlooking Jamestown Harbor, serving coffees, pastries, sandwiches, quiches, and salads. The view was better than the pasta salad, however.

Fillipo's Pizza (294-4467; 670 Ten Rod Rd., N. Kingstown/Wickford) Try "George's Special" — pizza with the works minus anchovies. Highly endorsed by many Wickfordites.

Gail's Galley (783-3550; 1157 Pt. Judith Rd., Narragansett/Pt. Judith) Get fresh fried seafood at the take-out window or eat in the charming dining room.

Harborside Grill (295-0444; 68 Brown St., N. Kingstown/Wickford) Three little breakfast and lunch eateries are in the middle of Wickford; this is the one locals recommend. Choose from a huge menu and eat at the counter or take it away.

J.L.'s Take Out (789-2020; State Pier off Great Island Rd., Narragansett/ Galilee) Great Island Rd. is packed with seafood restaurants and take-outs, but this is the most convenient to the Block Island ferry. Good fried everything.

PJ's Pizza & Restaurant (789-4950; 909 Boston Neck Rd./Rte. 1A, Bonnet Shores; also 789-4210; 865 Pt. Judith Rd., both in Narragansett) An essential pizza place with Greek overtones. Try the spinach and broccoli pies or the Greek cheese pizza. Cheap pasta dinners too. Delivery.

Seaside Café (789-2219; 114 Boon St., Narragansett Pier) The kind of unassuming spot you love. They've got breakfast, lunch, pizza, and vegetarian fare, and deliver anything, year-round.

Top o' the Morning (782-4075; 90 Middlebridge Rd., Narragansett) You could make the same breakfast and lunch fare at home, but it tastes better in this tiny, family-run bungalow overlooking the Pettaquamscutt River. Off the beaten track.

East Bay

Amaral's Fish & Chips (247-0675; 4 Redmond St., Warren) Eat in or take home superb fresh seafood fried in the lightest of batters. Wildly popular with the locals. Closed Sun.

Bristol House of Pizza (253-2550, 55 State St., Bristol) They deliver, but you'll have to go in person to decide between 25 kinds of pizza and 35 grinders; Greek specials like souvlaki and gyros too.

Cabral's Gourmet Chicken (253-3913; 585 Metacom Ave./Rte. 136, Bristol) Experts in rotisserie chicken way before it became trendy. Buy a whole bird for $5. Lots of other choices too, including chouriço pies, stuffed peppers, and stuffies.

Castigliego's (245-4640; 485 Metacom Ave./Rte. 136, Warren) A regular seafood palace, with stuffies, chowder, clam cakes, smelts, fried squid, lobster. Take it home or eat there in a small, pretty dining room.

The Hat Trick Restaurant (247-2930; 440 Child St., Warren) Try the Hat Trick Special: 3 eggs, pancakes, and sausages plus homefries for $3.33. Breakfast and lunch daily.

The Hope Diner (253-1759; 742 Hope St./Rte. 114, Bristol) The most recommended breakfast place in town. Lunch too.

Aquidneck

Atlantic Grill (849-4440; 91 Aquidneck Ave., Middletown) This is where guests at the Hedgegate B&B get the breakfast part of their stay, so you know it's good. A big breakfast and lunch menu, with take-out service.

Boston Chicken (849-8990; 258 Bellevue Ave., Newport) Although it's a Massachusetts chain, this rotisserie chicken is superb: moist, tender, and cheap. A big selection of cold salads, mashed potatoes, cornbread, and more to go with it.

Braga's (846-5374; 1397 W. Main Rd./Rte. 114, Middletown) Stop here for hot or cold grinders to take on a day trip from Newport. Also salads, burgers, and spaghetti, plus beer or wine if you eat in.

Café at Sayer's Wharf (846-9740; corner America's Cup Ave. and Sayer's Wharf, Newport) It's in the touristy part of town, yet locals come here for cold cuts, to get a drink at the open air bar, and to have a sandwich.

Flo knows her clams — get 'em here or at the original Flo's Clam Shack on Island Park in Portsmouth.

Craig Hammell

Flo's Clam Shack (Park Ave., Portsmouth/Island Park) Flo's is a RI fixture. A previous incarnation of the shack was seen floating out to sea in the 1938 hurricane — so you know Flo's has been around awhile. Terrific plump, fried clams, plus stuffies, chowder, and even burgers. You can tell this is vintage RI because they offer vinegar for the fries. There's another Flo's opposite First Beach in Middletown (847-8141). The new upstart has a larger menu — you can't get fried shrimp at the Portsmouth spot, only clams and fish.

Ocean Breeze Café (849-1750; 580 Thames St., Newport) Some like this place (not to be confused with Ocean Coffee Roasters), though others think it's a little sterile. Fresh muffins, homemade soups and chowders. B, L, D.

Pepperoni Express (849-6060; 7 Memorial Blvd., Newport) Good basic pizza and fast, reliable delivery. Also locations in Portsmouth (683-6230) and Middletown (847-2080).

Sakonnet

Four Corners Restaurant (625-1307; 3841 Main St./Rte. 77, Tiverton) An ordinary little sandwich joint open for breakfast, lunch, and dinner — but it's the only one of its kind for miles. Tell them if you don't want sugar in your tea or coffee.

Phoenix Pizza (624-8400; 750 East Rd., Tiverton) Choose from 12 kinds of pizza or make up your own. Also burgers, salads, and sandwiches. Free delivery.

Block Island

Bethany's Airport Diner (466-3100; State Airport, Center Rd.) One of those few places where Long Island commuters mix with Block Island locals. Serving breakfast fare, omelettes, burgers, and sandwiches. Stop here if you've biked all the way up the hill from Old Town Rd.

Block Island Burrito (466-2976, for take-out x2073; Water St., Old Harbor) Claims to have the world's largest burrito — it is pretty big, and very tasty. The nachos are only so-so. With tacos, fajitas, Spanish rice, chili.

Cappizzano's (466-2829, x5080; corner of Dodge St. and Corn Neck Rd.) Regular and gourmet pizza, calzones, grinders, Greek salads.

Island Pizza (466-2800; 3 Ocean Ave.) Delivers pizza or calzones to your dwelling or dock.

Old Harbor Take-Out (466-2935; Water St.) Couldn't be any closer to the ferry dock if it tried. Unusually good fare: try the pita sandwiches (Chicken Athena is delicious), fried seafood, or burgers. There's also a breakfast menu plus ice cream and frozen yogurt. Fresh Block Island blackberries on the sundaes are a nice touch.

Payne's Dock (466-5572; Payne's Dock, New Harbor) Slightly off the beaten path, most folks come here by accident. Don't — make a point of it. For under $4 the fried shrimp is a steal. Great chowder, clam cakes, hot dogs, ice cream, and homemade doughnuts till 6pm.

Rebecca's Seafood (466-5411; Water St., Old Harbor) Great clam cakes and spicy curlicue fries. You can also get burgers, sandwiches, and seafood dinners. Eat inside or at café tables under umbrellas.

WINERIES

In addition to visiting Bay area wineries, visitors can contact **The Wine Experience** (782-1478; PO Box 472, N. Kingstown/Saunderstown). It's a wine education organization that offers tastings, a wine-finding service, wine adventure packages, and more. Ask for Lynette Brodeur.

Sakonnet Vineyards (635-8486; 162 W. Main Rd./Rte. 77, Little Compton) Burrow deep down a dirt lane into beautiful countryside to reach the winery.

Keeping tabs on the vintage at Sakonnet Vineyards in Little Compton.

Craig Hammell

Sakonnet is the biggest — and from its medals, the best — winery in New England. Stroll through the grounds, take a tour of the caves, and stay for a tasting. The whites are best suited to Narragansett Bay soil and climate.

Vinland Wine Cellars (848-5161, 800-345-1559; 909 E. Main Rd./Rte. 138, Middletown) The winery is in a strip mall, but you can arrange to tour nearby Hopelands Vineyard where the grapes are grown (20 acres of vines overlooking the Sakonnet River — it looks like Bordeaux). Tastings and tours every hour.

Clamming it up at the annual Great Chowder Cook-Off at the Newport Yachting Center.

Pamela Petro

Seasonal Food Festivals & Rituals

The Newport and Narragansett Bay area is rich with food festivals of every imagining. Below are some of the major events. You can also find small local fairs, fondly referred to as "clamslurpers," almost every summer weekend.

Block Island Pasta Cook-off (466-2982) An all-you-can-eat opportunity to choose the best pasta on the Block. Mid-Sept.

Great Chowder Cook-Off (846-1600) Sponsored yearly by the Newport Yachting Center, this is a terrific chance to taste over 28 samples of clam and seafood chowder in one day (served up in tiny paper cups). Vote for your favorite. Mid-June.

Harvest Festival and Apple Pie Contest (783-5400) An annual tradition at the South County Museum in Narragansett, featuring jonnycakes, clam cakes, chowder, cider, and, of course, apple pie. Early to mid-Oct.

International Quahog Festival (295-2570) This decade-old Wickford event features a baked stuffed quahog (stuffies) cook-off, plus clam-shucking contests. Early Oct.

Lobstermen's Festival (783-1543) Yawgoo Bakes provides clam chowder, fresh fish, corn, burgers, and, of course, lobster, at this annual Narragansett event in Galilee. Late June.

Pick-Your-Own Look for strawberries in July, blueberries in Aug., and apples in Sept. and Oct. Locations include:

> *Delucia's Berry Farm* (635-2689; 96 Willow Ave., Little Compton). Strawberries, blueberries, raspberries.
> *The Berry Farm* (847-3912; 19 Third Beach Rd., Middletown) Strawberries.
> *Devecchio's Farm* (884-9598; 302 Potter Rd., N. Kingstown) Blueberries.
> *Quonset View Farm* (683-1254; 895 Middle Rd., Portsmouth) Strawberries and blueberries.

Taste of Block Island Seafood Festival (466-2982) Lots of "edibles from the ocean." Early June.

Taste of Rhode Island (846-1600) The biggest of Newport Yachting Center's food festivals. Appetizer samples from over 40 restaurants plus cooking demonstrations and a Parade of Chefs. Late Sept.

CHAPTER SIX
At The Helm
RECREATION

The word "yacht" comes from the Dutch for "sleek, agile craft." Yachts are to Narragansett Bay what coals are to Newcastle: this is their home, their breeding ground, it sometimes seems; and over the years racing yachts have brought fame and fortune back to the waters that gave them birth. Between 1893 and 1934 the Herreshoff Boatyard in Bristol designed and built more America's Cup defenders than any

Craig Hammell

Down to the beach with books, at Second Beach in Middletown.

other shipyard in the world. The tradition continues, and throughout the summer Narragansett Bay is alive with racing craft. From afar it must look like a giant clothesline, white sheets everywhere billowing in the wind.

Like most of Newport's signature sports, yachting arrived with Gilded Age vacationers in the late 19th century. James Gordon Bennett, who built the Newport Casino, was one of the most notorious — his personal yacht had a full-size Turkish bath and a miniature dairy. And, on land, "The 400" attacked wickets, shuttlecocks, and balls as earnestly as they did the waves. The first national tennis and golf tournaments were held in Gilded Age Newport, and sports such as polo, croquet, and fox-hunting were all raised to new levels of achievement.

Today Newport is still the place for international polo matches and even professional-level croquet — the New England Regional Croquet Championships are held at the Tennis Hall of Fame. Probably the best recreational activity on Narragansett Bay, however, is simply gazing at the natural magnificence of land and sea. The coast is often spectacularly rocky, as along the romantic shoreline of Beaver Tail State Park on Jamestown, or Brenton Point

State Park in Newport. But great swatches of sand poke through to offer some of the best beaches in New England. Bailey's Beach in Newport might have been the most exclusive when Mrs. Vanderbilt got her feet wet there, but today the crashing surf at Crescent Beach on Block Island, or the peace and quiet of Goosewing Beach in Little Compton, draw more attention.

So don't miss out on the time-honored pleasure of simply driving and taking in the scenery. Many of the bike rides outlined under Bicycling below are also suitable for car touring — cruise around with the windows down and enjoy a Bay breeze.

BASEBALL

From April through August, Rhode Island's own minor league team, the **Pawtucket Red Sox** — known simply as the Pawsox — play at McCoy Stadium just north of Providence (724-7300; 1 Columbus Ave., Pawtucket). Tickets are just a couple of bucks, and they sell ice cream in upside-down, miniature batting hats (reason enough for going). Several times a summer Pawsox players hold free clinics to teach kids how to bat, field, and throw: who knows? next year these guys might be in the big leagues. For information call 724-7300. To watch local leagues play, show up at **Cardines Field** in Newport (847-1398; W. Marlborough St.) — it's free.

BEACHES

Go on, get wet in the Ocean State. Beaches are what Narragansett Bay's 400 miles of coastline are for. Those listed below are all saltwater, and the fees, except where noted, are per car rather than per person. (Beach attendants start taking your money in mid-June and stop after Labor Day).

For **beachcombing** or shell-hunting, first visit the **Sachuest Point National Wildlife Refuge** Visitor Center in Middletown and study their display of local shells, to know what to look for (see State Parks & Wildlife Refuges below). The inside word is that **Brenton Point State Park** in Newport is good for oyster drills, periwinkles, and surf clams; **Roger Wheeler State Beach** in Narragansett has dog whelks, blue mussels, and moon snails; **Fort Getty** in Jamestown is often less picked-over than other spots and is good for slipper shells, mermaid's purses, and clam, quahog, and conch shells; finally **Purgatory Chasm** and **Sachuest Point** itself, both in Middletown, offer up sea urchins, and conch and clam shells. Happy hunting.

West Bay

Mackerel Cove (Jamestown) Along the causeway leading to the Beaver Tail peninsula, this isn't the place for people who like sheltered, hidden spots, but the water is shallow and warm, so it's great for kids. Half a mile long, with 150 parking spaces; $10/car. Lifeguard, restrooms.

Making their own fun on Narragansett Town Beach.

Craig Hammell

Narragansett Town Beach (Off Rte. 1A/Boston Neck Rd.) The long (half-mile), flat beach in the middle of Narragansett Pier. There's usually a crowd here, good waves, and boardwalk-style fun. Full cabana service plus a carpark; $5/car, or $4 walk-on fee.

Roger Wheeler State Beach (Narragansett) Off Sand Hill Cove Rd. in Galilee, a family-style place with good playground facilities. Full cabana service, 1650 ft. of beachfront, and a lot for 2000 cars; $8 weekdays, $10 weekends.

Salty Brine State Beach (Narragansett) Formerly Galilee State Beach, this is just west of Roger Wheeler. It's only 150 ft. long, but a major teen-spot-to-be-seen. Restrooms, parking for 100 cars; $8 weekdays, $10 weekends.

Scarborough State Beach (Narragansett) It runs alongside Ocean Rd. (for about 2000 ft.) on the way down to Point Judith — with your windows down you can smell the Coppertone. *Rhode Island Monthly* says "Big hair, hard muscles, more mousse and mascara than SPF 15." Two lots for 2900 cars, all facilities; $8 weekdays, $10 weekends.

East Bay

Bristol Town Beach (Colt State Park) So the Bay has ripples instead of waves, and the shore has pebbles instead of sand: the water still feels good, and the most it costs is $5 on weekends. 400 parking spaces; 300 ft. of beach. Full cabana service.

Aquidneck

Bailey's Beach (Newport) This small, unspectacular beach at the southern end of the Cliff Walk was the most exclusive spot as far as Gilded Age bathers were concerned. Go figure.

Easton Beach (Newport) Also known as First Beach, this is the gray strip of sand at the bottom of the Cliff Walk. It's three-quarters of a mile long and sometimes offers great surf (wetsuited surfers hang out here all year). A brand new cabana and pavilion complex was built in 1993; Hurricane Bob did in the last one. It gets crowded, but you can see the mansions and be seen. Parking for 737 cars; $5 weekdays, $10 weekends.

Fort Adams State Park Beach (Newport) This calm, clean beach offers peace and quiet, park facilities, and a superb view of Newport Harbor. It's small — 225 ft. — but a nice spot, and only costs $2 to park (423 cars).

Gooseberry Beach (Newport) This modest, privately owned beach out along Ocean Drive is open to the public; it offers great swimming with a protected cove for young children.

King Park Beach (Newport) Near the Ida Lewis Yacht Club off Wellington Ave., this little Harbor beach is an ideal spot for a picnic (it's really more park than beach). Free.

Sandy Beach (Prudence Island) Aptly named, it's the only one on the island. This lovely rim of sand, a mile and a quarter long, is on the northwestern arm of Prudence (about a 15 min. bike ride from the ferry landing at Homestead). It's absolutely undeveloped here — trees are thick right up to the sand. The state has more or less abandoned this beach but there's no reason not to use it: great views of the Newport and Jamestown bridges.

Sandy Point Beach (Portsmouth) At the end of Sandy Point Ave. off E. Main Rd./Rte. 138, this Sakonnet River beach is a sheltered, calm spot good for

Rowing your boat on the Bay.

Craig Hammell

young paddlers. It's a half-mile long, with full cabana service and parking for 150 cars; $5.

Second Beach (Middletown) Take Aquidneck Ave. to the end and head left, pass Purgatory Chasm sign, and wind up at Second Beach. Wide open sand and sea, with a land's end feeling here, despite the 1600-lot carpark. $10 weekdays, $15 weekends. Cabana service; one and a half miles of sand.

Teddy's Beach (Portsmouth) On Park Ave. in Island Park (very near the ruins of Stone Bridge), this is a small, quiet spot with only 575 ft. of shoreline and parking for 12 cars. No lifeguards, but the Bay surf isn't rough. Free.

Third Beach (Middletown) Head east from Second Beach and take a left to Third Beach (a right leads to Sachuest Point; see State Parks & Wildlife Refuges). It's secluded here and popular with families and windsurfers. Half a mile long; 200 cars; $10 weekdays, $15 weekends. Restrooms.

Sakonnet

Fogland Beach (Tiverton) Take Neck Rd. off Main/Rte. 77, turn right on Fogland Rd. (a beautiful drive). It's a pebbly Bay beach, but nicely marooned on a tiny peninsula. Parking for 250 cars, $4 weekdays, $6 weekends. A half-mile of shoreline with lifeguard and restrooms.

Goosewing Beach (Little Compton) A find, but beware, there's no longer direct access to Goosewing. So park at the town beach lot and walk eastward, crossing a little rivulet. Behind you are fields, cows, and an 18th-century stone barn; ahead is the Atlantic Ocean. A great place with 1300 ft. of shoreline.

Grinnell's Beach (Tiverton) Near the old Stone Bridge facing Island Park in Portsmouth just across the water, this is a teenager-hangout beach. A quarter mile of Bay sand, plus parking for 150; $4 weekdays, $6 weekends. Lifeguard, restrooms.

South Shore Beach (Little Compton) Also known as Little Compton Town Beach, it's a little tricky to find: head south on W. Main Rd./Rte. 77 almost to the end, turn left on Swamp Rd.; at the point Swamp makes a 90-degree bend to the left, take the road to the right (there's a small sign) to the beach — clean, secluded, quiet. Parking is $9 weekdays, $13 weekends. 1300 ft. of sand; lifeguard.

Block Island

Ballard's Beach (Old Harbor) Just south of the ferry landing at Old Harbor, the beach is right next to the big, noisy restaurant of the same name; it's sandy and good for fishing with half a mile of shoreline.

Black Rock Beach (West Side) Take the dirt lane (Black Rock Rd.) off Cooneymus Rd. past a fabulous old beach cottage called Bit o' Heaven. Keep going till you reach a spot to clamber down the cliffs, then you're all alone with the surf and sand. It's magnificent here, but isolated; be careful of hidden rocks when swimming. Half a mile of beach. Bring your dog and stay all day.

Crescent Beach (Corn Neck Rd.) This great, sandy swatch runs along Block Island's northeastern shoreline for two and a half miles, beginning in Old Harbor and encompassing **Fred Benson Town Beach** as well as **Scotch** and **Mansion Beaches** — the latter is the northernmost of the lot. The sand is clean and white, the water clear and cold. Park at the Fred Benson lot, or walk (it's easier to head down Corn Neck Rd. than walk in the sand — chances are a local will give you a lift). Mansion Beach is a personal favorite; the quarter-mile dirt road (a right off Corn Neck) is marked by a hedge of spruce trees; one of the nicest beaches in RI.

Fred Benson Town Beach (Corn Neck Rd.) Formerly called Block Island State Beach, this is the state-owned patch in the middle of Crescent Beach (see above). There's a bathhouse with full cabana service, a lot for 200 cars, and the only lifeguard on the island. Free.

BICYCLING

This is ideal cycling territory. Not only is the whole region fairly flat (the only hills that may tempt you off your seat are on Block Island, and even those are pretty mild), the scenery is never redundant. Southern Rhode Island can seem like an abridged version of the whole of New England — seascapes, farm scenes, and wooded areas all mingled together.

Rules for safe cycling are the same here as everywhere: use a headlight and/or reflector clothing at night, and wear a helmet. A tip: never trust Rhode Island drivers. They are especially infamous for failing to use turn signals. (There's a Don Bosquet cartoon of a used car salesman delivering the pitch: "And the turn signals are like new!") Finally, bring a decent lock and always use it.

The following are some recommended rides for each region, though for a thorough guide see *Short Bike Rides in Rhode Island* by Howard Stone (details are in the Bibliography section, *Information* chapter).

West Bay

The best choice for West Bay cycling is Conanicut Island (Jamestown's other name). Traffic jams here all occur on Rte. 138 — cars heading from the Jamestown Bridge to the Newport Bridge and vice versa. The rest of the island is a cyclist's paradise. On the southern end head down Beaver Tail Rd. to the lighthouse of the same name, or out to Fort Wetherill State Park on the eastern promontory. Or head up East Shore Rd. to the northern tip, then come down North Rd. on the western side; there's not much here but farms and a scattering of old houses.

East Bay

The East Bay Bike Path runs from Providence to Bristol — it's a great way to see the Bay.

Craig Hammell

The **East Bay Bike Path** is the crowning glory of Rhode Island's bicycle routes. It runs 14 and a half miles from Providence to Bristol, offering access to several parks and the Bay enroute; it also intersects a total of 49 streets, so obey the miniature stop signs, they're for real. The path is 10 ft. wide, paved with a center line for two-way traffic, and equipped with four-ft. shoulders (the rule is bikers to the right, walkers to the left, and dogs on leashes). Best of all, you don't even have to be in shape to go the distance — it's entirely flat. Stop at Quito's Seafood near the southern terminus (see Food & Beverage Purveyors, *Restaurants*). They've got great fried clams.

Or take a right on Child St. off Rte. 136 in Warren and follow it to Long La.; turn right and follow it to Touisset Rd., and then on to the Bay. This is East Warren, also known as the Touisset Section of Warren — realtors bill it as "Rhode Island's forgotten hamlet." It's true: there's nothing here but farms, stables, and, at the very tip of the Touisset peninsula, an old community of shingled beach houses (modest by Newport standards). The Bay opens before you, and the cycling is perfectly flat. Don't miss it.

Aquidneck

In Newport the **10 Mile/Ocean Drive** begins on Bellevue Ave. at the Tennis Hall of Fame and continues in a curvy, coast-hugging loop — take a break at Brenton Point State Park before winding up back in town at the Harbor. Or use

Biking by the Bay with the Newport Bridge in the background.

Craig Hammell

a bike to tour the side streets of the Point Section — a great way to get a good look at the colonial homes.

A route through eastern Middletown and Portsmouth, from Third Beach Rd. to Wapping Rd., finishing at Sandy Point Ave., offers great views of the Sakonnet River (Hopelands Vineyard at the southern end will make you think you're in Bordeaux — the vines supply Vinland Wine Cellars). The Island Park and Hummocks area of northeastern Portsmouth is also fun to explore by bike: it's a classic New England marshscape of water, boats, and seagulls. The best time is late September when the marsh reeds turn burnt umber.

On Prudence Island, the ferry schedule leaves you nearly a full day to explore, and there's hardly any traffic (though some roads are of tightly-packed gravel, so bring a cushion). Get a map from Marcie's General Store, then take off. The island is a tangle of woods and vines grown over abandoned fields; look for the old stone walls, and for deer — Prudence has the densest deer population in New England. Don't miss a tour of South Prudence Bay Island Park, an old military installation that now makes a perfect bike path.

Sakonnet

A suggested starting place is Tiverton Four Corners; take East Rd. into Adamsville, follow signs for Sneekers (a convenient restaurant and bar) into the Little Compton Commons, head north on W. Main Rd. to a left on Fogland Rd. (a brief detour to the beach here), then continue north on Neck Rd. which leads back into Tiverton Four Corners and, happily, Gray's Ice Cream. This is pristine countryside: you'll see horses, cows, gulls, farmstands, fields, and the sea, but only one traffic light.

Block Island

Cycle all the way out Corn Neck Rd. (about three and a half miles one way) to the North Light. Or follow West Side Rd. out of New Harbor and all around the western coast of the island; it becomes a ring road and will lead onto Mohegan Trail past the Southeast Light and Mohegan Bluffs to Spring Rd. and back into Old Harbor. Take a pack and spend all day — follow the dirt lanes west and south to the sea (Dorrie's and Grace Cove Rds., Black Rock Rd.).

EVENTS & ORGANIZATIONS

Narragansett Bay Wheelmen (831-1494) The Wheelmen is one of the biggest and oldest cycling clubs in the country; they hold organized rides every Sun. (and some Sats.), plus what's billed as "The Flattest Century in the East" on Sun. after Labor Day (traditionally 100 miles, though you can do 50 or 25; it starts in Tiverton). Their newsletter, *The Spoken Word*, lists all events. Send SASE to PO Box 428, Tiverton 02878.

Tour de Cure — Bike to the Bay through South County (789-4422, 800-548-4662) Experts and novices cycle 25, 50 or 100 kilometers to raise money for diabetes research. The start/finish is at Narragansett Town Beach; late May.

BICYCLE RENTALS & SHOPS

West Bay

Narragansett Bikes (782-4444; 1153 Boston Neck Rd./Rte. 1A, Narragansett/Bonnet Shores) A complete bike shop.

East Bay

Bay Path Cycles (254-1277; 13 State St., Bristol) At the southern end of the East Bay Bike Path (see above). Over 150 bikes on display. Repairs, rentals.

Aquidneck

Firehouse Bicycle Co. (847-5700; 25 Mill St., Newport) Sales, repairs, and rentals off Thames on Queen Anne Square (just find Trinity Church). Daily rates range from $10 for a one-speed to $25 for a bicycle-built-for-two.

Ten Speed Spokes, Ltd. (847-5609; 18 Elm St., Newport) Bicycle sales, services, and rentals; near Visitors' Bureau.

Block Island

You can rent a bike for the hour, day, or week at one of the following spots:

Block Island Bike & Car Rentals (466-2297; Ocean Ave.)

Block Island Boat Basin (466-2631, West Side Rd., New Harbor) Bike, moped, and car rentals.

Cyr's Cycles (466-2147; PO Box C, behind the Surf Hotel, Dodge St., Old Harbor) Bikes only.

Esta's Bikes (466-2651; Water St., Old Harbor)

Craig Hammell

Explore Block by bike.

The Moped Man (466-5011; Water St.) Also has mountain bikes, cruisers, and child seats as well as mopeds. Take a discount coupon if someone offers you one coming off the ferry.

Old Harbor Bike Shop (466-2029; Old Harbor) Bikes, mopeds, cars, and vans for hire.

Payne's Dock (466-5570; New Harbor) Bikes only.

The Seacrest (466-2882; High St.) Bikes only.

Mopeding Around and Carting Away

The new thing in Newport is **Cart Aways Electric Car Rentals** (849-0010; 16 Waites's Wharf, off Thames St., Newport). These little Danish-made whipper-snappers are all over town — especially out on 10 Mile/Ocean Drive, which is the recommended route. They look like motorized tennis shoes. Maximum speed is 45 mph, range is 40 miles, and they can accommodate two adults or one adult and two kids. Rentals by the hour or half-day ($20/hr.).

Or consider mansion-hopping on a moped. **Fun Rentals** (846-4374; 1 Commercial Wharf, off Thames St., Newport) offers scooters and double scooters by the week, day, or hour. It's not a bad idea in Newport, where parking can be a headache-and-a-half, but Block Island is another story. If your time or physical ability is limited, mopeds are the way to go, but otherwise Block isn't really the place for them. Bicycles are much better suited to the island's slow-speed charms — you miss a lot on mopeds and scare away wildlife. If you do rent one, watch out for the sand that accumulates at intersections — it's all too easy to wipe out.

For moped rental outfits on Block Island, see Bicycling above.

BILLIARDS

A new, trendy sport around the Bay.

Bumpers Billiards (848-7665; 999 W. Main Rd./Rte. 114, Middletown) Upscale pool in an "elite billiard center" — it's family oriented and attentive to etiquette. They offer 17 tables and lessons on tape or in person. $5 per player.

Greenwich Family Billiards (885-8833; 5600 Post Rd., E. Greenwich) Marathon pool-playing on Sat. before 6pm for $5; "Rock 'n' Pool" Sun. from 7pm, $6.

BIRD-WATCHING

Narragansett Bay and Block Island are on the Atlantic Flyway, so during spring and fall the area plays host to diverse species of song and shore birds and waterfowl — even the endangered peregrine falcon. Refuges (see State Parks & Wildlife Refuges below) attract over 60 species of nesting birds including the woodcock, osprey, great blue (and little green) heron, snowy egrets, cormorants, and the endangered piping plover. Bird-lovers have even seen pairs of bald eagles nesting on the southern shores of Narragansett Bay. **Ninigret National Wildlife Refuge Complex** (364-9124; Box 307, Charlestown, RI 02813), publishes a free wildlife calendar that notes the species to find during different seasons.

The birding event of the year is the **Block Island Bird Count**, sponsored by the Audubon Society and held during the first week of October. In the past, binoculared birders have spied up to 141 species of migrating birds (that's the record). Vans ferry groups from one end of the island to the other, hoping to catch sight of the white ibis, semipalmated sandpiper, lesser black-backed gull, and others. Call 231-6444.

BOWLING

West Bay

Kingstown Bowl (884-4450; 6125 Post Rd./Rte. 1, N. Kingstown)
Wickford Lanes (294-9886; Post Rd./Rte. 1, N. Kingstown)

Aquidneck

Aquidneck Lanes (846-2729; 173 E. Main Rd./Rte. 138, Middletown) Tenpin and duckpin bowling plus pro shop, snack bar, drinks.

Ryan Family Amusement Center (849-9990; 105 Chases La., Middletown) Candlepin and tenpin bowling; also at 266 Thames St., Newport (846-5774). See the Grab Bag section for other Ryan activities.

CAMPING

Hard to believe that woodlands still cover 60 percent of the most densely populated state in the union. Burrowed into these enclaves are a host of state, municipal, and private campgrounds. Remember to get a permit for every fire you build, and that there are no campgrounds on Block Island (where, ironically, you can burn beach fires to your heart's content). Rates usually run from $15 to $25 per night, depending on your equipment (tent or trailer). Most trailer sites include electric, water, and sewer hookups; general facilities usually feature hot showers, restrooms, dumping stations, and picnic tables. Extras are noted below.

West Bay

Fishermen's Memorial State Park (789-8374; 1011 Pt. Judith Rd./Rte. 108, Narragansett/Galilee) Of 147 trailer sites 40 include sewer hookups; also 35 tent sites. Tennis, basketball, horseshoe courts, and children's playground. Season: mid-Apr.–Oct. Reservations required; write in advance to Division of Parks and Recreation, 2321 Hartford Ave., Johnston, RI 02919.

Fort Getty Recreation Area (423-1363; Fort Getty Rd., Jamestown) A recommended spot on the spectacular Beaver Tail peninsula, with 25 tent and 100 trailer sites. Facilities include boat ramp, fishing dock. Memorial Day weekend–Columbus Day. PO Box 377, Jamestown 02835.

Long Cove Marina Family Campsites (783-4902; Long Cove Marina off Pt. Judith Rd./Rte. 108, Narragansett) 155 trailer and 25 tent sites. Facilities include the usual plus launching ramp, saltwater fishing, and dockage with 24 slips. One pet only, must be leashed. Season: May–mid-Oct.

Aquidneck

Melville Ponds Campground (849-8212; 181 Bradford Ave., off W. Main Rd./Rte. 114, Portsmouth) 57 tent and 66 trailer sites (33 have sewer hookups), featuring 116 fire rings and on-site fishing. Playground and beach privileges too. Season: Apr.–Oct. East Passage Yachting Center is just down the road.

Middletown Campground (846-6273; Second Beach, Middletown) The campground offers 36 trailer sites only, all with sewer hookups. Access to the beach — a favorite — comes with the deal. No pets. Season: mid-May–late Sept. 350 E. Main Rd., Middletown 02840.

Middletown Recreational Vehicle Park (846-9455; 132 Prospect Ave., Middletown) 40 sites; leashed pets only. Season: mid-Apr.–Oct.

Paradise Mobile Home Park (847-1500; 459 Aquidneck Ave., Middletown) 16 sites; public phone, but no pets or tents. Season: May–mid-Oct.

CHARTERS

Charter boats are available for fishing, whale-watching, and simply cruising around Narragansett Bay. Regularly scheduled sightseeing cruises ("sightsailing," as one promoter calls it) are noted under Tours. Chartering a boat refers to renting a crewed boat (the skipper remains onboard and in charge), and following an agenda of your own choosing or one recommended by the captain. It's your responsibility to get a group together (usually no more than eight) to share expenses. Several of the listings below also include "bareboat" charters — meaning that you hire just the boat and crew it yourself — though sail- and powerboat rental outlets are primarily noted under Sailing & Boating. Charter listings also include several-party fishing boats that depart for scheduled trips and generally take upwards of 20 passengers.

West Bay

The Frances Fleet (783-4988, 800-662-2824; PO Box 3724, Peace Dale, RI 02883) Deep-sea fishing (half and three-quarter day trips, plus extended trips to Georges Banks; call for special cod and bluefish dates); moonlight cruises, and whale-watching. Departs regularly from Galilee docks in Narragansett.

Morning Star **Charters** (295-5918; see Meadowlands B&B in *Lodging*) Options include two- and four-hour, day, and overnight cruises aboard the *Morning Star*. A two-hour sunset sail for six is $195. Breakfast, lunch, and/or dinner are served (BYOB).

Seven B's V (789-9250; Dock RR, Narragansett/Galilee) Custom 80-ft. yacht for special events, fishing, whale-watching, and moonlight cruises. Six passenger maximum. Sails from Galilee Charter Boat Docks.

Persuader (783-5644; 110 Avice St., Narragansett 02882) Join Capt. Denny Dillon aboard the *Persuader* for half and full day, and special evening trips. Will also do pick-ups on Block Island.

T.C. Charters (336-7054, 884-3460; Milt's Marina, 20 Water St., E. Greenwich) Sail aboard the 41-ft. party fishing boat *Desiderata*.

Aquidneck

Come Sail Away Yacht Charters, Ltd. (849-8123; Brown & Howard Wharf, off Thames St., Newport) Self-designed charters to the Bay islands, America's Cup racing waters, or all the way to Block; also offers two-hour Harbor tours and sunset sails (bread, cheese, fruit included with all sails, though BYOB). Maximum six people.

"Feelin Great" Charters (846-0724; 732-1726) Head out sport fishing (up to four people), or hire the 26-ft. *Bonito* for a Bay cruise (six people).

Myles Standish Charters (846-7225; 4 Smithfield Dr., Middletown) Offers both sport and bottom fishing plus sightseeing excursions aboard the *Mayflower*.

Newport Lobster Charters (849-8161; Bowen's Wharf, off America's Cup Ave., Newport) Lobster charters, Harbor tours.

Sakonnet

Sportfisherman (635-4292; Sakonnet Pt., Little Compton) This party boat sails on a schedule from Sakonnet Point; call Capt. Bud Phillips.

Block Island

G. Willie Makit Charters (466-5151; PO Box 1010, Block Island) Fishing charters offer inshore trips for bass, blues, cod, fluke, and pollack (six passenger maximum; four or eight hrs.), or offshore trips for tuna, shark, and marlin (four passengers; six or 10 hrs.). You've got to love the name.

CROQUET

Many inns have croquet sets for their guests to use — the Atlantic Inn on Block Island even has a course: wickets all ready and waiting. But if a friendly game of croquet turns your loved ones into cunning thrill-seekers who would rather send your ball flying into the bushes than win, take in a professional match instead. The **New England Regional Croquet Championships** are held at the International Tennis Hall of Fame (849-3990; 194 Bellevue Ave.) in early August. The best mallet swingers in the area compete for berths in the USCA National Open (that's the U.S. Croquet Association).

FISHING

If it swims in Narragansett Bay or Block Island Sound, odds are it's been caught by Rhode Island fishermen. And quite a lot swims here. Inshore, try fly and bottom fishing by boat, or surf casting; look for striped bass, blues, cod, pollack, tautog, mackerel, fluke (summer flounder), and flounder. Offshore, in serious sport fishing on the open seas, look for tuna, shark, and white marlin. The surf casting is good almost anywhere; ask the people at the bait shop what's running, what's good for catching it, and where. Don't forget essential fishing items: besides standard bait and tackle, bring a gaff, net, lots of rags, pail, knife, and a hip flask (full).

Most of the boats listed under Charters offer "deep-sea" fishing trips to inshore and offshore locations; some will even take you on an overnighter out to Georges Bank and other open-ocean grounds (note that the price of the charter includes bait and tackle — the crew will usually clean your catch for you too). There are two kinds of fishing charters: party ("head") boats take between 40 to about 110 passengers for bottom fishing excursions. You don't normally need a reservation and boats leave on a set schedule (usually 6am—2:30pm); sometimes you have to rent your tackle. Fishing charters require reservations and sail at your bidding — you get up enough people (usually between four to six) and plan your own route. Some of the best local spots include **Nebraska Shoals** off Charlestown for bluefish; **Coxes Ledge** east of Block Island for cod; near **Point Judith Light**, around Block Island, and **Matunuck Point** for bass.

Then there's always freshwater fishing for the compleat angler. A freshwater license is about $10 and is available at most bait and tackle shops. Trout season

The one that didn't get away.

Rhode Island Dept. of Tourism

opens on the second Sat. in April at sunrise; look for stocked ponds of brown, rainbow, and brook trout. For further license information call 277-3576 or 789-3094. Good bets are **St. Mary's** and **Melville ponds** in Portsmouth, and **Tiverton Trout Pond**.

Remember there's a general six-a-day state limit on any catch. There are special restrictions on stripers (at least 28", one per day); blues (10 per day); tautog, also called blackfish (keepers must be 12"); and flounder — throw it back — there is a total ban on keeping flounders, and you can be charged up to $500 for each flounder in your possession. (Know the difference between fluke and flounder: the latter have small, toothless mouths, while fluke have large mouths studded with sharp teeth.)

A note about **Block Island**: the best fishing here is about 100 ft. off shore, where small bait fish get "balled up," sending blues and stripers into a perpetual feeding frenzy. You can't miss at **Great Salt Pond** (New Harbor), but ask about other popular hot spots as well. See below for rowboat rentals. There are also 300 freshwater ponds on Block, which hold large mouth bass, pickerel, perch, and pan fish.

LESSONS

The Saltwater Edge (842-0062; Wellington Plaza, 550 Thames St., Newport) Expert guides will take you saltwater fly and light tackle fishing — or teach you how to do it.

Fin & Feather Lodge (885-8680; 95 Frenchtown Rd., E. Greenwich) Free fly casting instruction Sat. 9–12, weather permitting. Canoe rentals.

RENTALS, BAIT & TACKLE

For more options on bait shops, see the section on Marinas under Sailing & Boating below, and on Marine Supplies in the *Shopping* chapter.

West Bay

John's Bait & Tackle (885-3761; 135 Frenchtown Rd., N. Kingstown)

Quaker Lane Bait & Tackle (294-9642; 4019 Quaker La./Rte. 2, N. Kingstown) The obvious plus canoe and kayak sales and rentals.

Zeek's Creek Bait & Tackle (423-1170; 194 North Rd., Jamestown) Look for Zeek's "Hook, Line & Sinker" column in *The Jamestown Press*.

East Bay

Andrade's Bait & Tackle (253-1491; 629 Metacom Ave./Rte. 136, Bristol)

Aquidneck

Edward's Fishing Tackle (846-4521; 36 Aquidneck Ave., Middletown) A

*Fishermen harvest the sea at
Brenton Point in Newport.*

Craig Hammell

complete line of fresh- and saltwater tackle, plus live and frozen bait. Also try
Sam's Bait and Tackle down the street (848-5909; 936 Aquidneck Ave.).

Block Island

Twin Maples (466-5547; Beach Ave., New Harbor) Bait, tackle, and rowboat
rentals for Great Salt Pond. They sell lobsters here, too — but come early, they
sell out.

SHELLFISHING

The commercial fishing fleet out of Galilee owes its livelihood to lobsters,
but a host of other shelled and spiny creatures can be found in RI waters as
well. Non-RI residents are required to apply for a license from the Division of
Licensing in Providence (272-3576) before harvesting shellfish (not required for
Rhode Islanders). Non-residents are allowed half a bushel of scallops, and a
quarter-bushel each of quahogs, soft-shell and surf clams, oysters, and mussels
per day (except in shellfish management areas; RI residents are allowed twice
the take on all shellfish). Ask the bait shops where to go, but good bets for
clamming always include **Escape Rd.** in Galilee, **Fogland Point** on the Sakonnet River in Tiverton, **Bissell Cove** in North Kingstown, and **Great Salt Pond**
on Block Island. All you need is a rake and a bucket and a set of rules on sizes
— you can get these at most of the bait shops above.

If it's lobsters or nothing, for $20 residents only can buy a noncommercial
lobster license (five lobster pots a day) or a lobster driving license (five lobsters
per day). Again, get a set of rules, which is also available from the Division of
Law Enforcement (277-2284). Or better yet, visitors and residents alike can
build their own lobster trap at a class offered by URI on its East Farm location

(792-6211; Rte. 108, Kingston), near the Narragansett Pier. The class costs $55; if the trap doesn't work, use it as an end table.

SEASONAL EVENTS

Snug Harbor Shark Tournament (783-7766; Snug Harbor Marina, Gooseberry Rd., S. Kingstown) A quest for prize-winning sharks of all breeds. Mid-June. Immediately followed by the **Snug Harbor June Moon Madness Striper Tournament**. This is the region's only striped bass tourney, with separate competitions for surf casters and boat anglers. Entry form from Tournament Enterprises, Dept. SH, PO Box 803, Greenville, RI 02828. Note: South Kingstown is on the other side of Pt. Judith Pond from Galilee.

Block Island Billfish Tournament (466-2982; Block Island Boat Basin) Late July.

Tuna Tournament (737-8845; North Docks, Narragansett/Galilee) 1992 was the 35th year for this event with over 100 boats and 400 anglers. Early Sept.

The Green Spartina

You couldn't mind anything that came to its own place in a regular way. The seals went north in May, the terns came in, the striped bass came up the coast in schools. Real summer was bluefish, swordfish, tuna, sharks. When the water got to sixty-five degrees or so. And in the marsh, red-winged blackbirds, meadowlarks, and swallows. The spartina grew greener, everywhere there were new wicks of bright green. . . .

The kid was filleting the fish, his rod butt in a rodholder. Not a cloud in the sky, a perfect July day on a gentle blue sea.

They went out and hauled their pots, threw away the crabs, kept a few lobster. They ate supper at dawn, Campbell's tomato soup with chunks of bluefish. Dick made a sandwich with a fried hunk of fillet in it, plenty of mayonnaise, and a cold beer.

From *Spartina* by John Casey; Alfred A. Knopf, Inc., 1989. Winner of the National Book Award, 1989. Note: spartina is a sturdy genus of saltwater marsh grass that grows along the shores of Narragansett Bay.

GOLF

Newport was a pioneer in the realm of golf as well. In 1895 the city hosted the first national open golf tournament in the U.S.

The following golf clubs, courses, and driving ranges are open to the public. For custom club design, repairs, and used and new sales, try **Ocean State Golf** (295-5511; 7360 Post Rd./Rte. 1, N. Kingstown).

West Bay

Jamestown Country Club (423-9930; E. Shore Rd., Jamestown) 9 holes, 3344 yards, par 72, carts available. Snack bar, lounge.

North Kingstown Municipal Golf Course (294-4051; Quonset Access Rd., N. Kingstown/Quonset Point) 18 holes, 6300 yards, par 70, carts available. Snack bar.

Rolling Greens (294-9859; Ten Rod Rd., N. Kingstown) 9 holes, 3059 yards, par 35, carts available. Snack bar.

Woodland Golf & Country Club (655 Old Baptist Rd., N. Kingstown) 9 holes, 3180 yards, par 70, carts available. Lounge.

East Bay

Bristol Golf Club (253-9844; 95 Tupelo St., Bristol) 9 holes, 6060 yards, par 71, carts available.

Pocasset Country Club (683-2266; 807 Bristol Ferry Rd., Portsmouth) 9 holes, 2770 yards, par 34, carts available. Restaurant, lounge.

Aquidneck

Green Valley Country Club (847-9543; 371 Union St., Portsmouth) 18 holes, 6500 yards, par 71, carts available. Restaurant, bar.

Montaup Country Club (683-9882; Anthony Rd., Portsmouth) 18 holes, 6300 yards, par 71, carts available. Dining room, bar.

Tee Time Golf Practicing Center (841-8454; 1305 W. Main Rd./Rte. 114, Middletown) A 50-station driving range with covered and grass tees. Pro shop, private lessons.

HIKING & WALKING

The most famous place to walk here is, of course, the illustrious **Cliff Walk** (see Mansions in the *Culture* chapter). This three-and-a-half-mile trail is the Cadillac of walking paths, snaking around Newport's rocky coast with the ocean on one side and mansions on the other. But there are many other choices as well. In addition to the suggestions in the State Parks & Wildlife Refuges section below, also see Museum listings in *Culture* for more sites with hiking trails. Another source is Ken Weber's excellent *Walks & Rambles in Rhode Island* series (see the Bibliography in *Information*). The seasonal listings below contain energetic events for runners too.

West Bay

Beaver Tail State Park (Jamestown) Meandering trails follow the coast from one side of the headland to the other. The western route is probably too rigorous for kids, but it's more private and the views are superb; on the eastern shore note the granite blocks chiseled in delicate floral patterns — they were destined for a building in Virginia but went down in an 1859 wreck, only to be tossed ashore in the 1938 hurricane. The whole hike (rock-scrambling makes it a hike rather than walk) is three miles.

East Bay

Haffenreffer Museum of Anthropology (Bristol) A network of mapped nature trails runs like a maze through 500 acres of woodland overlooking Mt. Hope Bay.

Aquidneck

Cliff Walk Society (849-7110) Guided tours of the famed CW. Or if meandering isn't your speed, contact the **Cliff Walk Society Fitness Walking Club** (847-8961), which meets for one-hour brisk walks on Fri. afternoons.

Norman Bird Sanctuary (Middletown) Eight miles of well-marked trails lead through a variety of wildlife habitats and some spectacular sea-view scenery.

Sakonnet

Ruecker Wildlife Refuge (Tiverton) A mild one-and-a-half-mile walk through saltwater marshes and wooded uplands; the way is well-marked.

Block Island

The Nature Conservancy (331-7110), the **Block Island Conservancy** (466-2129), and the **Block Island Resident's Association** co-sponsor a series of guided nature walks late June–mid-Sept. Each walk has a designated meeting point and takes about one and a half hours. (466-2982 for more information.)

Clayhead Nature Trail (off upper Corn Neck Rd.; look for the parking area) This superb coastal trail begins at Corn Neck Rd. and heads east to the cliffs, then turns north all the way to Settlers' Rock (see Monuments & Memorials, *Culture*) at Sandy Point. A network of secondary paths, known as The Maze, offers scenic views and scores of sea birds. These trails are privately owned, but the public is welcome to hike them for free.

The Greenway (starting point at Nathan Mott Park, off Center Rd. opposite the Airport) This is a Conservancy-maintained two-mile network of trails that leads from mid-island to the southern coast. Its primary purpose is to provide a corridor for wildlife, but the terrain and the views are so compelling that it's a refuge for people too. A highlight is Rodman's Hollow, a glacial ravine forming a cornucopia of plant and animal life. The stone walls, dense copses, and sea vistas are stunning.

SEASONAL EVENTS

Block Island Bastille Day Race (466-2982; Weldon's Way, Old Harbor) Restaurant-sponsored waiters race for prizes. Mid-July.

Block Island Triathalon (466-2982) The Chamber of Commerce has entry forms. Early Aug.

Rhode Island Marathon (861-RACE) In Providence in early Nov.

HOCKEY

The Providence Bruins (known behind their backs as the Baby Bruins — Boston's Minor League team) skate at the Civic Center in Providence throughout hockey season. More people come to see them than any other professional hockey team in the country. Join the crowd. Call 273-5000 for tickets.

HORSEBACK RIDING & POLO

The Gilded Age lingers around Newport, but not so much in the mansions as out on the fields. The City by the Sea is still the polo capital of the world, and the **Newport International Polo Series**, which began in 1886 and was resurrected in 1992, packs in the fans. Matches take place every Sat. afternoon from July through early Sept. at Glen Farm, a restored farming estate on E. Main Rd./Rte. 138 in Portsmouth. (Banners mark the spot at the head of the long drive down to the playing fields: "Team U.S.A. vs. Argentina" — or the U.K., Egypt, Italy, and India, among others). This is Olympic-level polo and is taken very seriously, though the crowd is more casual than la-de-da. For more information call 847-7090 (tickets cost about $8). If you ride and are interested in learning to play polo, see the entry for **Glen Farm** below. They claim that after only a few lessons you'll be ready for the annual **Governor's Cup Match**, held at Glen Farm in mid-Sept. (call 846-0200).

The following stables offer trail rides, indoor ring riding, and lessons.

Aquidneck

Glen Farm (847-7090; Glen Rd., Portsmouth) Polo and riding lessons, plus trails through miles of farmland, woods, and beaches. Polo scrimmages on Fri. evenings and Sun. afternoons; polo clinic on Sat.

Newport Equestrian Center (848-5440, 847-1774; 287 Third Beach Rd., Middletown) Instruction at all levels, plus indoor ring for riding year-round. In season, trail rides on the beach ($55 for two hours). Riding camp in July, Aug.

Sandy Point Stables (849-3958; Sandy Point Ave., Portsmouth) Lessons, indoor/outdoor summer riding camp, and pony parties.

Upson Downs Stables (683-0453, 683-4838; White Horse Terr., Portsmouth) Riding lessons for $12 per hour; indoor ring riding.

Sakonnet

Roseland Acres Equestrian Center, Inc. (624-8866; 594 East Rd., Tiverton) Instruction for beginning, intermediate, and advanced riders. Indoor ring, polo lessons.

Block Island

Rustic Rides (466-5060; PO Box 842, West Side Rd., Block Island) Guided trail rides on the beach, plus pony rides for children. Call for information about their off-season special: two days of riding plus two nights accommodation.

SEASONAL EVENTS

Newport Rodeo (847-7090; Glen Farm, E. Main Rd./Rte. 138, Portsmouth) This is the real thing — a Texas-style rodeo that's part of the Professional Rodeo Circuit. Bull and bronco riding, barrel racing, team penning, steer wrestling, and trick riding.

SAILING & BOATING

Newport played host to America's Cup competition for 53 years. Then in 1983 the Aussies won it away; now Cup races are held in the home sailing grounds of the San Diego Yacht Club (until they lose, note some Newporters with fingers crossed behind their backs). So the Cup is gone, and with it the international yachting set — everyone from Ted Turner to the Aga Khan — who would arrive every four years to sail, spend, drink, and play.

But there's more to the legacy of America's Cup competition in Newport than America's Cup Avenue. Today, not-for-profit institutions such as the **Sail Newport Sailing Center**, as well as the **Newport Yachting Center** and the **Museum of Yachting**, attract a steady stream of prestigious sailing events to Newport's waters — a better state of affairs, in the long run, than one big bash every four years. From the **Michelob Regatta** to **Rolex's International Women's Keelboat Championships**, there's still a lot of glamour out on the seas.

The Lessons & Rentals listings below offer suggestions for instruction and bare-boat charters (sail-it-yourself rentals). And look at the Charters section, too — there is naturally some overlap between boat rentals and crewed charter offerings. Contact the Rhode Island Tourism Division (277-2601, 800-556-2484; 7 Jackson Walkway, Providence, RI 02903) for their comprehensive pamphlet *Boating & Fishing in Rhode Island.*

The America's Cup

Capt. Nat Herreshoff, Sir Thomas Lipton, Ted Hood, Harold Vanderbilt, Dennis Connor: these are just some of the names associated with the America's Cup, the oldest international sporting competition in the world. It all began in 1851, when Britain invited other nations to race yachts around the Isle of Wight. That competition was won by *America* (hence the America's Cup), whereupon the U.S. achieved a stranglehold on the once-every-four-years competition. Thomas Lipton (of tea fame) had to grin and bear it as all five of his *Shamrocks* were beaten by American defenders (*Shamrock IV* came the closest in 1920, but *Resolute*, skippered by Charles Francis Adams, came from behind to win). From 1893, when the daring design of *Vigilant* revolutionized yacht racing, through *Resolute* in 1920, all of the America's Cup defenders were designed and built by Capt. Nat Herreshoff at the Herreshoff Boatyard in Bristol (see *Culture* for more on the Herreshoff Museum and its new America's Cup Hall of Fame). Cup racing first came to Rhode Island waters in 1930 when the New York Yacht Club moved to Newport; it left with the Australians in 1983. The rest, as they say, is history.

The spirit of America's Cup racing lives on in Newport.

Craig Hammell

LESSONS & RENTALS

West Bay

Bob's Boat, Bait & Tackle (295-8845; 23 Brown St., N. Kingstown/Wickford) Sailing lessons.

Greenwich Bay Sailing Association (885-1231, 884-7700; East Greenwich Yacht Club, E. Greenwich) Offers a four-week beginner program for adults ($250), plus classes for kids, private lessons.

Mill Cove Yacht Sales and Charters (295-0504; 1 Phillips St., N. Kingstown/ Wickford) All levels of instruction on your boat or theirs. Also rents lasers and sunfish, and 16-ft. powerboats daily, plus 22- and 42-ft. sailboats either bare-boat or crewed. They'll sell you one, too.

West Bay Sailing (885-4532; Box 757, E. Greenwich) Lessons.

Aquidneck

The Recreation Department of Newport (in conjunction with Sail Newport) offers children's sailing lessons for $10 per four-week session. Call 846-1398.

Captain Ben Milam (353-4661; Goat Island, Newport) Capt. Milam offers a two-day, live-aboard course on his 30-ft. sailboat; champagne, breakfast, and lunch are included. $275 per person, June–Oct.

J. World Sailing School (849-5492; 24 Mill St., Newport) All levels of instruction, from beginning to championship racing. A weekend course costs $295.

Island Marine Yacht Charters (849-4820; PO Box 1230, Newport) Small boat rentals, repairs, and rides; also long or short term crewed charters on yachts up to 150 ft.

Long Wharf Yacht Charters (849-2210; Long Wharf Marina, off America's Cup Ave., Newport) Bare-boat rentals plus sport fishing and cruising charters; they also offer catering, and a B&B — see *Lodging*.

Museum of Yachting (see *Culture*) Educational programs include a school of yacht restoration, and courses in offshore navigation, celestial navigation, yacht design for sailors, and yacht surveying.

Newport-Barrington Sailing School & Cruises (246-1595; 5 Beaver Rd., Barrington 02806) Nine- and 13-hour sailing courses; cruises of the Bay. Apr.–Oct.

Newport Harbor Marine Charters (847-0703; PO Box 1454, Goat Island, Newport) Power- and sailboats up to 100 ft., either bare-boat or crewed. Also nine-ft. dinghies and daysailers for rent.

Oldport Marine Services, Inc. (847-9109; Market Sq., Newport) Sailing lessons.

Oldport Charter (846-5599; Sayer's Wharf, off Thames St., Newport) Offers sail- or powerboats from 28 to 50 ft., bare-boat or crewed. 20-ft. daysailer for rent.

Sail Newport Sailing Center (849-8385, 846-1983; Fort Adams State Park, off Harrison Ave., Newport) This non-profit group formed to preserve Newport's sailing tradition after the loss of America's Cup in 1983, and to promote public recreational sailing. Offerings include sailboat, rentals, tours, private and group instruction, and special events (see below). Open May–Oct.

Sight Sailing of Newport (849-3333; Bowen's Wharf, off America's Cup Ave., Newport) 23-ft. sloop rentals; 10-hour sailing courses.

Womanship (800-342-9295, Newport) Sailing lessons for and by women. Beginning classes offered from June–Oct. in three-, five-, and seven-day live-aboard programs. Special weekend courses, too.

Block Island

Block Island Club (466-5939; PO Box 147, Corn Neck Rd.) Sailing, windsurfing, swimming, tennis, and children's activities: they offer one-, two-, and three-week memberships.

Island Hobie Cat Rentals (466-5338; Cooneymus Rd., West Side)

MARINAS

These marinas offer public docking slips and/or moorings on and around Narragansett Bay. Most have "full service" facilities, which generally include electrical hookups, gas, diesel, and propane, bilge pumps, fresh water, ice, and telephone (those that are lacking are noted). Most have more, including a marine store, toilets, showers, and other amenities. Call for specifics, and to see if you'll need a reservation in high season.

West Bay

Anchorage is available in Point Judith Pond (a quiet, well-dredged basin — the **Rhode Island State Pier** at Galilee is here too), and there are three guest moorings behind the breakwaters in Wickford's outer harbor. Off Jamestown the best anchorage is in Jamestown Harbor, south of the ferry landing.

State and municipal launching sites abound on the Bay, such as this one at Jamestown Harbor.

Craig Hammell

Conanicut Marina (423-1556; 1 Ferry Wharf, Jamestown Harbor) 15 guest slips, 20 guest moorings; full repairs.

Jamestown Boatyard (423-0600; Racquet Rd., Jamestown) Five guest slips; full repairs (not many other amenities). Near Fort Wetherill State Park.

Long Cove Marina (783-4902; Old Pt. Judith Rd., RR#9, Box 76, Narragansett) 45 guest slips.

Pleasant Street Wharf (294-2791; 160 Pleasant St., N. Kingstown/Wickford) One guest slip, two guest moorings; minor repair work.

Wickford Bait & Tackle (295-8845; 1 Phillips St., N. Kingstown/Wickford) One guest slip; repairs. Bait and tackle.

Wickford Cove Marina (884-7014; Reynolds St., N. Kingstown/Wickford) Transient slips available; engine, hull, rigging repairs.

Wickford Shipyard (294-3361; 125 Steamboat Ave., N. Kingstown/Wickford) 12 guest slips; inner harbor.

East Bay

There are three state guest moorings at the extreme head of **Bristol Harbor** and a state pier on the eastern shore; you can also anchor in the **Warren River** (middle of Smith Cove).

Aquidneck

Potter's Cove off **Prudence Island** offers three state guest moorings — it's one of the best undeveloped anchorage sites in Narragansett Bay; there are five more state guest moorings off Prudence Bay Island Park, but these tend to be crowded. In **Newport Harbor** look for four state guest moorings on the south shore of Brenton Cove at the entrance to the smaller, inner cove, but the quietest anchorage is further out toward the head. Anchor south of the orange ball buoys between Fort Adams and the Newport Gas Co.

Bannister's Wharf (846-4500; Bannister's Wharf, off Thames St., Newport) 35 guest slips.

Brewer's Sakonnet Marina (683-3551; Narragansett Blvd., Portsmouth) 15 guest slips; the Hummocks area, northeastern Aquidneck.

Brown & Howard Marina (846-5100 in season, 274-6611 out-of-season) Transient and seasonal dockage for boats up to 250 ft., plus parking.

Christie's Landing (847-5400; Christie's Landing, off Thames St., Newport) 35 guest slips.

East Passage Yachting Center (683-4000, 800-922-2930; 1 Lagoon Rd., off W. Main Rd./Rte. 114, Portsmouth) On the grounds of the Navy's old PT Boat training ground (the Melville Grille & Lagoon Bar is also here; see *Restaurants*), this bills itself as the state's largest and most secure marina. Many guest slips; reservations accepted; all the usual amenities, plus shuttle van service to Newport.

Boats of all shapes and sizes in dry dock at the East Passage Yachting Center in Portsmouth.

Craig Hammell

Goat Island Marina, Inc. (849-5655; Goat Island, Newport) Guest slips and the usual.

Newport Harbor Hotel & Marina (847-9000 and 800-955-2558; 49 America's Cup Ave., Newport) 100 guest slips with all the works; engine, electrical, and minor hull repairs.

Newport Onshore Ltd. (849-0480; 379 Thames St., Newport) 75 guest slips.

Newport Yachting Center (847-9047; PO Box 549, America's Cup Ave., Newport) 3000 linear feet of guest slips. The NYC is a very active organization that sponsors many top-flight events (the Chowder Festival among them)

Pirate Cove Marina, Inc. (683-3030; 109 Point Rd., Portsmouth) Five guest slips, five guest moorings; full repairs. Island Park, northeastern side of Aquid-neck.

Stone Bridge Marina (683-1011; 41 Point Rd., Portsmouth) Two guest slips (nice view of the old Stone Bridge, at the foot of 15 Point Rd. Restaurant; see *Restaurants*). Island Park, northeast Aquidneck.

Sakonnet

There are several anchorage spots along the Sakonnet River. In Tiverton try the east shore (watch the strong current between the bridges in Tiverton Harbor); also try Fogland Harbor, though it's not particularly sheltered on the northern side. Sachuest Cove in the lower river is good except in north or east winds.

Block Island

Block Island Boat Basin (466-2631; PO Box 412, New Harbor) 100 guest slips.

Champlin's Marina (466-2641; New Harbor) 125 guest slips (it's part of a large marine and motel complex, so there's lots here, from tennis courts to a bakery).

Payne's New Harbor Dock (466-5572; New Harbor) 50 guest slips; try Dead Eye Dick's, the restaurant on the dock (see *Restaurants*).

Smuggler's Cove Marina (466-2828; New Harbor) 14 slips.

Town Moorings (466-5002; New Harbor) Moorings on a first-come, first-served basis; opposite Champlin's.

Town of New Shoreham Dock (466-2526; Old Harbor) 40 guest slips, right in the heart of things. Moorings in Old Harbor can get crowded.

SEASONAL SAILING & BOATING EVENTS

A representative selection of sailing events; any copy of the free publication *Best Read Guide: Newport* will give you more.

Annapolis to Newport Race (846-1000; New York Yacht Club, Halidon Ave., Newport) Early to mid-June.

Classic Yacht Regatta (847-1018; Museum of Yachting, Fort Adams State Park, Newport) A great chance to see the old beauties afloat. Early Sept.

Fool's Rules Regatta (423-1492; Jamestown Yacht Club, East Ferry Beach, Jamestown) 1993 was the 15th year of this silly sailing event. Construct your boat at 9am on the beach; use anything but standard marine materials; then race it 500 yards beginning at 11. Late August.

Newport International Boat Show (846-1600; Newport Yachting Center, America's Cup Ave., Newport) With over 300 boats and 400 accessory displays, this is the largest sail- and powerboat show in the Northeast. Catch the special promos, including free harbor cruises. Mid-Sept.

The Newport International Boat Show is the largest in the Northeast.

Courtesy Newport Yachting Center

Newport Regatta (846-1983; Sail Newport Sailing Center, Fort Adams State Park, Newport) 1994 is the 10th anniversary of this immensely popular, Michelob-sponsored event. Racing for 300 boats and 1500 people, plus socializing in the park afterwards. Mid-July.

New York Yacht Club's Annual Regatta (846-1000; New York Yacht Club, Halidon Ave., Newport) Open to IMS yachts. 1994 is their 140th year. Mid-June.

Rolex International Women's Keelboat Championship (846-1969; Sail Newport Sailing Center, Fort Adams State Park, Newport) Biennial event hosted by the Ida Lewis Yacht Club. Women-only teams from all over the world race in 40 to 50 J/24-class sailboats. Mid-Sept.

Craig Hammell

Boats find shelter at the Ida Lewis Yacht Club in Newport Harbor.

Block Island Race Week

This event began in 1965 with a good idea and a couple of entries; today Block Island Race Week is the largest sailing event on the East Coast. Over 5000 people wash up on the little island in over 300 sleek racing machines to compete in a score of different events, the highlight of which is the mid-week "Round the Island Race." By night there's a happy, noisy, carnival atmosphere; by day it looks like a rainbow has been ironed flat and stretched along the horizon — 360-degree views of brilliantly colored sails. For more information call the Storm Trysail Club, 846-1983; 914-834-8857. Held the last week in June.

Sail Newport Regatta for the Blind (846-1983; Sail Newport Sailing Center, Fort Adams State Park, Newport) Six teams compete; the skipper of each boat must be blind or visually impaired. Late Aug.

Sail Newport Sailing Festival (846-1983; Sail Newport Sailing Center, Fort Adams State Park, Newport) This free sailing event — harbor cruises offered on the rental fleet of J/22s and Rhodes 19s — has kicked off each summer sailing season for almost 10 years. The Museum of Yachting (next door) is free to anyone with a Sail Newport pass. The annual Barbecue Bash ($10 adults, $6 children) rounds out the day. The **Bank of Newport Memorial Day Regatta** is also held. Memorial Day weekend.

Wooden Boat Show (846-1600; Newport Yachting Center, 4 Commercial Wharf, off America's Cup Ave., Newport) The largest wooden boat show in the U.S. On land and in the water, 200 featured craft, plus demos, races, regatta, and children's boat-building lessons. Late June.

Green Bell #11

The place is unpromisingly called the Dumplings, guarded by Green Bell #11 lit at two-and-a-half-second intervals and moored in 165 feet of East Passage briny. There, afloat, I home in, and I can't recall a time, coming or going, when I've been unhappy to see that buoy.

. . . Within sight of Green Bell #11 I can hear B.B. King singing "I Got Some Outside Help (I Don't Really Need)" from the stage at Fort Adams , and hear (if the wind is just right) Miles Davis play with his back turned to the Jazz Festival crowd, and marvel at how lucky I am to listen for free (if you put aside the monthly payments and upkeep on my little pocket yacht), and get bombed by beer-filled balloons shot from a neighboring boat's water-cannon.

. . . And it isn't all downhill and upwind because where else but within sight of Green Bell #11 am I going to see Shamrock *play with* Endeavor*, while cruisers watch from the fantail of the* Q.E. Two*. . . .*

From *41'28"N. by 71'21"W.* by Geoffrey Wolff; a short essay published in *Rhode Island Monthly*, Jan. 1991.

STATE PARKS & WILDLIFE REFUGES

State parks are open from sunrise to sunset; naturalists are on duty only during summer months. Pets must be on leashes; toilets are usually available. For more on state parks contact the **Department of Environmental Management, Division of Parks and Recreation** (277-2632; 2321 Hartford Ave.,

State parks and picnic groves offer a variety of amenities, including observation towers, like this one on Rte. 1 in South Kensington.

Craig Hammell

Johnston 02919). At wildlife refuges, surf casting is allowed but no bicycles, motor vehicles, or kites. For more information call the Refuge Manager, 364-9124. A word of warning about **ticks**: wear protective clothing and *always* check for them afterward. Wood ticks are common, especially after paths have been mowed, but the tiny deer tick is the one to watch out for (the carrier of Lyme disease).

Narragansett Bay is a naturalist's dream: its rocky shores, coastal wetlands, and rolling dunes shelter hosts of indigenous and migratory animals. Environmental watch-dog groups, especially **Save The Bay**, preserve its integrity (and have helped restore it as well); for information on their programs contact them at 434 Smith St., Providence 02908 (272-3540). The highest preservation accolades, however, go to **Block Island**, named by the Nature Conservancy as "One of the 12 Last Great Places in the Western Hemisphere." The long-standing efforts of islanders to conserve open space and resist the temptations of tourism have been rewarded: the island remains home to 40 rare and endangered species, including some unique to Block Island. It used to call itself "The Bermuda of the North" — now it's become "Nature's Treasure on the Sea." For more on Block and the Bay, see Bird-Watching, and Hiking & Walking.

West Bay

Beaver Tail State Park (423-9941; Jamestown) At the southern tip of Conanicut Island, Beaver Tail is one of the best places in the state to set a Gothic romance: rocky, windswept, beautiful. **Beaver Tail Light** (see *Culture*) guards the point.

Fort Wetherill State Park (243-1771; Jamestown) From here look across the Bay to Fort Adams; both former military installations are still standing guard at the entrance to RI. Wetherill is on a small peninsula at the southeastern end of Jamestown; it offers a rocky shoreline, paths, and terrific views.

Goddard State Park (884-2010; Ives Rd., E. Greenwich) Right on Greenwich Bay, the park offers swimming, bathhouses, fishing, golfing, hiking trails, boat rentals, game fields, picnic areas, and a nature program.

East Bay

Colt State Park (253-7482; Hope St./Rte. 114, Bristol) This Bay beach park on the site of the former Colt estate and casino has a fishing pier, boat launches, bike and walking trails through woods and along the water, a sculpture garden, playgrounds, a 60-ft. observation tower in a converted silo, and a scenic, rocky coast. $4 parking fee.

Aquidneck

Exploring Brenton Point State Park on foot.

Craig Hammell

Brenton Point State Park (846-8240; Ocean Dr., Newport) Superb ocean views plus picnic tables, fishing, and a visitor center with a full schedule of nature programs. The sculptures are a monument to Portuguese navigators.

Fort Adams State Park (847-2400; off Harrison Ave., Newport) On the tip of the peninsula that shelters Newport Harbor, Fort Adams not only boasts the old fort (see Military Sites, *Culture*), but the best views in the state — to one side is the Harbor, the other Jamestown and the Bay. Swimming, fishing, boating, picnicking. Sail Newport Sailing Center and the Museum of Yachting are also here. $4 entrance fee.

Norman Bird Sanctuary (846-2577; Third Beach Rd., Middletown) Spy birds and other wildlife on 465 acres marked out by eight miles of trails. The reserve overlooks the sea and includes Hanging Rock — a natural wonder where Bishop Berkeley used to sit and meditate (see Whitehall House, *Culture*); you can see Hanging Rock from Second Beach Rd. Nature study programs year-round (and a Jonnycake Breakfast in May). Trail fee, $2.

Purgatory Chasm Not a state park or refuge, but worth seeing: where Paradise Ave. ends at Second Beach Rd. (also known as Purgatory Rd.), you'll see the Hanging Rock to your left and a small sign for Purgatory Chasm to the right. Park and follow the path to the sea: the chasm is a narrow cleft in the cliffs overlooking the ocean.

Sachuest Point National Wildlife Refuge (364-9124; follow Second Beach Rd. south to the right to land's end at Sachuest, Middletown) Impossible to believe that Newport is just two promontories away. This 242-acre refuge offers a three-mile maze of hiking trails (like green tunnels in summer) studded with wildflowers. Terrain includes salt marshes, grasslands, beaches, rocky cliffs, brushlands, and dunes — all resting areas for migratory birds. Visitor center; free.

Sakonnet

Ruecker National Wildlife Refuge (624-2759; Seapowet Ave., Tiverton) This 48-acre refuge offers hiking trails that wind through woodlands and an unforgettable salt marsh that's a habitat for herons, egrets, and osprey. Managed by the Audubon Society of Rhode Island. Free.

Block Island

Block Island National Wildlife Refuge (364-9124; Corn Neck Rd.) A 47-acre refuge of sandy beaches and rolling dunes at the tip of the Neck, on the western shore of Sachem Pond; look for herons, woodcock, osprey, cowbirds, and many other migratory birds. In summer it's a haven for tiger, swallowtail, and cabbage butterflies. No facilities; free.

Mohegan Bluffs (off Mohegan Trail on the southeast side of the island) Not part of a refuge or park system, but are simply magnificent sea cliffs — at nearly 200 towering feet, the highest in New England. The view is spectacular (and the nearest landfall is Africa). A famous battle took place here nearly five centuries ago between the Manisseeans and invading Mohegans: the latter lost and were pitched from the bluffs which still bear their name.

TENNIS

As a pastime, tennis is centuries old, the original "Sport of Kings" played indoors on court tennis courts. As an American institution, however, outdoor lawn tennis began at Newport. The first National Tennis Championship was held at the Newport Casino, now **the International Tennis Hall of Fame**, in 1881, where it remained until 1915 when the tournament moved to Forest Hills, NY. (Now it's ensconced in Flushing Meadows as that great Labor Day event, the U.S. Open.)

This doesn't mean that the Hall of Fame's 13 immaculate grass courts — incidentally, the only competition grass courts available for play in the country — lie languishing. Two major tournaments are held here each summer (see Seasonal Events below). If you feel your tennis togs (and your pocketbook) are up to it, book one of the grass beauties as a holiday treat, or call town halls for the location of municipal courts. Also see *Lodging* for inns, hotels, and B&Bs with tennis courts; these are often available to the public for a fee.

Aquidneck

International Tennis Hall of Fame (849-3990, 846-0642; Newport Casino, 194 Bellevue Ave., Newport) For information on the Hall of Fame and Newport Casino see Museums in *Culture*. Rent one of 13 historic grass courts from mid-May through early Oct. at $35 per person per 90 min. period; have your serve speed clocked by radar. Hard courts are a bargain at $20 per court per 90 min. Lessons are also available at $50 an hr. Pro shop. Wear white.

Tennis Indoor Club (849-4777; Memorial Blvd., Newport) $25 per hour per court. Regular hours are 6:30am–2pm, but if you reserve ahead they'll stay open for you.

Block Island

Block Island Club (see Sailing above).

SEASONAL EVENTS

While it's tempting to sit courtside at tournaments at the Newport Casino/Int'l Tennis Hall of Fame, go for the cheaper bleacher seats. The view is just as good, and if it's a hot July in Newport, the bleachers are the only place where you can catch a breeze. Bring a cooler plus seat pads, hats, sunscreen, and — this is a brilliant idea — old hairspray bottles filled with water to spritz yourself and others. All of the events below take place at the **International Tennis Hall of Fame**: see information above.

Miller Lite Hall of Fame Tennis Championships. The only professional men's tournament played on grass in the U.S. As part of the IBM/ATP tour it's an important stop, but doesn't draw top names — players are afraid of grass these days. Nonetheless, the quality of play is high. Early to mid-July.

Tennis Hall of Fame Enshrinement Ceremony. Held on semi-finals day (Sat.) of the Virginia Slims and Miller Lite tourneys, this hour-long event (speeches and exhibition matches) honors recent inductees. It's worth going just to see what Bud Collins will wear. Mid-July.

Tennis Hall of Fame Expo & Fair. Exhibits from the makers of top tennis accouterments. Mid- to late June.

Virginia Slims Hall of Fame International. Not the big Newport Virginia Slims tournament of yore, with the likes of Martina and Chris; it's now a four-day special event that attracts mid-ranking players. But you can't go wrong watching Pam Shriver and Zina Garrison-Jackson whack the ball. Early to mid-July.

TOURS

A diverse range of tours by air, sea, land, and on foot are noted below. The boats listed here offer sightseeing cruises with regularly scheduled departures; see Charters and Sailing & Boating for other sailing options. For Historic Walking Tours, see the Historic Buildings & Sites section of *Culture*.

BY AIR

Island Air Tours (884-3489, 800-Island Air; Newport State Airport, Middletown) Get a bird's-eye view of the mansions, the Harbor, and the Bay from the cockpit of a seaplane. Custom tours available.

Newport Helicopters, Inc. (846-8877; Newport State Airport, Middletown) Videographers, this is how you can get great footage of Newport; tours start at about $60.

BY BOAT

Block Island Harbor Cruises (466-2474; Champlin's Marina, New Harbor) Three tours of the Salt Pond daily aboard the *Debonair*. See Meals on Water etc. in *Restaurants* for information on the dinner cruise.

Southland (783-2954; Galilee Cruises, Inc., PO Box 522, Narragansett) Daily one hour and 45 minute tours of Galilee, Point Judith, and Jerusalem aboard this 64-ft. two-decker. Leaves daily (early spring–fall) from State Pier 3, Galilee; 11am, 1, 3, 5pm.

Spirit of Newport (849-3575; Newport Navigation, PO Box 3316, Newport) Departs every 90 min. for a one-hour cruise of the Bay and Harbor. Biggest boat in town — seats 200, with full bar. Leaves from the Newport Harbor Hotel & Marina (see *Lodging*) off America's Cup Ave.

Viking Queen (847-6921; Viking Tours, PO Box 330, Newport) Sail aboard the 140-passenger *Viking Queen* for a one-hour cruise of Newport. Tickets at Boat Dock, Goat Island.

Newport Sailboat Harbor Tours (683-2738, 246-1595; Goat Island, Newport) Scenic tours of the Bay and Harbor aboard 22- to 33-ft. auxiliary sloops. Goes right by the mansions. Apr.–Oct.

Oldport Marine Harbor Tours (849-2111, 847-9109; Sayer's Wharf off America's Cup Ave.) One-hour narrated cruises of Newport Harbor and lower Narragansett Bay.

Sight Sailing of Newport (849-3333; 22 White Terrace, Middletown) Board at Bowen's Wharf: daily sailing tours of the Bay and Harbor (one and two hours, or half and full day excursions).

Adventure (849-4820; Adventure Watersports, 2 Bowen's Landing, Newport) One-hour cruises six times daily; for $15 you can cruise Newport Harbor and get a crash-course sailing lesson.

Yankee Boat Peddlers (847-0298, reservations 849-3033; Christie's Landing, off Thames St., Newport) Four two-hour sailing cruises daily aboard the 70-ft. schooner *Madeleine*. Approximately $20 per person.

BY CAR OR BUS

Art's Island Tours (846-7880; 6 Barney St., Newport) Bus tours of Newport; cassette tapes for touring in your car also available ($7 with $20 deposit).

Driving Cassette Tape Tour of Newport (849-8048; Gateway Visitors' Bureau, 23 America's Cup Ave., Newport) Pick up one of these at the Visitors' Bureau and pop it in: a narrated tour of the mansions and Ocean Drive, complete with sound effects. (Good luck sticking to the right speed.)

The Paper Lion (846-5777; 24 Long Wharf Mall, off America's Cup Ave., Newport) Another auto tape tour of the City by the Sea. You can rent a tape player and cassette for the day, or order ahead by mail and get the tape (and map) for keeps for about $12.

Viking Bus Tours of Newport (847-6921; Gateway Visitors' Bureau, 23 America's Cup Ave., Newport) Narrated motorcoach tours (air-conditioned!) of colonial Newport, Bellevue Ave., and Ocean Drive. Departs daily 9:30, 11:30, 1:30.

ON FOOT

Cliff Walk Tours (848-5308) Guided walking tours of the famous three-and-a-half-mile path past the mansions, tailored to your interests. Some include box lunches or a stop at a four-star restaurant. 90-minute tours cost $100 for groups of 2 to 25.

Jane S. Jacques (884-8805; 30 Longfellow Dr., N. Kingstown) Custom-prepared tour guide service to Newport or elsewhere.

BY RAIL

Old Colony and Newport Railroad (624-6951; America's Cup Ave., Newport) The station is directly across from the Gateway Visitors' Bureau (this is the same line that serves the Star Clipper Dinner Train — see *Restaurants*).

Gaze at the Bay from 1890s-era parlor cars as the 1912 diesel chugs eight miles up the Bay to Portsmouth and back.

WATER SPORTS

There's no better way to explore Narragansett Bay's rocky coves than by kayak.

Craig Hammell

This section highlights sports in the water rather than on the water (here's hoping your sailing experiences don't fall into the former category). Fans of **Surfing, Windsurfing, Kayaking, Snorkeling, Scuba,** even **Parasailing** will all find something to keep them busy. It's easy to find lessons, sales, and rentals.

Divers will be heartened to hear that pros consider Narragansett Bay *the* place for some of the best dives in New England. There are two excellent spots off Jamestown, both with ample parking (important when lugging gear). **Fort Wetherill State Park** has two sheltered, southern coves and a rocky drop-off; look for flounder, tautog, eels, and squid. Nearby **Beaver Tail State Park** is also good though there's less visibility underwater (it's more exposed); rocky bottom, lots of seaweed and fish.

Surfers, listen up: WBRU (95.5 FM) broadcasts daily surf reports at 8:35am. The best surfing beaches are **Narragansett Town Beach** and **Second Beach** in Middletown (give **Easton [First] Beach** in Newport a try, too).

West Bay

Free surfing lessons are offered on **Narragansett Town Beach** mid-June–Labor Day. Weds. at noon (call The Watershed, 789-1954, for more information). The instructor's name is Peter Pan. (If you wait for not-so-great weather; you might get an individual lesson.)

The waters of Narragansett Bay offer some of the best diving in New England.

Craig Hammell

Anderson's Ski and Dive Center (884-1310; 97 Frenchtown Rd., E. Greenwich) Free diving lessons, if you are at least 12.

Ocean State Scuba, Inc. (423-1662, 800-933-DIVE; 23A Narragansett Ave., Jamestown) Diving rentals, sales, lessons, and boat dive charters. Also surf kayaking equipment — they call it "seagoing mountain biking."

Shark Watching (884-9115; Narragansett/Point Judith) Listed here because there is no separate category for insane ideas. Capt. Charlie Donilon will take 12 people for 10 hrs. on his 30-ft. boat *The Snapper*; some 30 miles out he baits the water and lowers you in a cage to get an up close and personal peek at the monsters. $670 per trip.

Warm Winds (789-9040; 26 Kingstown Rd., Narragansett Pier) Bodyboarding center plus athletic wear for men and women.

East Bay

East Bay Dive Center, Inc. (247-2420; 8 Church St., Warren) A complete diving facility with sales, service, rentals, instruction.

Aquidneck

Adventure Sports (2 Bowen's Landing, off America's Cup Ave., Newport) They do it all: rentals of bikes, motor scooters, powerboats, seacycles, sailboats, kayaks, and fishing rods; they also offer charters, lessons, guided tours, diving trips.

Alpine Ski & Sports (849-3330; Bellevue Plaza, off Bellevue Ave., Newport) Sales, rentals, and repair of diving equipment; lessons.

Atlantic Outfitters (848-2920; 17 Bowen's Wharf, off America's Cup Ave.,

Newport) This is the place to go for sea and surf kayaking — sales, rentals, and demos (surf kayaking refers to the sit-on-top style).

Dolphin Diving Services (848-9064; 26 Sherman St., Newport) Take personal diving lessons with a certified instructor from Brazil.

Island Windsurfing Sports (846-4421; 86 Aquidneck Ave., Middletown) They offer surfing, windsurfing, waterskiing, snorkeling, and boogieboard rentals, lessons, and sales. Also for sale are bikes, roller blades, and snowboards — plus active wear and limited volleyball and tennis equipment. Very hip and cool.

Newport Diving Center (847-9293, 800-DIVING-0; 550 Thames St., Newport) A true diver's haven, with gear, lessons, charters, repairs.

Ocean State Dive Charters and Instructions (683-3444; East Passage Yachting Center, Lagoon Rd., off W. Main Rd./Rte. 114, Portsmouth) Dive charters to RI, MA, CT, and NY; also night and lobster dives. Water pick-up service available. All levels of dive instruction and certification.

Redney's Surf Shop (846-2280; 89 Aquidneck Ave., Middletown) Surf and boogieboard sales and rentals plus men's and women's beachwear. They have a surf condition hotline — call 841-5160.

Water Brothers Surf & Sport (849-4990; 39 Memorial Blvd., Newport) Surf and skateboard sales and rentals with clothing and accessories.

Block Island

Block Island Club (see Sailing above).

Block Island Parasail (466-2474; PO Box 727, Old Harbor) The Parasail people's slogan is "Stay dry while you fly!" — you take off and land from the boat's deck.

SEASONAL EVENTS

Surfing Championships (789-1954) Rated ESA member competitions for all ages at First (Easton) Beach in Newport, and Narragansett Town Beach in Narragansett Pier. Call for dates.

Swim the Bay (272-3540) Swimmers have been breaststroking their way from Newport to Jamestown for almost 20 years now. Check-in is at 9, starting time is at 11am for this two-mile swim across the Bay — you get lunch on the beach when you finish. Pre-registration is mandatory. Mid-Aug.

WHALE-WATCHING

Don't miss the opportunity to go out and see the big fellas here: humpbacks, finbacks, right whales (the rarest on the Atlantic seaboard) and tiny minke whales are all to be seen in Rhode Island waters — not to mention sharks, dolphins, sea turtles, and a host of birds. All whale-watching cruises leave from the Galilee docks in Narragansett (see the Charter listings above), and take an average of five hours. The season runs from July through early Sept., and each trip costs approx. $30 per adult. No matter how hot it is on the mainland, be sure to take a sweater or windbreaker — temperatures will drop at sea. Also bring a camera, sunglasses, a hat or scarf, and sunscreen. Most boats provide food and beverages.

GRAB BAG

miscellany of fun things to do, many ideal for kids.

West Bay

Adventure Land (789-0030; Point Judith Rd./Rte. 108, Narragansett) The only miniature golf course in RI with waterfalls and caves and islands. Also bumper boats, batting cages, and a state-of-the-art go-kart track.

Canopy Club (294-2021; 7835 Post Rd./Rte. 1, N. Kingstown) Darts! Tues.–Sun. 4pm–1am, with a tournament Sat. night.

Fiddlesticks (295-1519; 1300 Ten Rod Rd., N. Kingstown) Miniature golf; a pail of balls costs 3 bucks. Also baseball and softball batting cages.

Frosty Drew Observatory (No phone: Ninigret Park, Charlestown) Not quite on the Bay, but very close by: pick a clear Fri. night and go see the stars — best time is when the moon is in its first quarter. For general astronomical news call Sky Hotline (726-1328), for information on meteor showers, comets, what ever is up there.

Kingston Balloon Company (783-9386; Kingston) Kingston isn't a Bay town, but this is too good to leave out: flights start an hour before sundown for a balloon's eye view of sunset over the Bay. About $200 per person.

Narragansett Bowhunters (295-7228; 1531 Ten Rod Rd./Rte. 102, N. Kingstown) Archery: indoor league Sun. afternoon and Mon. nights plus free beginner instruction Sun. 9–12.

Narragansett Ocean Club (783-6120; 360 South Pier Rd., Narragansett Pier) Indoor roller skating with loud music and shrieks.

East Bay

Country Dance Instruction (253-1010; King Philip Inn, 400 Metacom Ave./Rte. 136, Bristol) Certified dance instructors will show you how to do the

Texas Two-Step in the King Philip's Massasoit Room (see *Lodging*). Wear your boots if you've got 'em.

Ernie's American Karate Academy (253-6409; 20 Gooding Ave., Bristol) Self-defense instruction in American-style karate; weight room too.

Greg's Skate Rental (431-1030 days, 245-7522 nights; 240 Market St., Warren) Inline skate rentals with equipment.

Kiddko (245-0044; 632 Metacom Ave./Rte. 136, Warren) Video games, kiddie rides, pool tables, and junk food.

Aquidneck

Children's Night (846-1398; Newport Recreation Department) Every Thurs. evening in season at 6:30pm — free entertainment with music, magic, puppets, and stories.

Old Tyme Photos (846-1433; 404 Thames St., Newport) Dress up in Victorian togs and look silly in a sepia-toned photo. A great twist on the family portrait.

Newport Butterfly Farm (846-3148) Two 12-ft. flight areas house over 25 species of native "flutter-bys" bred by Marc Schenck, who will lead you on a personal one-and-a-half-hour tour of his unusual farm; he also sells monarch, swallowtail, and caterpillar garden kits. Call for a reservation and avoid wearing strong perfume (attracts bees) or red (the butterflies love it and will roost on you).

Ryan Family Amusement Center (849-9990; 105 Chases La., off Rte. 114 behind Ames Shopping Center, Middletown; also 846-5774; 266 Thames St., Newport) Miniature golf, bowling (see Bowling above), video games, and a sports pub.

Jai Alai

Jai Alai (pronounced Hi-a-lie) means "Merry Festival." It's a fast-paced game played with a basket that players fasten to their forearms, used for catching the ball and whipping it against the wall. It has also been well described as "handball at 100 mph." Jai Alai originated in the Basque region of Spain, though it's mainly played today in Latin America — plus the Jai Alai frontons in Rhode Island, Florida, and Connecticut. The idea is to bet on different players as you would on a horse race. Speaking of which, **Newport Jai Alai** (849-5000, 800-556-6900; 150 Admiral Kalbfus Rd., Newport) also offers live, simulcast racing from tracks all over the country. And these aren't the only ways to win (or, it must be said, lose) money: there are over 400 video poker and video blackjack games to boot. The Newport Jai Alai fronton is at the foot of the Newport Bridge (free admission coupons are generally available at the **Gateway Visitors' Bureau** on America's Cup Ave.).

CHAPTER SEVEN

Not a Mall in Sight
SHOPPING

Many years ago Lincoln Steffens said that Rhode Island was a state for sale — cheap. While that may still be the case in some quarters (the banking and credit union scandals of recent years come to mind), today the towns around Narragansett Bay have set up shop for themselves, selling everything from antique scrimshaw to costume jewelry, hip clothing, bodyboards, and T-shirts. Lots and lots of T-shirts. And very little is cheap.

Not surprisingly, Newport dominates the pack when it comes to shopping. The town is brimming with stores of all description, but be warned that the turnover rate is ferocious. Rents are high and many little

Craig Hammell

Master furniture-maker Jeffrey Greene crafts pieces "fit for the 18th-century home," which he displays at his Wickford shop The Ball & Claw.

boutiques can't sustain the swings of a seasonal economy; the same, to a lesser degree, is true of Block Island. The shops listed below are examples of the kinds of stores typical of the area; it's inevitable that some of them will be history by the time you visit. On the other hand there are some constants, including the gift shops at historic houses and museums; a selection of these are also noted below. Museum shops often have unusual items of excellent quality unavailable anywhere else. Some of us always look forward to shopping at the end of every cultural experience.

Newport may be conveniently organized into distinct shopping areas. **Belle-**

Thames Street shopping.

Craig Hammell

vue Avenue shops tend to be fairly swanky, with superb commercial architecture along the Casino block — though there's an Almacs supermarket directly across from the Tennis Hall of Fame, and Bellevue Plaza is home to chains like Alpine Ski and Sport, and Radio Shack. **Thames Street** has a dual personality: upper Thames, from Washington Park to Trinity Church, can give the impression that Newport has cornered the market on T-shirt shops, while lower Thames attracts interesting boutiques with quality wares. The shops along the wharves — Brick Market Place (near Long Wharf), Bowen's and Bannister's wharves and Perry Mill — have a high turnover rate (Crabtree & Evelyn is here, if that tells you anything). **Spring Street** is a favorite area: not too fancy, not too trendy.

The architecture of Thames Street in Newport provides a pleasant setting for shopping.

Craig Hammell

There is shopping beyond Newport, however. **Wickford village** in North Kingstown (here identified simply as Wickford), has a high concentration of top-quality shops without a high concentration of shoppers. What it lacks in restaurants (it's a dry town), it makes up for in galleries, boutiques, and antique shops. On the other side of the Bay, **Tiverton Four Corners** has the largest number of shops in the Sakonnet region. As promised, there are no malls here. The Mill Pond complex — the only thing approaching a group of stores not occupying a historic home — is housed in weathered shingle buildings next to an old grist mill; fields make up the background.

General stores have been included under Food & Beverage Purveyors in the *Restaurants* chapter.

ANTIQUES

New England is known for its antiquing and Rhode Island is no exception. Newport in particular has both a regional and an international legacy to draw from: not only the China trading days of the 18th and 19th centuries, but also the Gilded Age, when expensive baubles of every description filled the mansions. Many items from both periods are now for sale in shops and galleries throughout town, and they set an impressive standard: quality can be dizzyingly high, with prices to match. Much here is of Asian or European origin, rather than colonial or Early American. Shops in Newport are concentrated on **Franklin, Spring**, and the lower stretch of **Thames St.**, as well as **Bellevue Ave.** Contact the **Newport Antique Dealers Association** (20 Franklin St., Newport 02840) for a set of pamphlet guides to members' shops.

Beyond Newport, Warren is the best place to go, though there are antique shops all throughout the Narragansett Bay region.

West Bay

Antique Boutique (884-6767; 527 Main St., E. Greenwich) A collection of old and new bric-a-brac plus jewelry and Christmas items. Another location at 5707 Post Rd./Rte. 1 has new wares only. Prices and quality are both good.

Apple Antiques (295-8840; 8045 Post Rd./Rte. 1, N. Kingstown) A nice selection of furniture and small items, just down the road from Smith's Castle (see *Culture*).

Gallery 500 (885-6711; 500 Main St., E. Greenwich) Like a yard sale, only in a shop.

Mentor Antiques (294-9412; 7512 Post Rd./Rte. 1, N. Kingstown) Look for the red British phone box outside: English furnishings and more.

Wickford Antique Centre (295-2966; 16 Main St., Wickford) A big space with mostly small antiques and vintage clothing; right around the corner is

Wickford Antique Centre II (295-2966; 93 Brown St.), which concentrates on furniture and art.

East Bay

Alfred's Antiques (253-3465; 331 Hope St./Rte. 114, Bristol) Custom mahogany furniture, crystal, and fine china. Check out Alfred's Annex down the street (297 Hope): mainly small items on consignment.

The Center Chimney (253-8010; 44 State St., Bristol) High level, fairly expensive country antiques.

Joe's Antiques (254-1520; 278 Hope St./Rte. 114, Bristol) Good prices, lots of stuff ranging from junk to finds.

Warren Antiques

Warren has been described as "an architectural gem waiting to be polished." This means that rents are still affordable (the chic boutiques haven't arrived yet), and there are bargains to be found, especially in the realm of antiques. More antique dealers cluster in Warren than anywhere else in Rhode Island. Many have set up shop on **Water Street**, others in the new **Warren Antiques Center** in the renovated Lyric Theatre Building.

Warren Antiques Center (245-5461; Corner of Main & Miller Sts., Warren) 150 dealers are represented in this attractive old theatre. There's great diversity in merchandise, but not so much that it overwhelms (and very little junk). Smaller items are displayed in lovely old oak cases. (And there's an Ocean Coffee Roasters in the lobby — an excellent local chain selling coffee and baked goods.)

Water Street, a venerable old street along the Warren River, is home to a number of antique shops. (The Nathaniel Porter Inn, Tav Vino's, Bullock's, and the Wharf Tavern are here as well; see *Restaurants*.) A selection:

The Lady Next Door (831-7338; 196 Water St.) Art Deco collectibles, Fiesta ware, and toys.

Christie and Hadley Antiques (245-2711; 164 Water St.) A range of items and periods, with estate jewelry too.

Onnie's Yesterday Shop (245-7631; 72 Water St.) Vintage nostalgia and general antiques.

There are a number of other shops in town as well, mostly on Miller and Main (Rte. 114) streets:

Be Bop A Lula (no phone; 342 Main St.) Great kitsch, from velvet Elvis paintings to vintage '40s clothing.

Main Street Merchants (253-5603; 508 Main St.) Sift through the junk for the treasures; good prices.

Full Circle (245-9206; 47 Miller St.) It's a small space but the merchandise is well-selected; strong on decorative arts and one-of-a-kind items.

The Square Peg (no phone; 51 Miller St.) This is the one that started the Warren antique craze — an eclectic paradise.

Aquidneck

A&A Gaines (849-6844; 846-0538; 40 Franklin St., Newport) A superb shop: Chinese porcelains, nauticals, clocks, and top-quality 19th-century furniture. Prices to match.

Alice Simpson Antiques (849-4252; 40-1/2 Franklin St., Newport) Specializes in Victorian silver plate, textiles, and jewelry. Reasonable prices.

Almy House Antiques (683-3392; 980 E. Main Rd./Rte. 138, Portsmouth) A comprehensive, country-style antiques shop between Old Almy Village and the Benjamin Fish Common (park at one little complex and walk to the other).

Antiques at the Drawing Room of Newport (841-5060; 221 Spring St.) Merchandise as high-falutin as the name: Baccarat chandeliers, Hungarian pottery, all manner of museum-quality 19th-century furnishings.

Antiques, Etc. (849-7330; 516-518 Thames St., Newport) Something for everyone, from old toys, jewelry, linens, and glass to furniture. A good spot to hunt.

Benjamin Fish House Antiques (683-0099; 934 E. Main Rd./Rte. 138, Portsmouth) A fine collection of furniture and small items, with some exceptional ship models, lanterns, and artwork. The house was built in 1793. Fair prices up and down the scale.

The Burbank Rose (849-9457; 111 Memorial Blvd., Newport) See *Lodging* for the B&B of the same name; the shop offers small antiques, collectibles, and sports memorabilia.

Buxton Moreno Antiques (849-2928; 233 Spring St., Newport) A general assembly of collectibles and decorative art.

Cory Farm Antiques (683-4991; 3124 E. Main Rd./Rte. 138, Portsmouth) Several rooms of fine, country antiques.

Courtyard Antiques (849-4554; 142 Bellevue Ave., Newport) Packed to the gills with an eclectic mix, some good, some not.

Eclectics (849-8786; 5 Lee's Wharf, Newport) Antiques, crafts, books, maps, and prints. This shop down at the end of the wharf has a nice feel to it.

Gallery 176 Antiques, Inc. (847-4288; 83 Spring St., Newport) Small items concentrating on silver, glass, china, jewelry — somewhat pricey.

JB Antiques (849-0450; 33 Franklin St., Newport) Furniture, paintings, and accessories, all top quality, such as an eye-catching Arts and Crafts pottery piece painted with scenes from the Bayeux Tapestry.

Jill Oltz–H. Weber Wilson Antiques (846-7010; 24 Franklin St., Newport) Garden furniture and architectural elements, from lighting fixtures to doorknobs and stained glass.

John Gidley House (846-8303; 22 Franklin St., Newport) A small space with high prices and excellent items ranging from marble fireplace mantels to oil lamps and furniture.

Mainly Oak, Ltd. (846-4439; 489 Thames St., Newport) Good quality oak furniture, restored on the premises.

Newport Antiques (849-2105; 471 Thames St., Newport) A cluttered haven of estate jewelry, coins, and a variety of china and collectibles.

Patina Antiques (846-4666; 32 Franklin St., Newport) Decorative arts, Americana, silver, copper, and furniture.

Smith Marble Ltd. (846-7689; 44 Franklin St., Newport) English and European antiques; specializes in china and silver, with some large pieces of furniture.

Stock and Trade (683-4700; 2771 E. Main Rd/Rte. 138, Portsmouth) Antique furniture and collectibles; check out **The Eagle's Nest** in the back.

The Talking Machine Emporium (849-5360; 42 Spring St., Newport) Antique radios, wind-up phonographs, records (needles too — remember them?), and more talky-era collectibles.

Triton Antiques (847-6077; 160 Spring St., Newport) Unlike most Newport antique shops, Triton carries New England country and primitive items.

NEWPORT ANTIQUE FESTIVALS

Newport Antiques & Collectibles Festival (617-863-1516; at Glen Farm, E. Main Rd./Rte. 138, Portsmouth) 400 dealers at a gala outdoor antiques event. First weekend in June.

Newport County Antiques Week (846-7010; The Newport County Antique Dealers Association, PO Box 222, Newport) Features shows, tours, lectures, and shop events. Last week in April.

Of Furniture and Clocks

Before the Revolutionary War, Newport craftsmen achieved a standard of excellence unequaled anywhere else in the colonies. The Townsend and Goddard families, in particular, led the way with exquisite furniture that today commands towering prices. The Nicholas Brown desk, a Townsend-Goddard piece that belonged to the Brown family of Providence, was auctioned by Christie's in 1989 for $11 million: the highest price ever fetched by an artwork other than a painting. If that leaves you out of the bidding, stop by the **Newport Historical Society, the Hunter House,** and especially the **Samuel Whitehorne House** (see *Culture*), to view examples of Townsend-Goddard furniture. You can also stroll by the houses these master cabinetmakers erected for themselves, all in the **Point Section** of town. Christopher Townsend's home and workshop complex was built at 74-76 Bridge St. in 1725, with another for Job Townsend at 68-72 Bridge, sometime before 1758. John Goddard was originally apprenticed to Job, but he went on to cabinetmaking fame and glory himself and built 81 Second St. More of the families' homes are throughout the area.

Nearby, at 16 Bridge St., is the 1725 home of William Claggett, Newport's equally famous master clockmaker. Claggett was a mechanical genius of the first order, and many of the clocks and organs he built are still working. You can see for yourself at the **Seventh Day Baptist Meeting House** (see *Culture*).

Sakonnet

The Cottage at Four Corners (625-5814; 3848 Main Rd./Rte. 77, Tiverton Four Corners) A top-drawer gallery with matching prices: antique furniture, quilts, and small items are beautifully displayed along with local handcrafts and exhibited artwork.

Granny Smith's Emporium (635-2591; Commons, near Wilbur's Store, Little Compton) A cooperative antique shop with everything from kitchen stoves to autographs. New items too: baskets, kitchenware, pottery.

Peter's Attic (625-5912; 3879 Main Rd./Rte. 77, Tiverton Four Corners) A comprehensive selection without sky-high prices, including lots of glassware and mirrors made from old window frames. Note that Tiverton's only public toilet is behind Peter's.

Block Island

The Island Exchange (466-2093; Ocean Ave.) Revolving collection of antiques and used everything.

BOOKS, CARDS, & MUSIC

In addition to the following book shops, another source for Bay-related reading is **Lamont Books Press** (423-3816; PO Box 493, Jamestown 02835), which produces a fun series of children's books about Newport (a great pre-vacation gift to help children feel at home once you get here). **Island Books** in Middletown carries the series, as do other local shops — or order by mail. For more on books about the area or by Rhode Island authors, see the Bibliography section in *Information.*

West Bay

The Bookstore in Wickford (294-3285; 99 Brown St., Wickford) Recent fiction and non-fiction hardcovers, children's books, and a selection of paperbacks.

Rookiemania (789-3597; 12A Pier Marketplace, Narragansett Pier) Baseball cards and sports memorabilia.

Sound Wave (789-9570; Salt Pond Plaza, Point Judith Rd./Rte. 108, Narragansett) The best selection of tapes and CDs around: imports plus classical, jazz, rock, rap, reggae, you name it.

East Bay

Two Guys Sportscards & Comic Books (247-2780; 420 Main St., Warren) The name says it all.

Aquidneck

The Armchair Sailor (847-4252; 543 Thames St., Newport) An utterly superb shop specializing in marine and travel books. Also seafood cookbooks, children's, magazines, much more. Complimentary coffee and tea, too.

B. and B.'s Baseball Cards & Comics (683-3323; 3001 E. Main Rd./Rte. 138, Portsmouth) Just what it says.

The Book Bay (846-3033; 201 Brick Market Place, off America's Cup Ave., Newport) Plenty of RI and Newport material that will enrich your visit to the area. A good selection of new releases, gift books, paperbacks, and magazines as well. You can get a copy of *Newportopoly* here ($19.95 — the Visitors' Bureau has it too).

Island Books (849-2665; Wyatt Sq., 575 E. Main Rd./Rte. 138, Middletown) This is one of the few serious, non-specialty bookstores in the Newport & Narragansett Bay area. The selection isn't huge but it's well chosen, from classics to the latest fiction titles as well as best-sellers. Also children's books and a good display of local works.

Little Red Lighthouse Children's Books (683-4443; Benjamin Fish Common, 934 E. Main Rd./Rte. 138, Portsmouth) A very good children's book shop, with up-to-date titles and classics.

The Newport Book Store (847-3400; 116 Bellevue Ave., Newport) Excellent old and rare material; specialties include Americana, military, and RI.

Papers (847-1777; 178 Bellevue Ave., Newport) Cards, loose writing paper, Crane's stationery, and gifts.

Simons & Simons (848-0339; 223 Spring St., Newport) An inviting, eclectic little shop that offers framing and hand-painted mats, marbleized papers, books on subjects from polar exploration to religion, records, and hand-colored prints.

But does it have a price tag?

Craig Hammell

Sakonnet

A&R Books & Collectibles (624-8947; 2474 Main Rd./Rte. 77, Tiverton) A nationally-known mail-order dealer in baseball books and cards and sports art has opened a retail shop behind Helger's Produce Market (see Food Purveyors, *Restaurants* chapter); get your soft ice cream after you browse.

Books from Four Corners (624-4311; Mill Pond Shops, 3964 Main Rd./Rte. 77, Tiverton Four Corners) A nice display of local history and fiction by RI authors, with a small selection of paperbacks, cards, and children's books too.

Block Island

Book Nook (466-2993; Water St., Old Harbor) Beach reading stuff: paperbacks, magazines, newspapers. It's a good idea to reserve ahead for the Sunday *New York Times*.

CHILDREN'S

West Bay

Juggles (885-4578; East Greenwich Marketplace, 5600 Main St./Rte. 1, E. Greenwich) Children's toys. Another location is called **The Toy Cellar**, at 7 Main St., Wickford.

Teddy Bearskins (295-0282; 17 Brown St., Wickford) A great children's clothing store; infants through pre-teens.

Aquidneck

Adurables (683-0067; Benjamin Fish Common, 934 E. Main Rd./Rte. 77, Portsmouth) Children's clothing.

Gentle Jungle (849-8210; Bowen's Wharf, off America's Cup Ave., Newport) Stuffed animals galore, plus toys too.

Peppermint Patti's (848-0738; 117 Brick Market Place, off America's Cup Ave., Newport) Children's clothing and toys.

The Walrus and the Carpenter Toy Store (849-0012; Eastgate Center, 909 E. Main Rd./Rte. 138, Middletown) Don't miss this one: toys for every child, and some adults as well. There's a terrific collection of unusual rubber stamps, plus books, and a full range of toy horses. (Next to Andrew's Restaurant.)

Sakonnet

Little Purls (625-5990; Mill Pond Shops, 3964 Main Rd./Rte. 77, Tiverton Four Corners) Top-of-the-line children's clothing.

Block Island

The Little Works (466-2033; Corn Neck Rd.) Toys, children's clothing, puppets, other great items to occupy a rainy day.

CLOTHING & ACCESSORIES

West Bay

Big Kahuna Clothing Co. (783-1990; 4A Pier Marketplace, Narragansett Pier) Cool active clothes and beachwear.

Canvasworks (295-8080; 10 Main St., Wickford) Custom-made canvas bags.

Green Ink (294-6266; 17 Brown St., Wickford) Elegant, interesting, and pricey contemporary women's clothes, shoes, and accessories.

Village Reflections (295-7802; 5 W. Main St., Wickford) Both classic and semi-funky clothes and accessories for women. Interesting prints.

East Bay

Boomerang (245-9810; 259 Water St., Warren) One of those great budget-saving shops with used children's clothing. **Village Resale**, with second-hand and vintage clothes for adults, is at the same address.

Corner Place Coat Outlet (247-1040; 462 Main St./Rte. 114, Warren) Coats for everyone, at great prices. Lots of children trying on ski jackets.

Jamiel's Shoe World (245-4389; 471 Main St./Rte. 114, Warren) Come here first if you're looking for shoes: it's an old-fashioned shoe store with new-fangled merchandise. How about a pair of suede Esprit sandals for $34 (regularly $42)? Also Nickels, Rockport, athletic shoes, and more.

Aquidneck

Belle de Jour (848-2130; 400 Thames St., Newport) Hip, stylish women's clothing; very contemporary.

Cabbage Rose (846-7006; 493 Thames St., Newport) Funky new and used women's clothing and hats.

Chico's (849-8286; 219 Brick Market Place, off America's Cup Ave., Newport) Great women's clothes; unusual prints in 100% cotton. Expensive, but worth it.

Cole-Haan Co. Store (846-4906; 206 Bellevue Ave., Newport) Men and women's leather footwear and accessories. Very upscale.

Edna Mae's Millinery (847-8665; 424 Thames St., Newport) Great hats made by hand from vintage and new materials.

Island Canvas (847-8987; 223 Brick Market Place, off America's Cup Ave., Newport) Locally made canvas bags and backpacks. Two-year guarantee.

Lily's of the Alley (846-7545; 64 Spring St., Newport) A friendly shop with comfortable-earthy-contemporary women's clothes. Good prices, lots of cotton prints.

Ma Goetzinger's (683-9400; 2908 E. Main Rd./Rte. 138, Portsmouth) An excellent women's clothing and shoe shop with good quality contemporary and classic styles, all by itself on Rte. 138. Recommended, though prices are on the high side.

Native American Trading Company (846-8465; Spring St., Newport) An exceptionally fine shop featuring rugged, sturdy stuff — principally men's outerwear. All the hats, coats, backpacks, and leather goods are authentic — made by the companies that made such things first. Items from all over the world. Also fine Native American art objects.

Sole Desire (846-0067; 131 Brick Market Place, off America's Cup Ave., Newport) A good little shoe store; they even had the red, pointy-tipped cowboy boots a friend had his heart set on.

Suit-Systems (847-7848; 359 Thames St., Newport) Computer-measured swimwear for men and women (do you really want a computer to know your measurements?).

Team One Newport (848-0884, 800-847-4327; 547 Thames St., Newport) Very serious sailing gear, plus swimwear and sports clothes too. Call ahead for their catalogue.

Timberland (846-4410; 16 Bannister's Wharf, off America's Cup Ave., Newport) Wonderful sturdy leather hiking boots and accessories.

Tropical Gangsters (847-9113; 375 Thames St., Newport) Way cool clothing and accessories for men and women.

The Weathervane (849-6219; Long Wharf Mall, off America's Cup Ave., Newport) Good, middle-of-the-road women's clothing at reasonable prices. If the temperature drops, pick up a cotton sweater here.

Sakonnet

Pond Lilies (624-2594; Mill Pond Shops, 3964 Main Rd./Rte. 77, Tiverton Four Corners) An above-average source for stylish women's clothing, from dresses and sweaters to coats and jewelry.

Sakonnet Purls (624-9902; 3964 Main St./Rte. 77, Tiverton Four Corners) Order a custom-knit sweater, or choose from a fine variety of yarns to make your own. Needlework too.

Block Island

Bare Necessities (466-2669; Water St., Old Harbor) "The home of the Block Island Izod." Although a $43 shirt doesn't seem to qualify as a bare necessity.

Été (466-2925; Dodge St., Old Harbor) Hip and cool clothes to identify that you went to Block Island. A favorite is "Block Island — Laissez les bon temps rouler."

Madhatter (Chapel Cottage, Chapel St., Old Harbor) Men's, women's, and children's hats, and sunglasses too.

Oceans & Ponds/The Orvis Store (466-5131; Ocean Ave.) Orvis is America's oldest mail order company; here you can get all manner of outdoor gear without paying for postage — Timberland hiking boots, Orvis jackets, Nautica swimwear, and much more. Also eclectic merchandise like weather instruments, Caribbean spices, and the official, hand-sewn Block Island flag. Fishing charters and canoe and kayak rentals too.

Seascape (466-2202; Water St., Old Harbor) Good quality sports clothing and swimwear above the Star Dept. Store.

The Shoreline (466-2541; Water St., Old Harbor) Great outdoor and casual clothing for women and men (Putumayo, Patagonia, and more). Another location is on Ocean Ave. (466-5800).

CRAFT GALLERIES & STUDIO

West Bay

Arts & Crafts of the Americas (6 Main St., Wickford) Predominately Mexican and South American handcrafted wares.

The Ball & Claw (295-1200; 1 W. Main St., Wickford) An exceptional shop showcasing the exquisite craftsmanship furniture-maker Jeffrey Greene lavishes upon pieces designed for, as he puts it, "the 18th-century home." Recommended.

Tailored Craft (885-1756; 211 Main St., E. Greenwich) A small gallery with Native American crafts and Southwestern jewelry.

Wrigley Designs Studio & Shop (884-9886; 6 King St., E. Greenwich) Painted earthenware and more; the most innovative and original crafts in town.

Aquidneck

The Coop: Newport's Artisan Cooperative (848-2442; 99 Spring St., Newport) A favorite craft gallery in Newport, with fascinating works by local handcrafters in everything from tin to wood and fabrics. Ask to see the "Bio Book" for a blurb on each artist. Tin pieces by James Reynolds are terrific.

Craig Hammell

A window on life beneath the waves, Bowen's Wharf, Newport.

The Erica Zap Collection (849-4117; 477 Thames St., Newport) Top-quality international crafts.

MacDowell Pottery (846-6313; 220 Spring St., Newport) A small place with a good selection of serviceable pottery, plus cards and gifts. Watch the potter at work.

Newport Scrimshander (849-5680, 800-635-5234; 14 Bowen's Wharf, off America's Cup Ave., Newport) Scrimshaw has fallen into disfavor — it's the art of engraving on ivory — though no elephants died for the scrimshaw exhibited here. The owner works mostly with prehistoric mammoth and walrus ivory. Jewelry and collectibles.

The Quilt Artisan (846-2127, 800-736-4364; Aquidneck Green, 747 Aquidneck Ave., Middletown) New and antique quilts, plus quilting supplies and classes. Call for a workshop schedule.

Sue Cannon Clay Studio (452 Thames St., Newport) Sue works mainly with cobalt glazes, inspired by similar English glazes brought to Newport by 18th-century colonists. She sells out of her studio.

Thames Glass (846-0576; 688 Thames St., Newport) At the end of lower Thames is a wonderful glassblowing studio and shop: everything from vases, paperweights, and perfume bottles to goblets and candlesticks.

Thames Street Pottery (847-2437; 433 Thames St., Newport) Pottery thrown on the spot, plus work in wood, clay, and glass from artisans around the country. Native American pottery too.

Tropea-Puerini (846-3344; 391 Thames St., Newport) A fine craft gallery with cutting-edge wares.

Sakonnet

The Metalworks, Inc. (624-4400; Main Rd./Rte. 77, Tiverton Four Corners) Heating and ventilation systems are created here, as are very nice copper and brass lanterns.

The Windmill (624-1818; 3988 Main Rd./Rte. 77, Tiverton Four Corners) This little shed behind Sakonnet Purls offers hand-painted and glazed ceramic tiles plus Byzantine and modern-style mosaics. Order a custom-made address tile or pick up a wrought-iron table with a mosaic-patterned top.

Block Island

Block Island Blue Pottery (466-2945; Dodge St., Old Harbor) Very attractive baking dishes, mugs, bowls, and more, displayed in a c. 1790 home.

Pottery by the Sea (466-5069; Dodge St., Old Harbor) Good standard pieces.

The Red Herring (466-2540; Water St., Old Harbor) Handcrafted items and home accessories from around the island and the country selected with a sure eye; above The Shoreline.

Watercolors (466-2538; Dodge St., Old Harbor) All handcrafted gifts and jewelry, including pottery by local RISD graduates, tile-work tables, seaglass vases, and more.

GIFTS

West Bay

Askham & Telham, Inc. (295-0891; 12 Main St., Wickford) High quality gifts and home accessories; look for the lovely needlepoint pillows.

Different Drummer (294-4867; 7 W. Main St., Wickford) A neat little shop with cards, jewelry, locally made gifts, rubber stamps, and T-shirts.

The Green Door (885-0510; 378 Main St., E. Greenwich) A top quality, eclectic shop with vintage linens, quilts, glass and tin ware, and more; folk art and craft offerings too.

Jamestown Designs (423-0344; 17 Narragansett Ave., Jamestown) Fine quality gifts, handcrafted jewelry, and cards; original and reproduction prints of island scenes. Look for delicate, hand-thrown stoneware by island potter Irene Parthenis — she calls her work "All Fired Up."

J.W. Graham (295-0757; 26 Brown St., Wickford) Crafts and other unusual handmade wares, principally for the home.

Robin's Nest Gift Shoppe (885-7717; 36 Main St., E. Greenwich) Country accessories, candles, and "Victorian" gifts. Much the same selection is on hand down the street at **Gracefully Yours** (442 Main).

Santa's Galleria (782-8244; 2A Pier Marketplace, Narragansett Pier) Christmas specialty items; standouts include nutcrackers and a host of reproduction Victorian glass ornaments; plus gifts and jewelry.

Twenty Water Street (885-3700; 20 Water St., E. Greenwich) Upscale gifts, antiques, nautical apparel, and 20 Water St. souvenirs; in the same building as the restaurant (see *Restaurants*, Warehouse Tavern).

The Wooden Horse (789-3050; Mariner Square, Point Judith Rd., Narragansett) Christmas items plus candles and country gifts; some nice Advent calendars.

East Bay

Linden Place Gift Shop (253-0309; 500 Hope St./Rte. 114, Bristol) See *Culture* for the historic home Linden Place; it supports the best gift shop in town, including pewter ware, local handcrafts, books, and nautical items.

Maria's Gift Shoppe (245-4543; 463 Main St./Rte. 114, Warren) Maria calls it The Wedding Center, and that's just what this is: a great spot to pick up crystal, china, silver, etc. at reasonable prices.

Aquidneck

Cabbages & Kings (847-4650; 214 Bellevue Ave., Newport) "Gifts and decor designed for gracious living" — an upscale gift shop.

Cadeaux du Monde (848-0550; 140 Bellevue Ave., Newport) Unusual art and artifacts from South America, Asia, and Africa.

The Old Almy House (1016 E. Main Rd./Rte. 138, Portsmouth) This place goes on and on, with everything from country store provisions (penny candy and coffee beans), to candles, cookbooks, and gifts; the antiques are upstairs and the "Christmas Fantasy" shop is at the back.

The Newport Preservation Society Museum Store (849-9900; off America's Cup Ave., Newport) A fine selection of museum reproductions from Newport and around the world.

Sakonnet

Country Cabin (624-2279; Mill Pond Shops, 3964 Main Rd./Rte. 77, Tiverton Four Corners) Country-style gifts and handmade items (including quilts), plus some antiques.

Block Island

Mermaids Boutique (466-2299; lower Dodge St.) Gifts, sundresses, and jewelry, plus mermaid squirt guns and wonderful one-off items like sandals ornamented with plastic grapes and chili peppers ($34).

The Spindrift (466-2596; Corner Dodge St. & Corn Neck Rd.) Gifts, jewelry, clothes, and some memorable items including a set of lobster Christmas lights and PooPets: self-fertilizing sculptures made of manure.

HOUSE & GARDEN

West Bay

The Aunt's Attic (783-4569, 783-3470; 966 Boston Neck Rd./Rte. 1A, Narragansett/Bonnet Shores) A terrific source for used furniture and household accessories; antiques too. Recommended.

The Ball & Claw (See Craft Galleries & Studios above.)

Farrago (885-6960; 101 Main St., E. Greenwich) A tiny shop with unusual household items and gifts.

Joint Venture Woodworking (295-5308; 2549 Boston Neck Rd./Rte. 1A, N. Kingstown/Saunderstown) Custom handcrafted furniture, sign carving, architectural and marine mill work; **The Strip Joint**, in the same building, repairs fine furniture.

Rocco's Used Furniture and Things (295-5551; 2507 Boston Neck Rd./Rte. 1A, N. Kingstown/Saunderstown) A junkyard with exceptional flair, decorated with everything from buoys to a Cinzano café table umbrella.

The Shaker Shop (294-7779; 16 W. Main St. at the Brown Street Bridge, Wickford) Handmade Shaker-style furniture and accessories. Beautiful and expensive.

Topiaries Unlimited (294-6990; 30 W. Main St., Wickford) Unusual sculpted shrubs, plus potting supplies and flowers.

Wild Goose Chase (885-4442; 312 Main St., E. Greenwich) Painted furniture with a Southwestern flair. Well worth a look.

Aquidneck

134 Spring Street (848-5394; Newport) Funky art furnishings and home accessories. How about a leopard-skin ice bucket or a bunch-of-grapes chandelier? Also jewelry, hats, and more. A great place.

The Aardvark (849-7232; 475 Thames St., Newport) The address refers to a jumbled antique shop, but four doors down is a yard full of great statuary, from imposing to campy and downright silly.

Art Reflextions, Inc. (683-2300; 2922; E. Main Rd./Rte. 138, Portsmouth) Not only do they import Oriental rugs, they make them too. Look for the end-of-summer sale.

Bellevue Florist (847-0145; 159 Prospect Hill St., Newport) This elegant little shop tucked down a tiny side street off Bellevue looks like it belongs in Lon-

Statuary from the Aardvark in Newport might be the perfect, if heavy, souvenir.

Craig Hammell

don. They carry only a small selection of wicker and home accessories, but it's worth a peek.

Bill's Lawn Ornaments (683-1017; 1960 E. Main Rd./Rte. 138, Portsmouth) Birdbaths, picnic tables, sheds, even dog houses.

The Christmas Tree Shop (841-5100; Aquidneck Center, Rte. 138, Middletown) These shops started as a Cape Cod phenomenon but are expanding across southern New England. Despite the name, you can find everything here from French glassware to Barbie Doll clothes to brassware from India. Their slogan "Don't you just love a bargain?" is apt — these are very low prices. And yes, they carry Christmas stuff too.

Crosswinds Gallery (683-7974, 800-638-8263; Old Almy Village, 980 E. Main

Rue de France offers French elegance in Newport, featuring home fashions and accessories.

Craig Hammell

Rd./Rte. 138, Portsmouth) A wonderful shop exclusively devoted to weather-vanes and cupolas, with a smattering of wind chimes for sound effects.

Rue de France (846-3636; 78 Thames St., Newport) This little gem would be at home on the Ile St. Louis in Paris — it's a revelation in Newport. Reams of French lace, fabrics, household items, much more. Write for their catalogue.

Sakonnet

Courtyards (624-8682; 3980 Main Rd./Rte. 77, behind Mill Pond Shops, Tiverton Four Corners) They advertise "garden ornaments and artifacts," and outside you'll find lots of sundials, birdbaths, and statuary; inside look for crafts, jewelry, and dried herbs hanging from the ceiling.

JEWELRY

West Bay

Browne and Co. (295-2420; 14 Main St., Wickford) A very fine jewelry shop (and a good bet if your watch battery dies), plus original Nantucket lightship baskets, scrimshaw, and antique clocks.

Harbour Galleries (884-6221; 253 Main St., E. Greenwich) Antique and estate jewelry sold in a c. 1775 building.

Howard's Jewelry and Gifts (789-5020; Mariner Square, Point Judith Rd./Rte. 108, Narragansett) Good prices on traditional jewelry and gifts (Hummels, porcelain, etc.).

Turquoise Door (783-4720; 18A Pier Marketplace, Narragansett Pier) Specializes in Southwestern jewelry.

East Bay

Bargain Unlimited (253-8215; 437 Hope St./Rte. 114, Bristol) Stand with your back to Hope Street and you'll think you're in the Garment District of New York. The owners make most of what you see: a glittering, sparkling, spangling treasure trove of costume jewelry plus hair ornaments, scarves, and handbags. Wow.

Aquidneck

Firenze Jewelers (849-7070; Bowen's Wharf, off America's Cup Ave., Newport) Estate and antique jewelry.

Geoclassics (849-5587; 61 America's Cup Ave., Bowen's Wharf, Newport) Jewelry and other pretty things at this gem and mineral shop.

J.H. Breakell & Co. (849-3522; 69 Mill St., Newport) A very fine silversmith's shop: all the exquisite pieces you see are designed and forged on the premises. Don't miss this one — send ahead for the catalogue.

Block Island

Jennifer's Jewelry (466-2744; Dodge St., Old Harbor) Costume and fine jewelry, Chinese and Japanese pearls, scrimshaw, estate items.

KITCHEN

West Bay

Craig Hammell

Ceramist Thomas Ladd's work is available at Wickford Gourmet's Kitchen & Table shop.

Wickford Gourmet's Kitchen & Table (295-9790; 31 W. Main St., Wickford) A great gourmet shop (see *Restaurants*) has a great kitchen and gift shop next door. Look for ceramic work by renowned local potter Thomas Ladd.

Aquidneck

Kitchen Pot Pourri (847-5880; 42 W. Main Rd./Rte. 114, Middletown) All manner of kitchen supplies and accessories.

The Runcible Spoon (849-3737; Bellevue Ave., Newport) Elegant — and expensive — kitchen and table wares and gifts.

Sakonnet

Stone Bridge Dishes (635-4441; PO Box 218/Stone Church Rd., Little Compton/Adamsville) A superb kitchen shop just up the road from the Rhode Island Red Chicken Monument; from garlic presses to Quimper pottery from France, this is the place. Copper weathervanes, too. Go early and have breakfast at The Barn (see *Restaurants*). UPS shipping.

MARINE SUPPLY

West Bay

Arnold's Boat Shop (884-4272; Water St., E. Greenwich) Sales and repairs.

Conanicut Marine Services, Inc. (423-1556; 1 Ferry Wharf, Jamestown) This may be one of the most comprehensive ship's stores in the world: from marine hardware to gear for every kind of weather imaginable, plus gifts, rafts, dinghies, and more. Also a full-service marina, repair shop, and boat yard.

East Bay

Shannon Yachts (253-2441; 19 Broad Common Rd., Bristol) Builders of 28-, 38-, and 50-ft. ocean and cruising yachts.

Water Street Yacht Shop (245-5511; 259 Water St., Warren)

Aquidneck

Aquidneck Island Marine (847-0101; 134 Aquidneck Ave., Middletown)

Fawcett Designs Inc. (849-0653; Bowen's Wharf, off America's Cup Ave., Newport) Custom yacht design and sales.

J.T.'s Ship Chandlery on Thames Street has everything from sound charts to rope cables — and more.

Craig Hammell

J.T.'s Ship Chandlery (846-7256; 364 Thames St., Newport) Nautical heaven. This shop has it all, from serious marine hardware to clothing, charts, books, even cool plastic champagne glasses for your yacht (or your home).

Nautor's Swan (846-8404; Bowen's Wharf, off America's Cup Ave., Newport) Yacht sales and brokerage; parts distribution center.

Sakonnet

Cove Market & Marina (635-8003; Sakonnet Point, Little Compton) Down at land's end in southeastern RI is a little market where you can find antiques and consignment items, newspapers, T-shirts, ice cream pops, and a friendly dog. Marine supplies too.

Riverside Marine (625-5181; 211 Riverside Dr., Tiverton) Get your rods, reels, lines, bait, soda, cigs, and gifts here; ramps $5 a day.

Block Island

Block Island Boat Basin (466-2631; West Side Rd., New Harbor) A general store for boats, with everything from clothing to paperbacks, ice, marine hardware, and 85 slips.

Block Island Marine (466-2028; High St., New Harbor) Nautical hardware and more.

PHARMACIES & NEWSSTANDS

West Bay

Baker's Pharmacy (423-2800; 53 Narragansett Ave., Jamestown) Suntan lotion, beach toys, magazines, newspapers, and more.

East Bay

Buffington Pharmacy (253-6555; 495 Hope St./Rte. 114, Bristol) An old-fashioned drug store, with everything from gifts and souvenirs to candy and ice cream. Aspirin too.

Delekta Pharmacy (245-6767; 496 Main St., Warren) A superb old-fashioned apothecary shop straight from the 1880s (see Food & Beverage Purveyors, in *Restaurants* chapter, for fountain service). Great smells and sights, including soaps, perfumes, and locally crafted items. It's a prescription center, too.

Duffy's News (253-9851; 467 Hope St./Rte. 114, Bristol) Newspapers, stationery, magazines, and the like.

Marshall's News Stand (245-1627; 504 Main St./Rte. 114, Warren) Open from 6 to 6.

Aquidneck

Bellevue News (847-0669; 111 Bellevue Ave., Newport) A great little newsstand with magazines, candy, the works.

Carroll Michael & Co. Pharmacy (849-4488; 115 Bellevue Ave., Newport) Make a point of stopping here — it's more like a gallery than a shop, with exquisite displays of perfumes, soaps, gifts, and other elegant, luxurious items (prescriptions, too). They decorate with great flair at Christmas.

Block Island

Block Island Pharmacy (466-5825; High St.) In addition to prescriptions and such, the largest video library on Block, plus paperbacks, magazines, camera supplies, TV and VCR rentals, a fax machine, and a Notary Public.

SOUVENIRS & NOVELTIES

West Bay

Earnshaw Drug, Card, & Gift Shop (294-3662; 63 Brown St., Wickford) Okay, so they do prescriptions too, but the emphasis here is on RI souvenirs.

Fanta Seas (783-8400; 40A Pier Marketplace, Narragansett Pier) Good quality Narragansett souvenirs: T-shirts, hats, gifts, more.

Town Hall (423-7200; 93 Narragansett Ave., Jamestown) The town sells the official Jamestown flag for $35. What better souvenir could you get?

Aquidneck

J.J. Newberry's (846-5918; 144 Thames St., Newport) This old five and dime chain is the best place to get stuff that says "Newport." Also give **Scrimshaw Souvenirs** a try, just down the way.

Nickels (849-8470; 87 Thames St., Newport) Look for the big frog out front. This shop defies description: from feather boas to beaded curtains, it's a hoard of funny, campy stuff. Cards, too.

Operculum (849-6292; Bowen's Wharf, off America's Cup Ave., Newport) Really an overgrown shell shop, with gifts and souvenirs from, as they put it, "the oceans of the world."

The Souvenir Stop (849-6717; 115 Brick Market Place, off America's Cup Ave., Newport) Big-time Newport bric-a-brac and clothing. If it's too crowded, head to **The New Store** (101) a few doors down.

The Nickels frog on Thames Street in Newport welcomes shoppers.

Craig Hammell

Block Island

Star Department Store (466-5541; Water St., Old Harbor) A wonderful place to wander around: Block Island souvenirs, T- and sweatshirts, beach toys, even sportswear. The old wooden floor creaks as you browse. For BI souvenirs, also try **Esta's Gift**s (466-2651) further down the street.

SPECIALTY

West Bay

Bagpiper (783-0555; 32A Pier Marketplace, Narragansett Pier) A smoke shop with Irish imports, flasks, and more.

The Hour Glass (295-8724, 800-585-8724; 15 W. Main St., Wickford) An excellent clock shop with kaleidoscopes, weather instruments, sundials, and other mechanical gems.

Northeast Brewers Supply (789-9635; Mariner Square Mall, Pt. Judith Rd., Narragansett) Everything you could desire to brew your own, plus European-style sleeve glasses.

The World Store (295-0081; 16 W. Main St., Wickford) From environmental gifts to fossils, books, ant farms, and Swiss Army knives.

Yankee Saddler (885-1910; East Greenwich Marketplace, 5600 Post Rd./Rte. 1, E. Greenwich) An all-horse store featuring riding gear, toy horses, and memorabilia.

East Bay

American Tourister Factory Outlet (245-7098; 91 Main St./Rte. 114, Warren) Take home your souvenirs in new luggage: suitcases, briefcases, and travel accessories. They'll ship anywhere in the U.S.

Don's Art Shop (245-4583; 543 Main St./Rte. 114, Warren) Art and drafting supplies.

Photo World (253-2248; 433 Hope St./Rte. 114, Bristol) If you drop your camera at Blithewold Mansion or the Herreshoff Museum, this is where to have it fixed. Film and processing too.

Aquidneck

Arnold Art Centre (846-3349; The Polo Center, 700 Aquidneck Ave., Middletown) There is another location at 210 Thames St. in Newport, but the parking is easier here and the staff is great: all the art supplies you'll need.

The Christina Doll Collection is handcrafted by a Newport native.

Craig Hammell

The Christina Doll Collection/Peggy Mulholland, Inc. (846-8372; 365 Thames St., Newport) Exquisite, limited edition, handmade dolls. Very expensive but absolutely stunning. Christina dolls are also available at **Miniature Occasions** (849-5440, 800-358-4285; 57 Bellevue Ave.), which also sells custom-made Raggedy Ann and Andys, and offers classes in doll- and dollhouse-making (five sessions, 2 to 3 hours each). Call ahead to see what's being offered.

Ebenezer Flagg Co. (846-1891; 65 Touro St., Newport) Their logo says "We Make or Procure Any Flag." A great flag-maker's shop with a colorful, international collection. Bring a design and they'll make one for you.

Newport Hobby House, Ltd. (847-1515; 235 Spring St., Newport) From car and plane models to masterful, miniature wooden ships, toy train sets, and

Kim Damon, owner of Newport Hobby House, Ltd., with a model of a Booth Bay lobster boat.

Craig Hammell

much more. Their specialty is a host of sailboat models in wood, plastic, and fiberglass; kits range from 18 to 55 inches (for display or for sailing with radio control). If you can't find your own sailboat model on the shelves, have blueprints made and master shipbuilder Don Gray will build it for you (he builds the real thing too). If you want to see some of Gray's work in action, head down to Melville Pond on Sundays to watch members of the Aquidneck Island Model Yacht Association race their flotilla.

Newport Needleworks Ltd. (847-9276; 210 Bellevue Ave., Newport) Interesting needlepoint design kits, including local scenes of the Marble House Doors and The Elm's Gate.

Sakonnet

Dog Portraits by Brooks Wall (635-4225; Little Compton) Bring a photo and artist Brooks Wall will paint (in oil, acrylic, or watercolor) a portrait of your pooch.

Four Winds, Inc. (624-4549, 800-638-8943; 149 Nanaquaket Rd., Tiverton) Self-described as "RI's Premier Flag Company," they stock 332 flags and banners from all over the world, plus seasonal and historical flags as well. Or come with your own design.

Block Island

Block Island Historical Society Shop (466-2481; Ocean Ave. at Old Town Rd.) Don't miss the small museum or the shop: exclusive reprints of old postcards, plus great T-shirts.

SPORTING GOODS

West Bay

The Soccer Depot, Inc. (295-1045; 755 Tower Hill Rd./Rte. 1, N. Kingstown) Exclusively soccer paraphernalia — the works.

East Bay

Gob Shop (245-4800; 465 Main St./Rte. 114, Warren) Sporting goods plus clothing and athletic footwear.

Aquidneck

Aquidneck Island Sporting Goods (847-7317; 796 Aquidneck Ave., Middletown) Clothing, footwear, and gear.

Blue Sky's Kite Connection (846-KITE; 207 Brick Market Place, off America's Cup Ave., Newport) Single line and stunt kites, windsocks, and assorted paraphernalia.

High Flyers Flight Co., Inc. (846-3262, 846-2960; 492 Thames St., Newport) Another kite shop; if you miss it, continue up Thames to #468 and you'll find yet another, **Flying Colors Ltd.**

Sports N Stuff (848-0889; 1134 Aquidneck Ave., Middletown) A complete sporting goods store with gifts, baseball cards, and sweats too.

Block Island

Block Island Kite Co. (466-2033; Corn Neck Rd.) Kites, windsocks, rafts — anything that will blow in the wind or float on the water.

Island Sport Shop (466-5001; Weldon's Way, Old Harbor) Surf, cycle, fitness, and more.

CHAPTER EIGHT
The Nitty-Gritty
INFORMATION

Craig Hammell

Yacht racing is one of Newport's favorite pastimes.

This compact reference source will come in handy for planning a trip or in mid-vacation. It covers the following topics:

AREA CODE/ZIP CODES/TOWN HALLS

The area code for all of Rhode Island, with a few exceptions, is 401. Zip codes and town hall telephone numbers are listed below. Note: the official name for Block Island is New Shoreham.

Town	Telephone	Zip Code
Block Island	466-3200	02807
Bristol	253-7000	02809
East Greenwich	886-8665	02818
Jamestown	423-7220	02835
Little Compton	635-4400	02837
Adamsville		02801
Middletown	849-2898	02842
Narragansett	789-1044	02882
Newport	846-9600	02840
North Kingstown	294-3331	02852
Portsmouth	683-3255	02871
Prudence Island		02872
Tiverton	624-4277	02878
Warren	245-7340	02885

BANKS

The following banks are well represented in the Narragansett Bay area. All are members of international ATM networks, which are noted below.

Bank	Telephone	ATM Networks
Bank of Newport	273-6620 or 800-234-8586	Cirrus, Yankee 24
Citizens Bank	849-6444 or 800-922-9999	Cirrus, Yankee 24
Fleet Bank	846-7400 or 800-445-4542	NYCE, Cirrus
Hospital Trust	847-2280 or 800-662-5086	NYCE, Yankee 24, Plus
Shawmut Bank of RI	800-742-9688	Cirrus, NYCE, Yankee 24
The Washington Trust Company	466-7710 (Block Island) or 782-1000 (Narragansett)	Cirrus, Yankee 24, Plus

BIBLIOGRAPHY

The following books represent the tip of a great literary iceberg of what's been written about Newport and Narragansett Bay. The Newport Library's Newport Room is a great place to start reading.

Books You Can Buy

AUTOBIOGRAPHY, BIOGRAPHY & REMINISCENCE

Gavan, Terence, *The Barons of Newport.* Newport, RI, Pineapple Publications, 1988. 88 pp., photos, $7.50. Chatty history of the Gilded Age gang.

Botkin, B.A., ed., *A Treasury of New England Folklore.* New York, American Legacy Press, 1989. 618 pp. Reminiscences, legends, ghost stories and other tales of New England, state by state.

McEntee, Grace Hall, *Where Storms Are Beautiful.* Pastoral Publishers, 1993. 167 pp., $12.95. Tales of a teacher who lives on Prudence Island and commutes to the mainland by fishing boat everyday.

O'Connor, Lucy, ed., *Jonnycakes and Cream*, 1993. Forty-five oral histories of Little Compton, Rhode Island, supplemented by news clippings, photos, and poems by area residents.

CHILDREN'S BOOKS

Lamont Press Books: a series of 8 children's books about the Narragansett Bay area, published by the Lamont Press in Jamestown, RI. Paperback, $4.50 each. One title is *Newport Houses*, illustrated by Richard Carbotti.

COOKBOOKS

The Hammersmith Farm Cookbook, 1990, 242pp. Illustrated recipes from Jackie O's childhood home.

Murphy, Martha, *The Bed & Breakfast Cookbook: Great American B&Bs and Their Recipes from All 50 States.* Owings Mills, Maryland, Stemmer House Publications, Inc. A great cookbook and guide from a Narragansett B&B owner.

Shernam, Barbara, *The Island Cookbook.* Favorite Recipes Press, 199pp., $14.95. Highlights the cuisine of Block Island, Newport, Jamestown, Prudence, Nantucket, and Martha's Vineyard.

The Society for the Propagation of the Jonnycake Tradition, eds., *The Jonnycake Cookbook.* 1972, $7. Many ways to cook and serve Rhode Island's favorite food.

FICTION

Casey, John, *Spartina.* Alfred A. Knopf, Inc., 1989. This story of a Rhode Island fisherman won the National Book Award in 1989.

Rice, Luanne, *Blue Moon.* Viking, 1993. A novel about a troubled family in the fictional fishing village of Mount Hope, RI.

Wolff, Geoffrey, *Providence.* Penguin Books, 1986. A fast-paced crime novel set in Providence, though the characters roam around Narragansett Bay.

HISTORY

Conley, Patrick T., *An Album of Rhode Island History, 1636–1986.* Virginia Beach, Virginia, The Donning Company, Pubs. 1992. 288 pp., photos, $29.95. Illustrated history of the state; great early photos and prints.

Hale, Stuart O., *Narragansett Bay: A Friend's Perspective.* Rhode Island Sea Grant, URI, 1988 (second edition). 130pp., illustrations, soft cover, $12.95. Social history of the Bay.

McLoughlin, William, G., *Rhode Island: A History.* "The States and the Nation" Series, American Association for State and Local History, New York, W.W. Norton & Co., 1986. 240 pp., $9.95. Intelligent and readable paperback covering RI events and ideas.

Quinn, Alonzo W., *Rhode Island Geology for the Non-Geologist.* Providence, RI Department of Natural Resources, 1976. 63 pp., photos and illustrations. Concise, understandable history of RI geology.

RECREATION

Birdwalks in Rhode Island: Exploring the Ocean State's Best Sanctuaries. Woodstock, Vermont, Backcountry Publications. 144pp., paperback, $9.95.

McCabe, Catherine O., *Cyclist's Guide to Block Island.* Booklet with three island tours.

Breakwaters are great places to fish and explore.

Craig Hammell

Stone, Howard, *Short Bike Rides in Rhode Island.* Chester, Connecticut, Globe Pequot Press, 1988 (third edition). 241 pp., with illustrations and maps. A terrific resource for bicycle touring in the Ocean State.

Weber, Ken, *Walks & Rambles in Rhode Island: A Guide to the Natural and Historic Wonders of the Ocean State.* Woodstock, Vermont, Backcountry Publications, 1993 (second edition). 166pp., maps, photos, $11. Forty self-guided walking tours throughout Rhode Island. Also see his *More Walks & Rambles in Rhode Island*, 1992.

TRAVEL, ART, ARCHITECTURE, & PHOTO ESSAY

The Artistic Heritage of Newport and the Narragansett Bay. Exhibition Catalogue, William Vareika Fine Arts, 1990. Full color illustrations, soft cover, $5.95. The exhibition was held to benefit Save the Bay; everyone benefits from the charming catalogue.

Gannon, Tom, Newport, *Rhode Island: A Guide to the City by the Sea.* The Countryman Press, 1992 (second edition). 174pp., illustrations.

Gavan, Terence, *Exploring Newport.* Pineapple Publications, Newport, 1992, $8.95. 111-page guide to Newport's historic attractions, planned as a series of walking tours. Restaurant and lodging information at the back.

Guinness, Desmond and Julius Sadler, *Newport Preserved: The Architecture of the 18th Century.* New York, Viking Press, 1982, 152pp, illustrations. The story behind the conservation and restoration of Newport's colonial heritage.

Mulvaugh, Jane and Mark Weber, *Newport Houses.* New York, Rizzoli, 1989. 220pp., color photos. The domestic architecture of Newport, from colonial clapboards to the mansions. Introduction by Robert Stern.

Newport Mansions: The Gilded Age. Foremost Pubs., 1982. A photo extravaganza by photographer Richard Cheek, with text by Tom Gannon.

Smith, Clyde H., *Coastal Rhode Island.* Foremost Books, 1987. 128pp., $35. A stunning, all-photo coffee table book that shows off the beauty of the Bay.

Welch, Wally, *The Lighthouses of Rhode Island.* Apopka, Florida, Lighthouse Publications, 1987. 34 pp. Full-color booklet with descriptions of all the lighthouses in the state.

BLOCK ISLAND

Berrigan, Daniel, *Block Island.* Unicorn Press, 1985. 102pp.

Livermore, Samuel, *History of Block Island, Rhode Island.* Block Island Committee for Republication for the Block Island Tercentenary, 1961 (originally published 1877). 371pp., illustrations. This is *the* history of the island: you can read it in the library, though copies are still for sale.

Ritchie, Ethel, *Block Island Lore and Legends.* Block Island, F. Norman Associates, 1955. 93pp., illustrations. An indispensable glimpse of island folklore.

Wilkinson, Chilton, *Saltbound: A Block Island Winter.* New York, Methuen, 1980. 263pp., illustrations. Life "on-island" throughout the seasons.

Books You Can Borrow

Bacon, Edgar Mayhew, *Narragansett Bay: Its Historic and Romantic Associations and Picturesque Setting.* New York, G.P. Putnam's Sons, 1904. Old-time recollections of the Bay.

Davis, Hadassah and Natalie Robinson, *History You Can See.* Providence, RI Publications Society, 1986. Historical anecdotes rooted in familiar scenery.

Hazard, Thomas Robinson, *The Jonny-Cake Papers of 'Shepherd Tom': Together with Reminiscences of Narragansett Schools of Former Days.* Boston, The Merrymount Press, 1915. Classic account of 19th-century Rhode Island life by a famous reformer (causes ranged from abolition to women's suffrage) and businessman.

O'Connor, Richard, *The Golden Summers: An Antic History of Newport During its Years of Glory.* New York, G.P. Putnam's Sons, 1974. 344 pp., photos. Just what the title says.

Pierce, John T., Sr., *Historical Tracts of the Town of Portsmouth, Rhode Island.* Portsmouth, RI, Hamilton Printing Co., 1991. 114 pp., photos and illustrations. Quirky historical facts about Portsmouth.

CLIMATE, WEATHER, & WHAT TO WEAR

Despite meteorologists' tag for Rhode Island weather — "humid continental" — it's never as hot and muggy here in summer as, say, in New Jersey or Washington D.C., nor does it stay bitterly cold in winter for very long. The average mean temperature is 50 degrees F, with January logging in as the coldest month (28 degrees) and July as the hottest (72 degrees). There is one factor that belies these seemingly moderate temperatures, however, and that is wind. Block Island especially, but the Bay towns as well, can be extraordinarily windy places: expect everything from gentle zephyrs to big blows, and note that it's always cooler and windier offshore (so especially if sailing or boating is in your plans, bring a waterproof windbreaker and wear light layers beneath it).

Casual is the one adjective that describes dress in and around Newport. There's literally no place on Block Island that won't let you in the front door in jeans (even the spiffiest restaurants), and the same goes for most of Newport's restaurants, though there are a few exceptions (the White Horse Tavern and the Inn at Castle Hill require jackets and ties). Comfortable walking shoes are a necessity (with soles that can negotiate cobblestones), as are sunglasses: the glare factor is high here, with reflected sunlight off the sea.

EMERGENCY NUMBERS

Town	Ambulance	Fire	Police
Block Island/ New Shoreham	911	466-3220	466-3220
Bristol	911 or 253-6611	253-6611	253-6900
East Greenwich	911	884-4211	884-2244
Jamestown	911	423-1313	423-1212
Little Compton	635-2323	635-2323	635-2311
Middletown	911	847-3636	846-1104
Narragansett	911	789-1011	789-1011
Newport	911 or 846-2211	846-2211	847-1212
North Kingstown	911 or 294-3344	294-3344	294-3311
Portsmouth	911	683-1155	683-2422
Tiverton	624-4242	624-4242	624-3222
Warren	911 or 245-3411	245-3411	245-1311

HANDICAPPED SERVICES

Most state facilities in Rhode Island, such as parks and campgrounds, offer access for the physically impaired. See the *Lodging* and *Restaurants* chapters for information on individual establishments. The following organizations can provide more detailed information on handicapped services in the Narragansett Bay area:

Deaf Interpreters (800-525-0770)
Information for the Handicapped: Tips on Tape (831-1131)
Rhode Island Governor's Commission on the Handicapped (277-3731)
Rhode Island Relay (800-RI-55555)

HOSPITALS

The following hospitals provide emergency room services:

Newport Hospital (846-6400; Friendship St., Newport)
Rhode Island Hospital (277-4000; 593 Eddy St., Providence 02903)
Roger Williams Hospital (456-2000; 825 Chalkstone Ave., Providence 02908)
South County Hospital (782-8000; 100 Kenyon Ave., Wakefield 02879)

Westerly Hospital (596-6000; 25 Wells St., Westerly 02891)
Women and Infants Hospital (274-1100; 101 Dudley St., Providence 02905)

MEDIA

One of the best ways to learn about a place is to read the local paper: from police briefs to the high school lunch menu, it can give you a real feel for life in a particular corner of the planet. The following publications are but a selection of what's out there. In summer, especially, a host of free weekly and monthly magazines flourish as well (such as *Ocean State Traveler*), all of which contain up-to-date reviews and information on seasonal events. An indispensable source of information state-wide is *Rhode Island Monthly* (421-2552; Narragansett Media, Inc., 18 Imperial Pl., Providence 02903). Every year the June issue offers a Beach and Summer Guide, and the August issue rounds up the "Best and Worst of the Ocean State."

PUBLICATIONS

The Block Island Times (466-5533/2222; PO Box 278, Block Island)
Bristol Phoenix (East Bay Newspapers: 253-6000; One Bradford, Bristol)
East Greenwich Magazine (885-3447; 655 Main St., East Greenwich)
Jamestown Press (423-3200; 42 Narragansett Ave., Jamestown)
Narragansett Times (789-9744; 187 Main St., Wakefield)
Newport Daily News (849-3300; 101 Malbone Rd., Newport)
Providence Journal-Bulletin (East Bay offices: 846-0600; 28 Pelham St., Newport; 245-8600; 529 Main St./Rte. 114, Warren) The largest paper in the state. Restaurant reviews appear on Fridays.
Sakonnet Times (683-1000; 2829 E. Main Rd./Rte. 138, Portsmouth) Covers Little Compton, Tiverton, and Portsmouth.
The Standard-Times (294-4576; 13 W. Main St., North Kingstown) "Jamestown's Hometown Newspaper."
Warren Times-Gazette (245-6002; 72 Child St., Warren)

RADIO

WADK-AM 1540, Newport; News, talk.
WALE-AM 990, Providence; Local talk shows, including "Closet Free Radio," one of the few gay and lesbian radio shows in the U.S., Mon. and Fri., 6–8pm.
WBLQ-FM 99.3, Block Island-South County; adult, contemporary, soft rock.
WBRU-FM 95.5, Brown University; pioneering alternative rock.
WCTK-FM 98.1, Providence; country.
WHJY-FM 94.1, Providence; album rock.
WKRI-AM 1450, West Warwick; adult, contemporary.

WOTB-FM 100.3, Middletown; jazz, new age.
WPJB-FM 102.7, Narragansett; adult, contemporary.
WPRO-FM 92.3, Providence; Top 40.
WRIU-FM 90.3, URI; most eclectic mix of music in the state, from reggae to
gospel.
WWBB-FM 101.5, Providence; oldies.
WWRX-FM 103.7, Providence, Westerly; classic rock.

TELEVISION

WLNE-TV Channel 6, Providence; CBS
WJAR-TV Channel 10, Providence; NBC
WPRI-TV Channel 12, Providence; ABC
WSBE-TV Channel 36, Providence; PBS

POST OFFICES

Town	Telephone and Address
Block Island	466-7733; Dodge St.
Bristol	253-6100; 515 Hope St./Rte. 114
East Greenwich	884-2610; 176 First Ave.
Jamestown	423-0330; 75 Narragansett Ave.
Little Compton	635-2332; 2 Meeting House La.
Middletown	846-1283; Commercial.
Newport	847-2329; Federal Bldg., Thames St. (Broadway Station: 846-0444; 195 Broadway).
North Kingstown	294-4641; 234 W. Main St.
Portsmouth	683-1320; 95 Chase Rd.
Tiverton	624-4772; 600 Main St./Rte. 77
Warren	245-5039; 53 Child St.

PUBLIC RESTROOMS

This list contains possibly the most crucial information in *The Newport &
Narragansett Bay Book.*

Block Island: parking lot at Old Harbor ferry landing.
Bristol: none.
East Greenwich: none.
Jamestown: Recreation Center on Conanicus Ave. (restrooms in separate
structure facing Union St.); seasonal.
Little Compton: Town Hall (40 Commons).

Middletown: None.

Narragansett: In the Pier Marketplace complex next to the Public Library, corner of Kingstown Rd. and Caswell; seasonal.

Newport: Gateway Visitors' Bureau, 23 America's Cup Ave; Cardines Field, corner of America's Cup Ave. and Broadway; Mary Street Parking Lot; former Newport Armory at 365 Thames St.

North Kingstown: between Brown St. and Wickford Harbor.

Portsmouth: Sandy Point Beach Bath House; seasonal.

Tiverton: Port-o-Potty behind Peter's Attic Antiques, 3879 Main Rd./Rte. 77, Tiverton Four Corners.

Warren: Town Beach; seasonal. Hugh Cole Pavilion at the playground on Hugh Cole Rd. (off Child St.); seasonal.

REAL ESTATE

If Rhode Island feels like home to you maybe you should live here. Call the **Rhode Island Association of Realtors** (785-3650) for a list of real estate agents in the area of your choice. If you're interested in renting, the association can also direct you to agents who handle seasonal rentals (though don't over-look the classified ads of local papers: sometimes they're the best source for rental information).

Sailing on Newport Harbor.

Craig Hammell

ROAD SERVICES

The number to remember is **800-AAA-HELP**: AAA's 24-hour Emergency Road Service hotline. If you're looking for information rather than immediate assistance, try one of these regional offices:

AAA Narragansett (789-3000; 14 Woodruff Ave., Narragansett)
AAA Newport (841-5000; 99 East Main Rd./Rte. 138, Middletown)
AAA Providence (272-7000; 55 Dorrance Ave., Providence)
AAA Warwick (736-0001; 501 Centerville Rd., Warwick) The main office for Rhode Island.

TOURIST INFORMATION

FISHING & HUNTING REGULATIONS

For questions about fishing or shellfishing, hunting, boating restrictions, or coastal resources, contact the **Rhode Island Department of Environmental Management** (789-3094: general number), and in particular the **Division of Fish and Wildlife** (277-3075).

TRAVELER'S AID

Newport Council for International Visitors (846-0222, 846-5314; PO Box 3032, Newport)

Traveler's Aid Society of Rhode Island (521-2255; 177 Union St., Providence, 02903)

VISITOR INFORMATION

Rhode Island Tourism Division, Office of Economic Development (277-2601; 800-556-2484; 7 Jackson Walkway, Providence, RI 02903) For statewide information; the free *Rhode Island Visitor's Guide* is published every April, and is an excellent resource for attractions and seasonal events.

Rhode Island Welcome Center (539-3031; bet. Exits 2 and 3 on Rte. 95 near the Connecticut border) Open daily year round; lots of brochures plus human assistance.

REGIONAL ORGANIZATIONS

Block Island Tourism Council (466-5200, 800-383-BIRI; PO Box 356, Block Island)

Newport Gateway Convention & Visitors' Bureau (849-8048, 800-548-4662; 23 America's Cup Ave., Newport) An essential stop: they have a reservation service and plenty of resource material on Newport and Aquidneck.

South County Tourism Council, Inc. (789-4422, 800-548-4662; PO Box 651, Narragansett)

CHAMBERS OF COMMERCE

Block Island Chamber of Commerce (466-2928; Drawer D, Block Island). Ask for Alva, she's very helpful.

Bristol County Chamber of Commerce (245-0750; PO Box 250, Warren)

Narragansett Chamber of Commerce (783-7121; PO Box 742, Narragansett)

Newport County Chamber of Commerce (847-1600; PO Box 237; Newport)

North Kingstown Chamber of Commerce (295-5566; PO Box 454, North Kingstown)

Craig Hammell

Rhode Island Red Memorial, Adamsville.

Index

LODGING BY PRICE CODE

Lodging Price Codes:

Inexpensive   Under $50
Moderate $50 to $100
Expensive $100 to $180
Very Expensive   Over $180

WEST BAY

Moderate
Jamestown B&B
John Updike House
Lionel Champlin House
Meadowland B&B
Mon Reve
Monte Vista Motor Inn
The Morans' B&B
Murphy's B&B
The 1900 House B&B
The Old Clerk House
Stone Lea B&B
Totus Tuus
White Rose B&B

Moderate–Expensive
Historic Home B&B
The 1773 Narragansett House

Moderate–Very Expensive
Bay Voyage Inn

Expensive
Dutch Inn
The Village Inn

EAST BAY

Moderate
Joseph Reynolds House
King Philip Inn
Nathaniel Porter Inn
Rockwell House Inn
William's Grant Inn

AQUIDNECK

Inexpensive–Moderate
White Cap Cabins

Moderate
Bluestone B&B
Brown's B&B
The Burbank Rose B&B
The Country Goose B&B
The 1855 Marshall Slocum Guest
    House
Flower Garden Guests
Founder's Brook Motel & Suites
Hedgegate B&B
Merritt House B&B
Polly's Place B&B
Portsmouth Ramada Inn & Confer-
    ence Center
Seaview Inn

Moderate–Expensive
Admiral Benbow Inn
Atlantic House B&B
Bannister's Wharf Guest Rooms
Bethshan B&B
Brinley Victorian Inn
Culpeper House B&B
Hammett House Inn
Howard Johnson's Motor Lodge
Hydrangea House
Jailhouse Inn
La Forge Cottage
The Melville House
Pilgrim House
Rose Island Lighthouse
Royal Plaza Hotel
Stella Maris Inn
Stoneyard B&B
Windsong B&B

Moderate–Very Expensive
The Clarkeston
Elm Street Inn
Mill Street Inn

RESTAURANTS BY PRICE CODE

Restaurant Price Codes:

Inexpensive	Up to $15
Moderate	$15 to $25
Expensive	$25 to $35
Very Expensive	Over $35

WEST BAY

Inexpensive
Aunt Carrie's
Cathay Garden
Champlin's Seafood
Gregg's
Jigger's Diner
Junction 40 Restaurant & Pub
Ocean View Chinese
Peppers
Snoopy's Diner
Twin Willows
Wickfod Gourmet

Inexpensive–Moderate
Frank & Johnny's Restaurant &
    Pizzeria
Mandarin

Moderate
Casa Rossi
Chez Pascal
Jamestown Oyster Bar

Moderate–Expensive
Angel's
Red Rooster Tavern
Schoolhouse Café
The Steak Lodge
Walter's
Warehouse Tavern

Expensive
Bay Voyage Inn
Coast Guard House

Spain
Trattoria Simpatico

Expensive–Very Expensive
Basil's

EAST BAY

Inexpensive
Aidan's Pub
Balzano's
Bullock's
Old Venice Restaurant
The Sandbar

Moderate
Redlefsen's Rotisserie & Grill
S.S. Dion
Tav-Vino/The Blue Collar
Wharf Tavern

Expensive
The Lobster Pot
Nathaniel Porter Inn

AQUIDNECK

Inexpensive
Annie's
Anthony's Shore Dinner Hall
Burkey's 5th Ward Diner
Mexican Café
Reidy's Family Restaurant
Tito's Cantina
Wharf Deli & Pub

Inexpensive–Moderate
Eastside Mario's
International Café
Salas'

RESTAURANTS BY CUISINE

SHOPPING BY AREA

About the Author

Marguerite Harrison

Pamela Petro began her association with Rhode Island in 1978 as a freshman at Brown University. After graduation she worked in Washington D.C. and New York and received an M.A. from the University of Wales, before moving back to Providence in 1988 to begin work as a freelance writer. Since then she has become a regular contributor to *The New York Times* Travel Section, writing about everything from farmhouses in Iceland to historical cities in Brazil, and also writes for a variety of other publications from *The Atlantic Monthy, Islands,* and *American Heritage* to *Endless Vacation* and Welsh literary journals. She loves dogs and wishes she had another Karmann Ghia convertible.

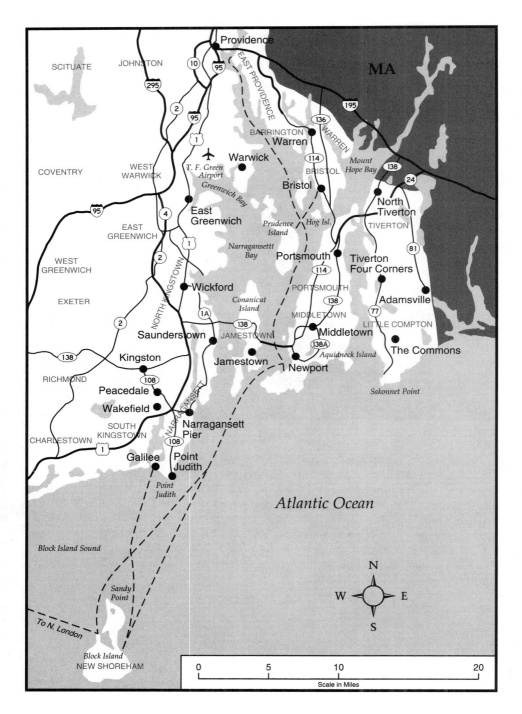

Newport and Narragansett Bay

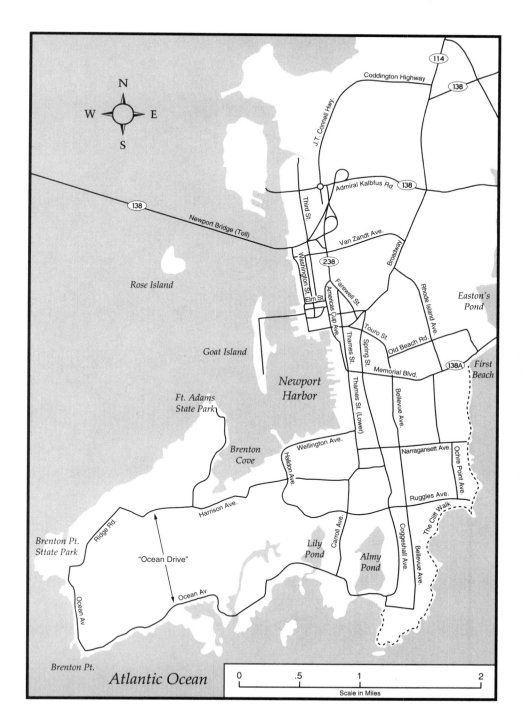

Newport

NOTES

NOTES